SING ME A CIRCLE:
LOVE, LOSS, AND A HOME IN TIME

Sing Me a Circle:
Love, Loss, and a Home in Time
By Samina Najmi

Winner of the 2024 Aurora Polaris Award

Copyright © October 01, 2025 Samina Najmi

No part of this book may be used or performed without written consent of the author, if living, except for critical articles or reviews.

Najmi, Samina
1st edition

ISBN: 978-1-949487-48-0
Library of Congress Control Number: 2025930899

Interior design by Natasha Kane
Cover design by Joel W. Coggins
Author Photo by Azfar Najmi
Editing by Cynthia Via and Kris Bigalk

Excerpt credit: Naomi Shahib Nye, "No Explosions" from *The Tiny Journalist*. Copyright © 2019 by Naomi Shihab Nye. Reprinted with the permission of The Permissions Company, LLC on behalf of BOA Editions, Ltd., boaeditions.org.

Trio House Press, Inc.
Minneapolis
www.triohousepress.org

For my Ammi, Suraiya Jabeen, who inked her yearnings in long, lined notebooks every day—before either of us knew to call them personal essays

And for my chickadees
Maya and Cyrus
this love song

Table of Contents

Part 1

Triptych	3
I. Of Fan Belts and Fathers	
II. Rubina Najmi, Who Fights Her Way In—and Out	
III. One Flew Over the Schoolgirls' Heads	
The Straight Lines of a Circle	9
I remember you in fragments	18
Abdul	19
Blind Date	36
Greenford's Gift	38
fragment 2	59
Fireworks, or the Bombing of Karachi	60
Surayia's Schools	66
Apa	73
Sky-dying	77
The Little Room on the Roof	80
fragment 3	88
fragment 4	89
Burglar in Braids	90
Monsoon Muse	95
The Najmi Creation Story	100
Story of a Storyteller	103
fragment 5	109
fragment 6	110

Part 2

Amma	113
Sweet-and-Twenty	126
fragment 7	133
fragment 8	134
Quarantine Song	135
The Cat Connection	139
Hiding Osama Bin Laden	150
Membership Dues	155
Teaching as a Pakistani American Muslim Feminist	160
fragment 9	170
fragment 10	171
The Cab-Driver and I	172
She Leaves Me, She Leaves Me Not	177
Applause	183
Ring In the New	184
World Cup Mama	204
The Sky That Didn't Fall	209

Part 3

Benign Baggage	213
fragment 11	224
First Thanksgiving Without Them	225
Here—And There—Lies Home	229
Yellow Coat	236
Mourning Dove	244
Café Convo	245
Trinità	246

fragment 12	255
Brew	257
One Summer in Gaza	259
Seduced by the Story	273
The Crow and the Keys	281
Memoir in Dust	288
Learning Distance	290
Teaching as a Pakistani American Muslim Feminist: Ten, Twenty Years On	295
fragment 13	301
Between Cave and Canyon	302
Acknowledgments	313
A Note of Thanks	317
About the Author	321

Part 1

Triptych

I. *Of Fan Belts and Fathers*

Someone who identifies as darksoulofdeath2 has a post on *Yahoo! Answers* asking what a fan belt is. The post has elicited responses ranging from mirth to indignation, as well as a couple of patient attempts to engage with the query seriously. Darksoulofdeath2 has offended some, not because everyone is expected to know what a fan belt is but because the question, instead of being posed under *Yahoo! Autos*, appears on the site's *Martial Arts* page.

"You mean like in a car? You've got to be kidding me. I've seen some questions posted in the incorrect section by accident, but damn!" says Bujinkan Ninja.

Another response begins teasingly but goes on to offer a concrete description: "It's a Black Belt . . . that is attached to pulleys (one of which has a fan blade mounted to it that's attached on the water pump) that as the belt spins it will turn the fans pulley blowing air onto the vehicles radiator" [sic].

Then there's the commentator who offers eight solid sentences of knowledgeable description and advice, only to end with the warning: "Don't ask auto questions on the martial arts page unless you like rude answers. Some of us lack a sense of humor."

But I may be the one person to whom a fan belt question on a martial arts page makes sense. *A fan belt is a Black Belt. . .* Spend a little time browsing on the website of *Black Belt Magazine* and your hazy sense of the philosophy behind traditional East Asian martial arts is confirmed: it's about discipline, courage, and humility. Far from representing a Darwinian survival contest, the traditional martial arts emphasize rectitude and chivalry. They teach us about duty, loyalty, and sacrifice. And the *sifu* who models these virtues for us, who teaches by example, is in the Chinese tradition seen as a father.

Black Belt, fan belt, father. This is where they converge, in a memory.

I'm not among the knowledgeable when it comes to cars (or martial arts). But I've never had to ask what a fan belt is, what it does, or what it is capable of. When I first heard the term—at fourteen, from my father—I learned of its dark power. I learned that such power is indifferent to its reach. And I learned how variably we humans respond when we find ourselves in the grip of its tyranny.

It must have been a Saturday in 1978, shortly after we acquired our second-hand, dark blue Toyota Corolla, because only my father had to head out to work that day. It was a winter's day by Karachi standards, which is to say that the sun warmed the morning up into the fifties. We were still huddled under our thick cotton blankets when Abbu's shapely hand waved goodbye and he headed downstairs. We heard the metal gates of our house clank open, the car door slam shut, the engine start, purr, and stop. Funny sound, not really a purr at all—more like a strangled sort of gruffness. It restarts, same unfriendly sound, then stops. The car door opens again, and then a long silence. Panic in our hearts now. Abbu is a heart patient whose parents died young; his own death has always seemed possible to us. Besides, he is prone to fainting—a phenomenon I now know in myself and my son as a vasovagal tendency, often triggered by the sight of blood, but mostly inexplicable. My two siblings and I toss off our blankets and run out to the balcony, our mother behind us.

There's Abbu, standing at the hood of the Toyota that never

made it out of the gates. It's still parked in the small space between the concrete stairway and the metal gates that remain open in anticipation of its exit. Abbu's head is bent over the open hood of the engine. We're relieved, then curious. We run down the concrete stairs, still in our pajamas.

"What's the matter with the car, Abbu?"

Abbu doesn't respond. His gentle brown hands continue to fumble around in the engine. When he finally looks up, we see the mix of pain and revulsion on his face. Then our eyes fall on the amorphous black and white fluff in his hands—black and white with red streaks.

"Kittens," he says. "Caught in the fan belt. Look what the blades of the fan can do."

The kittens are in pieces.

Seeking shelter in the car engine, oblivious of the danger in their place of refuge.

We scream and fly back up the stairs and into our blankets. We have quite forgotten about Abbu's vasovagal vulnerability, what the sight of blood can do to him. Or maybe we know that self-indulgence is not an option for him in this moment. That he wouldn't abandon the scene if he could. Maybe we expect him—trust him—to stay put and deal with the bloody aftermath. To do his duty with chivalry, sparing us. To be the *sifu* who models discipline, courage, and sacrifice. Whatever the case, we leave Abbu standing there, alone by the open gates, holding the kitten bits in his shapely hands.

II. *Rubina Najmi, Who Fights Her Way In—and Out*

She's a three-pound, fifteen-ounce baby, born too soon.

Born October 30, 1966, before she's ready for the world or the world is ready for her. First in our family to be born in the Western hemisphere. The doctors at London's Hammersmith Hospital send her mother home without her.

"This baby's only chance is the incubator," they say.

What a hopeful word, incubator. Where good things, bright things, happy things hatch. The promise of feathered dreams taking flight.

So the baby first sees the world through a sheet of glass. Reaches out her dark brown hands, this way, that way, there's cold, hard glass. Glass between her and the warmth of human flesh, between her and the pulse of another heart. Because human contact could kill her, don't you know?

Glass that makes gawkers of the family. They look from a distance but must not touch. For a month she lies in an incubator in a room in a hospital—box within box within box.

But the newborn is a fighter. She fights for her breath and lives. And the doctors tell the mother: "This child is a survivor."

The survivor grows up in Karachi, a dark, brilliant child who never smiles in photographs. She's a toddler who eats fistfuls of dirt, a tween who throws things at her younger brother, a teenager who fights with her parents and believes she is a bad influence on her little sister; who spends weekends brooding in her room, the door shut and nobody knocking. She cries as she watches *Chariots of Fire*, its Olympic runners who reach the finish line against all odds. She becomes the first girl in the family to win a scholarship to a college in America.

In eighteen years her family has grown cold, hard, and aloof. They watch from a distance but refuse to touch.

Three months before it's time to leave for Smith College

in Massachusetts, the survivor gets up on a chair in the bedroom of her Karachi home. She ties one end of her long cotton dupatta to the ceiling fan, the other around her neck, and kicks the chair from under her.

III. *One Flew Over the Schoolgirls' Heads*

One hot and sticky day in Pakistan's coastal city of Karachi, the girls of the Cambridge section at St. Joseph's are filing back into their classrooms after recess. Exhausted from the Herculean endeavor to push through the mob of girls outside Abdullah's or Mrs. Velo's snack bars clamoring for chili chips, Ice Cream Soda, or milk toffees, we collapse on the wooden benches of our eighth-grade classroom, envying those whose seats are directly beneath the ceiling fans. Our forty-odd pairs of hands reach for water bottles even if the water in them is already tepid. The air circulated by the ceiling fans is much too warm, but in time it will work its magic: our uniforms will unglue from our backs, the semicircle of sweat beneath our short sleeves will fade, and the rivers edging our temples and hairlines will begin to evaporate.

It's time for Senior Miss Fikree's geography class. Through the haze of humidity and the pungent odor emanating from our semicircled sleeves—an odor whipped around the room by the ceiling fans—we command our minds to grasp how high and low pressure systems develop in the atmosphere.

Suddenly a sparrow swoops in through the open door, sending the girls aflutter. What on earth is the little bird doing here, among us? How disruptive, how foolish! Was it tempted indoors by the relative cool of our high colonial ceilings or overpowered by a freak, exploratory impulse? Doesn't it know that some risks are not worth taking, some curiosities and yearnings best buried within us?

Within seconds the sparrow has realized its mistake. But unable to see its way out despite multiple possibilities of escape, it becomes a winged frenzy. It darts from one end of the classroom to the other in blinding flashes, to the gasps of the girls, who duck their heads, cover their ears, shut their eyes. Nobody wants to witness this degree of desperation. We all know it doesn't have to be this way. But none of us knows what to do about it, not even Miss Fikree, and in any case, it all happens so fast. Next thing we know the intruding bird—so small, so afraid, so out of place—has fluttered straight into a ceiling fan and sliced itself between the blades that continue in their own circular frenzy. Down comes the sparrow, a bloodied pulp on the classroom floor. It lies as still now as it had pulsated with frantic life a moment before. An ounce of flesh and feathers at our feet.

I wonder now why we hadn't all jumped to switch the fans off the moment the sparrow flew in among us. We might have saved its life. Could our own physical comfort have made us indifferent to the threat it faced? Perhaps the spectacle of the bird's vulnerability simply paralyzed us. Or did the danger fail to register because we failed to imagine it?

I think about the sparrow's flight and fall, its impetuous, audacious venture into our world. I wonder if it had a moment's regret. Decades later, I can hear the desperate flapping of its fragile wings. But I have no memory of its cry.

The Straight Lines of a Circle

When my son, Cyrus, was a year and a half old, I took him and Maya to Karachi, Pakistan, where we stayed until he was almost two. It was 2003, some months after the US occupied Iraq, and, for a time, my American life no longer felt tenable. We lived with my father in the home I grew up in, across the street from my mother and her husband. I taught part-time at Meadow Secondary School, which Ammi had founded in 1975 when we first returned to Karachi from west London. In the time that I left Cyrus in Abbu's care, and sometimes even while I was home but focused elsewhere, my toddler would pick up one of his crayons and proceed to draw circles on the walls. The living room was his preferred canvas and purple his color of choice. He'd clamber up the couch, reach a little, and get to work on his mural. One day his crayon even found its way to Abbu's bedroom. Three feet of wall below his mirror became a scribbled mess.

I expressed my horror. Abbu's face, however, shone with excitement.

"Samina!" he said. "Look at those perfect circles. Aren't you amazed that he drew them without a compass? Just look!"

In the five months that we lived with Abbu, his walls were covered with circles of diverse colors and sizes, often overlapping in intricate patterns. All his life so reverential toward property and so mindful of appearances, my father didn't care what visitors might think of his vandalized walls. His grandson's genius remained on display long after the flesh-and-blood reality of him had returned to Massachusetts.

There's a passage in Maxine Hong Kingston's *The Woman Warrior* that focuses on the roundness of things in the Chinese village she is describing. However many times I read the memoir, I linger over this paragraph. Sometimes I ask my students at Fresno State what they think of when I say the word "circle." Their responses vary: cycles, they say; the absence of beginnings and endings, non-hierarchical structures, community, wholeness. I ask if they see themselves forming the circle hand in hand with others, as they did in elementary school, perhaps, or are they the person around whom the ring forms? Are they enclosed, trapped, or kept safe by that circle? Do they see themselves as the lone individual standing outside it altogether—looking in or looking away?

I've been thinking that all linearity is circularity in disguise. You have to zoom out to see the shape, and you do it through the lens of time.

We talk about geography in my Asian American literature class, and such terms as "East," "West," and "Middle East." The question *East of what?* yields a discussion of imperial perspective and the colonial power to name the earth. But those histories aside, I'm struck by the fact that if you go far enough West, you end up East.

I can uproot myself from the land that gives me context, journey five thousand miles westward to Boston, then a further three thousand miles to Fresno, to end up about as far as I can possibly be from where I first began. But after all that dogged progression, I look up to find myself retracing parts of a circle my parents drew before me.

This fall it will be thirty years since I left Karachi—left home, parents, friends—for the privilege of studying literature at an American university. A tuition waiver, stipend, and teaching fellowship made it possible for me to leave, accompanied by an unemployed husband I had insisted on marrying as an undergraduate. When you leave home as a student, you're focused on a specific educational goal, small and unremarkable in the grand scheme of things. But the pursuit of that degree shapes the entire trajectory of your life. It determines the personal choices you make—divorce, new marriage, children, divorce reprise. Whether or not you're ready for U.S. citizenship, you need the Green Card in order to live with your American husband and build a life with him, and you need the marriage in order to obtain the green card. Before you know it, there are homes and mortgages and babies, even as you return to the MLA Job List every fall in search of a tenure-track position that will enable you to do more than adjunct work with that doctoral degree for which you left home in the first place.

Like all summaries, that one is unfair. And in any case, a summary presupposes linearity—a beginning, middle, and end—where there really is none.

Zoom out and you can see that, unique as I thought my situations were, my parents had faced comparable choices long before I did. First, they left Patna, India—my mother as a child, to what was then East Pakistan, now Bangladesh, and my father, barely eighteen, to Karachi. The bloodbath of the 1947 Partition still fresh in collective memory, my parents crossed the border by rail into an idealistic future in newly created Pakistan, where they had no familial context for their lives. Then as a married couple with two children, they left their young country in 1966 for London, the former seat of empire. That's the mocking irony of generations of postcolonial lives, that you fight off your colonizers only to be forced to seek them out again for the economic and political stability of which they robbed you, this time in an alien and mostly hostile landscape. If irony had a physical shape, it would be round.

All points on a circle are always the same distance from the center.

So my parents lived their immigrant lives in London as others have before and after them: leaning on the support of family who had preceded them there, two growing families in my aunt and uncle's two-and-a-half bedroom home in the suburb of Greenford; the tireless factory hours, the clerical jobs, the pursuit of English, the building of their professional profiles. All with a view toward returning to Karachi on a sounder footing, the dream of a home of their own deferred because this was London, an aberration, a detour, not where they were meant to be, but a point on the arduous path of becoming. Land of opportunity, neither the first, nor the last. And return to Karachi they did, eventually, as did my aunt and uncle's family. My parents' first attempt, just after my seventh birthday in June 1970, failed. Two years later, financial worries compelled them to head back to London for another couple of years before they returned to Karachi "permanently." In that time, my father acquired his M.Phil. in physics but had to forgo the Ph.D. in order to support his family and return to teach physics at Urdu Science College, where he went on to serve as principal for fourteen years before he retired. While in London, my mother went from assembly line coffee-packing to discovering her gifts as an elementary school teacher. Chalk Hill Primary School tried to keep her, but Ammi gave it up to return to Pakistan and, as it happened, began her own preschool in the living room of our two-bedroom Karachi home. English Playhouse grew with my younger sister, year by year, until one day it stood, preschool through high school, as Meadow Secondary School, on "real" school grounds. My own teaching career originated as a part-timer at Meadow when I was seventeen. You see what I mean by the circularity of things.

So it's true that my parents had remarkable careers as educators in Karachi. Also true that somewhere along the way they lost sight of each other, and their 23-year-old marriage ended in divorce—a scandal in the Karachi of the eighties. Ammi left our neighborhood, but she moved back to our lane within two years to be closer to my fourteen-year-old sister. It was in 1985, when her niece, Rubina, born in Greenford when I was three years old, took her own life. It was the summer before she was to leave for Smith College in Massachusetts. Thirty-three years before Maya leaves home for college.

Ammi left without leaving. She remained either next door to Abbu or across from him for twelve years.

Now a sophomore on the STEM pathway at Edison High School in Fresno, California, Cyrus no longer draws circles on walls. But he is immediately interested in the geometry of my thoughts on circularity.

"There's a lot you can do with that," he says, encouragingly. "For instance..." He grabs a scrap of paper and draws a small circle with a line touching it. "That line is tangent to the circle." He hopes he has handed me a metaphor, and of course he has. A tangent touches fleetingly at a certain point, without intersecting, without altering the shape of anything, and both the line and the circle go on as if that brief point of connection never happened.

Too many of those to make sense of. It's easier to wrap my head around a chord, that line that connects one point of a circle with another. The segment it creates is not the whole circle but contained within it, an integral part of the whole. My marriage of eighteen years to Maya and Cyrus's father, for instance; or friends and places that form us at specific moments in time.

There's nothing like being the middle generation to make the whole circle visible.

Abbu died five years ago in Karachi, the shape of his one, individual life complete. His three children were eight thousand miles away, each having obtained the Ph.D. that had remained beyond his grasp, and stayed on to have American children. He lived to see me move my young family from Boston to Fresno for a tenure-track job, lived to see me achieve that tenure, come home to Karachi one last time on my sabbatical in the spring of 2012. Abbu lived to see my first forays as a memoirist, offering up the prequels to my own memories in long-distance phone calls. I wonder if he heard in those first essays the echoes of his own words authoring the lives of his ancestors. On every visit to the US in the last six years of his life, he would write the story of his family, longhand in Urdu. He wrote so that we, the descendants scattered across the globe, would know where we came from. Then in the last weeks of his life, he had his granddaughter Maya's novella published in Karachi, so she would see herself as a writer.

Did my father, the son of a poet, see writing as my inheritance—a family tradition we held on to across time, space, and language?

My mother the essayist, and my aunt the poet are preceded by their father, the railway doctor who wrote poetry. Balkhi is the clan name they share with the 13th-century Persian poet Rumi, who, as a boy, fled with his family from Balkh, in present day

Afghanistan, when the Mongols invaded. Their caravan traveled west until they found a home in Anatolia. The Sufi poet-teacher's name pinned him to place and political geographies: he was both Balkhi, "of Balkh," and Rumi, "of Rome," a subject of the eastern Roman empire. Yet through eight centuries, his words have translated across space and time, legible to the human heart.

My mother, aunt, and I have a more immediate literary ancestor in their mother, my grandmother Kaneez Fatima, the lifelong invalid who was also a memoirist. Amma's hand penned family history in her notebook over the course of twenty years, never to be published in her lifetime. Truth-telling like Abbu, and a gifted storyteller to boot, Amma told vivid tales of people and places she had loved, then lost to death or displacement. People and places she had gone on loving for the rest of her life.

We are a family in which too many died young—in Patna, Chittagong, and Karachi; on land and in the skies. In bedrooms, in mental asylums, in shelters for the homeless. Buried far from where we began, too far from our parents and siblings, our children and grandchildren. We are a family that has sought its moment in Asia, Africa, Europe, and North America. In the Northeast, the South, the Southwest, and West Coast of the United States. We are a family anchored on the page, in Urdu, in English, in poetry, and in prose—words we have written for no-one but ourselves. To read us is to read of homes that eluded us, and of homes we denied to others.

In the last phone conversation I had with my father, six days before he died, he was focused on the writerly possibilities that had opened up for his daughter and granddaughter. Abbu's voice was aglow with the knowledge that Maya and I had both just held our very first literary readings in faraway Fresno. I read in the Spectrum Gallery at the annual Rogue Festival, under the auspices of Fresno State's Chicanx Writers and Artists Association, at exactly the same time that twelve-year-old Maya was reading her winning entry in the Wild About Books contest at A Book Barn. I like to think that Abbu found a pleasing symmetry in the image, assurance of our family's roots in paper.

Ammi was about the age that I am now when rheumatoid arthritis first began to contort her life and eventually forced her to give up the school she had founded three decades prior. I see her treading the earth with precarious step, her toes at grotesque angles formed by the auto-immune disorder. In her seventies, she has made what is likely to be her final migration, from Karachi to San Diego, from the Indian Ocean to the Pacific, to live with my sister, Sadia, and her family. She takes psychology courses at San Diego City College, volunteers among senior citizens with dementia, and cherishes the addition of her new granddaughter, Amara. The arc of Ammi's life has followed her children's, to California.

This fall, my firstborn will leave home, too.

When Maya was little, her life and mine formed concentric circles, having different radiuses but the same center—a bodily reality while I carried her in my womb. But what mother would want to contain her daughter's life within her own, even if she could? The concentric quickly gives way to the overlapping and intersecting patterns of so-called Apollonian circles, magnificently complex and beautiful to the eye. I don't have the mathematical grasp that Apollonius of Perga had over two thousand years ago. But I do understand the geometric beauty of overlapping and intersecting lives, especially those of mother and daughter. And those "pencils of circles," as they are so picturesquely called, become more visible the further you zoom out through the lens of time.

In Urdu, the word *kal* means "yesterday." And we use the same word for "tomorrow."

Maya will be leaving for college just as I mark the thirtieth anniversary of the day I left Karachi. I know that she is impatient to experience the world beyond home, as I was. All the second-guessing that is a parent's inevitable lot—what I did right, what I might have done better, what I wish had been mine to give her—is subsumed by a single question: *Did I love her enough?*

Enough to let her go.

Like Ammi and Abbu before me.

I remember you in fragments

Your eighteen years in scraps and scatterings.

Some are Kodak-generated memories,
like my earliest one of you, of us. London, Shepherd's Bush, 1966:
I sit holding you in my three-year-old arms,
a small dark bundle in a lemon blanket.
Holding a milk bottle to your tiny mouth.
I'm too young to know how you fought to live,
preemie baby released from an incubator.

My very first first cousin on both sides, you are to me
a baby sister to love and love me back.
I am your big Baji, and you're given a name
to rhyme with mine.
Rubina, Samina.

Big sister, big hopes, big promises.

I hold you. I hold you,
But not tightly enough.
Kodak itself a memory.

Abdul

for my Abbu

As a professor of multiethnic U.S. literature at Fresno State, I often teach the writings of immigrant authors. We ponder what it means to speak of "home" and belonging, and their opposites: homelessness, exile, and the experience of displacement so layered that people can spend their lifetimes unpeeling, unfolding, and repackaging it.

In my family, the layers of displacement are multigenerational: my grandparents' post-1947 migration from Bihar, India, to the port city of Karachi in the new Muslim state of Pakistan, followed by their move from East Pakistan before it became Bangladesh in a second bloody secession. My parents and their siblings chased after the red balloons of their dreams in Sindh and Punjab, in Denmark, Nigeria, and Malawi, and in suburban London, heart of the former empire that had, for better or worse, held their families together. As young adults, my own siblings and I scattered to different parts of the New World in the 1980s, while the puritanic General Zia-ul-Haq, with dark shadows beneath his eyes, took hold of Pakistan as a toddler might grab a wind-up toy, and reset it on a more orthodox, Saudi-aligned course.

But these family histories of migrations and the search for belonging are easy to recount. The story that never makes it into my classroom centers on a man who was family but not family, dependable and dependent, central to our lives yet inhabiting its peripheries. Present, but irrelevant to me.

Abdul had been working in our extended family in Karachi long before I was born. If he had a family name, I never asked what it was, and nobody seemed to know his early history. Family lore has it that an uncle of my father's discovered Abdul as a young waiter at Karachi's Nigaar Hotel shortly after Partition. Detecting the rhythms of his own birthplace in Abdul's singsong Bihari accent, my great-uncle offered him domestic employment, and Abdul exchanged his life among Karachi go-getters for the promise of room and board with fellow Bihari immigrants. A self-respecting but ultimately willing heirloom, Abdul served in this or that branch of the family as our vagaries dictated. Each time prospects overseas lured domestic employers like my parents away from Pakistan, Abdul adapted to new masters and mistresses, new working conditions, new rules, new beds.

  Shortly after my parents' marriage in Lalmonirhat, in present-day Bangladesh, my mother left her family to join my father in Karachi, over a thousand miles away. Here he lived with his sister Anwari and her husband Izhar, in the appropriately named neighborhood of Bihar Colony. Built by post-Partition immigrants and refugees on land assigned to them as compensation for their losses in India, Bihar Colony's most salient characteristic was the foul smell that emanated from its neighboring tanneries. By the time my mother arrived there in 1962, it boasted electricity but no gas, running water, drainage or sewage system. The inhabitants relieved themselves in collective chamber-pots of sorts in their backyards. Each household would wait for the jamadar to carry the pot out, empty it who knew where, and bring it back to resume its function in the backyard. When I was born, my mother washed my cotton diapers in water delivered to the house in sheepskin mashak sacks.

  Abdul had a place in my father's Bihar Colony home long before my mother did. He had been working there back when my father and aunt lived with their two other brothers, Idris and Ilyas, the siblings ranging in age from teens to early twenties. Their parents no longer alive, their grandmother cast a caring eye over them in this new land of Pakistan, where they had arrived on separate trains, with different destinies. They lived together: five members of a family who had left ancestral lands in India on the strength of a religious ideal—and Abdul, who had left the same patch of India for his own reasons. Their Bihar Colony home saw my uncle Idris's marriage, the birth of his first two sons, Ashar and Farrukh, and his subsequent employment in the Ministry of Labor in Islamabad; it saw my uncle Ilyas's—Chotepapa's—departure for school in Copenhagen and accountancy in London, and my great-grandmother's death from lung cancer. It also witnessed the marriages of my Phupijan, Anwari, as well as my father, and became home to their spouses. Through these years, Abdul occupied a room outside, in the courtyard. When my mother joined the family, Abdul welcomed the new bride but shooed her out of the kitchen, making it clear—much to Ammi's relief—that cooking was *his* turf.

Bihar Colony kept Abbu and his sister together until I was fifteen months old, at which point my parents, with Abdul and me in tow, moved to a flat near the zoo. Gandhi Garden—one of the few Karachi neighborhoods whose name still preserves its pre-Partition memory—became my brother Amir's first home. Phupijan and Phupajan settled into faculty housing at Karachi University, where Phupajan taught Library Science. Abdul joined them there when my parents moved to England.

Though Abdul had held me as a baby and maneuvered my stroller happily on the unpaved roads of my first neighborhood, I have no memory of him before the age of seven. In 1970 we had just returned from England, where my father obtained his graduate degree in physics and Ammi trained as an elementary-school teacher. In the initial months of what turned out to be a two-year sojourn in Karachi, we stayed with Phupijan and her growing family, which already included Asif and Shazia. I would see Abdul busy in the kitchen of their campus home. He was dark and gaunt, and even in this early memory, he has salt-and-pepper hair and a permanent stubble. Back then, he also wore a permanent frown, along with a cotton loongi wrapped around his thin hips and legs. Though he lived in the house, I don't remember where he slept. He was sullen and mysterious, and I felt a little scared of his scowl.

When my parents' attempt to re-root us in Karachi failed, we returned to Greenford, now with my baby sister Sadia, who was born eight months before the 1971 war with India. There I remember hearing that a change in Pakistani currency had rendered all of Abdul's savings, stashed away in secret pockets, obsolete. He had had only one ambition: to travel to India and revisit the birthplace he had left behind in his youth. But after losing his savings to an economic whim of the state's, he never spoke of going back to India again.

A couple of years later, my parents ended their second stint in Greenford, determined to make Karachi home again, and some twelve years later Abdul circuited back to us. My father's Kazmi cousins and Sajjad Phuppa, with whom Abdul had been living comfortably for many years, were migrating to America, and were anxious to find Abdul a new home. By the time Abdul moved into our home, 379-A/1, in December 1986, our twin Greenford families—my parents' family and Chotepapa and Khalammi's, who followed us back to Karachi—had fractured beyond recognition. It had been a year-and-a-half since we had lost Rubina. We were reeling in different directions, not knowing how to comfort ourselves or one another. A year before Rubina's death, Ammi had sought a divorce from Abbu and moved out of 379-A/1. But now, after Rubina's suicide, she lived as Sheikh Sahib's tenant next door to my father, unable to fully commit to the school-teacher from Mauritius whose love had served as a catalyst for the divorce, yet unable to return to Abbu, who would gladly have welcomed her back. My angry young man and I shared Sheikh Sahib's ground floor with Ammi, married but unable to support ourselves financially. Meanwhile, Amir had graduated from Stanford at the age of twenty and begun his first job in Palo Alto. The family was untethered.

It was my mother who offered to take Abdul in. He could sleep in the living room, she said. Sajjad Phuppa was relieved and grateful. But when Ammi took Abdul to meet my grandmother in her Kashana apartment, Abdul was disoriented and thought he might have to live there. Although he remembered Amma well from her time in Gandhi Garden twenty years ago, he took one look at the apartment complex and declared that Ammi's house was too big and too crowded for him. Ammi got him to stay with us at Sheikh Sahib's for a couple of nights, but he didn't want to be there.

"I want to live in Haroon Sahib's house," Abdul said.

And so he came to live in our Gulshan home, where Abbu and Sadia occupied the bedrooms on the upper level of 379-A/1 while English Playhouse claimed the downstairs. (Soon I, too, would move back into my old bedroom with my husband, until we left for Boston.) There was no room for an additional person, but Abdul had voiced a clear preference for living at 379-A/1, in my father's employment, and Abbu couldn't deny him.

The balcony overlooking our lane served as Abdul's bedroom. He refused to sleep on a mattress and preferred a traditional charpai bed instead with criss-crossed ropes like a hammock, held tightly together by a rectangular wooden frame on legs. My father installed a wall fan directly above Abdul's bed and a thick awning that provided shade on summer afternoons. In the winter, it served as a buffer from the cold when Karachi Decembers forgot their accustomed gentleness. Abdul kept a small tin trunk under his charpai that contained everything he owned, including gifts of new clothes from us that remained new because he never wore them. For twelve years, including all my time as a graduate student in Boston, our balcony served as Abdul's home. My father eventually built him a room of his own, in the part of our backyard where a fig tree once thrived, but my memory of Abdul binds itself to the balcony.

When Abdul wasn't chopping onions and simmering meat curries in our cubicle of a kitchen—the kitchen that had been part library and part playroom in its former life—or making his way to Kamran Market for some household item we needed, he liked to look out from the balcony. He had an astonishing way of lying on his charpai with head raised seven or eight inches off the pillow, hands clasped behind the thin stem of his neck, and knees bent, as though in imminent readiness to do sit-ups. Holding that posture for hours, he could see the level rooftops of the single-story homes on our street, neighbors walking up the stairs to their roofs to catch the cool evening breeze, gift of the Arabian Sea. He looked down at the passersby: mothers rushing their children between the marketplace at one end of the street and Maymar Apartments at the other; men as old as he, making their bent and patient way to Masjid-e-Noor, the Mosque of Light. (Though my father walked to the masjid five times a day in response to the muezzin's calls for prayer, Abdul chose to accompany him only once a year for the holiday prayer at Eid.) Looking, Abdul saw Allah's business meld with the business of Kamran Market. Butchers feathered dead chickens while the live ones looked on; mounds of mangoes lay ambering on the fruit seller's cart, and children lined up at Mr. Book, clamoring for the brightly colored stationery in protective plastic sheaths that gleamed with Karachi's dust.

Now and then, Abdul went to the barber's. He would study his hollow cheeks and deeply lined face in a hand-mirror while the barber's radio played filmee songs loud enough for the entire neighborhood to sing along. Abdul returned from these visits cropped and clean-shaven, and maybe even inclined to take a shower. Nobody knew why he was so averse to showering, but my parents, like all of Abdul's employers before them, seemed to have long relinquished any attempts to coax or coerce him into it. The same went for any attempt to persuade the socks off his feet: no matter how unbearably hot and humid the season, Abdul wore his socks, eschewing shoes unless he was going out.

Some mornings Abdul would come in from the balcony flashing a big grin at my father. One hand raised and fingers spread, he'd swivel his wrist from left to right in the time-honored South Asian gesture of negation and announce: "I'm not working today." Sometimes he volunteered that he was going to his old stomping grounds in the old part of the city, Saddar, to see a movie—Urdu or English, it didn't much matter because he couldn't hear very well anyway. On these occasions, Abdul would be dressed in his tin-trunk best, unaccustomed black shoes polished to perfection. He would then retrieve several of the rupees saved from his monthly salary. My father made a point of paying him in crisp new bills, knowing that Abdul prized cleanliness in cash, if not in his person, and Abdul would tuck these bills into a cloth pouch.

Over the years, he constructed many such pouches, stitching each addition onto the long cloth belt that held the independent units together. (After Abdul's death, my father would discover this uniquely designed belt of monied pouches among the contents of Abdul's tin trunk. The ten-rupee bills had become obsolete, but the rest of the currency was good enough to form a substantial donation to local charities and a madrassa.) Ready for his day about town, Abdul would pocket the bills, hail a rickshaw—no lowly public buses for him!—and be off. Though we worried that he might get lost, Abdul always found his way home at the end of the day.

Oblivious of the world as Abdul seemed to be, he surprised us occasionally with his grasp of social conventions. One afternoon, teenaged Sadia, outfitted in spandex, was exercising in the family room when Chotepapa happened to visit. Just as he was about to enter through the side door, Abdul rushed towards it and promptly slammed the door in my uncle's face. At the time, his sense of propriety amused us. It is only now that I realize the full implication of that gesture: not only did Abdul seek to protect my sister's modesty like an old-time gallant, but the slamming revealed that he considered himself more of an insider to our family than the uncle we saw as our second father.

Today, as I try to recall Abdul's passions—with a curiosity I lacked when we lived under the same roof—three things emerge in sharp relief: television soaps, tea, and cigarettes.

Abdul loved to watch the latest TV "drama serial" with us. While we planted ourselves on the couches and armchairs, Abdul rooted himself to the floor, some three feet away from the television screen. From time to time, he would interrupt the show to ask if the beautiful woman on the screen was our acquaintance Miss

So-and-So. He surprised us with his comparisons to long-departed relatives, or to people my parents had known years ago in Bihar Colony or Campus. Occasionally, he would point to a handsome young man in a romantic scene and tell us shyly, through a tooth-free smile: "See that man? That's me."

But my greatest connection with Abdul centered on our common love of strong, hot tea, no matter how warm the day. He would come in from the balcony and, eyes shining brightly, ask: "Should I make some chai?" Most of the time I said yes because I wanted it, and sometimes I said yes so he could justify making himself a cup. He made his way to the kitchen and put his favored kettle on the stove. It was a small, aluminum kettle with a handle that was neither heat-resistant nor firmly attached to the body of the container, and a lid that had an independent life, falling out entirely if you poured at too steep an angle. The kettle wavered threateningly as you guided boiling hot water out of its spout and at the same time tried to keep the lid from unleashing its scalding breath on your hand. Abdul, who dismissed any glossy whistling kettles that my mother or I tried to foist upon him, would grasp the overheated handle with one of his many rags, his thin, unsteady hand dangling the kettle over the teapot. Loose Lipton tea leaves awaited as he poured the hot water into the teapot and placed an embroidered tea cozy over it to keep it warm even if he himself was sweltering. While the tea steeped, he heated the buffalo milk my father had purchased that very dawn from what used to be Fateh Ally Sahib's dairy farm. Then out came the mismatched china cups, into which Abdul poured the rich, aromatic tea through a strainer. If it caught the light while he poured, the tea would glitter like a garnet waterfall. Then Abdul plopped milk and sugar into each cup to suit his own taste. He often carried several cups of tea as they chattered with their companion saucers on a tray, an ensemble that trembled its way to the living room.

Abdul made many, many cups of tea—for Abbu, for our guests, for his friend Bakhshu, the chaprasi peon at Urdu Science College where my father was now principal, and for me as I prepared to teach my Compulsory English class at Karachi University, having been hired as a part-time Co-operative Teacher shortly after my graduation. In the days after my father came home from the Cardiovascular Hospital, Abdul made twenty or thirty cups of tea a day for the colleagues and relatives who came to see him. Only once in a long while, if Abdul lay sick on his charpai, staging a prolonged hunger strike, did Abbu or I make a cup of tea for him and bring it to the balcony.

Abdul's third passion, for cigarettes, was as non-negotiable as his aversion to showers or his proclivity for socks. He welcomed the minty Marlboros I brought him on visits home from Boston and savored what he described as the cool, cool sensation of puffing on them. But it was the beeri that commanded his undying loyalty. Beeri, the poor man's cigarette throughout South Asia, shaped by the hands of rural women and children. Abdul's beeris were dry tobacco leaves rolled to resemble a cone. Deadly as any smoke, and Abdul loved them.

For me, the beeri ignites a memory that I'd rather not claim.

It was a few years into graduate school at Tufts University in Boston that I took a year's leave and returned to Karachi. I had fled from my marriage to the angry young man, wanted to evade the complicated new relationship emerging on the horizon, and had begun to question my doctoral ambitions. Then as now, I believed that when we're uncertain of the road ahead, the wisest course is to trace our steps back home, however we define it, and stay until we find our bearings again. My home in Karachi had contracted: my siblings, too, had flitted off to the US, and while English Playhouse still occupied the lower level of 379-A/1, Ammi herself no longer lived there. Abbu and Abdul were now the only individuals still together—two lonely men, whose separate destinies anchored in one home.

I returned from Boston to find that Abdul had taken to smoking his beeris in our poorly ventilated kitchen, rather than on the balcony.

"Abdul, please smoke outside," I'd say. Abdul would nod, and maybe head for the balcony and maybe not. In any case, he'd be puffing away on his beeri again another day. I was young and wounded, smarting from my own sense of powerlessness as a woman, and uncertain of my place in the world. One afternoon, the simmering resentment caught fire.

Studying from hefty anthologies of American and British literature for the oral exam that awaited me at Tufts, I could smell the air, suddenly grown pungent, as it wafted into my bedroom. This time I set my three-inch tome aside and marched towards the kitchen, a woman with a mission. I could feel the heat rising to my face like a fiery tidal wave, my heart thumping. Abdul was standing very still in the kitchen, his gaze fixed on some faraway vision beyond the window-screen, a beeri lodged in his long, dark fingers. He stood enveloped in its smoke and in the haze of his own thoughts. Though I used the polite second-person "aap" to address him, my voice grew shrill and unfamiliar to my own ears.

"How many times have I asked you not to smoke in the kitchen, Abdul? How *many* times?" I demanded. "But you just won't listen, will you? If you don't give a damn about your own health, you have no right to make the rest of us sick with that smoke!"

My voice trembled uncontrollably, like Abdul's hands when they carried teacups, and startled him out of his reverie. Dark clouds began to gather on his face, and for a moment he looked like the frightening figure of my childhood. Wrist swiveling and voice quivering with pain, he exclaimed: "Is this not my home, then? Is this *not* my home?"

And with that, he walked out of the kitchen with his beeri, towards the balcony.

I had wrung the question from him, the question that undergirded the flux of all the years. More cry than question, it reverberated with the faraway sound of Abdul's sandaled footsteps as he wandered, a young man, from India to Pakistan, Bihar to Karachi; from one home to the next, until those feet came to rest on our balcony.

Next thing I knew, Abdul was rummaging through his tin trunk, to return from the balcony a few minutes later with an armload of miscellaneous objects. He flung them onto the dining table at which I now sat, trying to assure myself that I had done the right and reasonable thing.

"Take *this* that you brought me!" Abdul said, hoarsely. "And *this* — and *this* — and *this*," as scarves, hats, mugs, and mint Marlboros accumulated in a shamefaced heap before me. Abdul had kept these Boston tokens over the years and remembered the giver long after the purchase had been forgotten. In a flash of recognition and remorse, I pressed my palms against each other, the most visible gesture of supplication I knew.

"Forgive me, Abdul!" I pleaded—once, twice, three times—as he turned his back on me and headed out towards the balcony again.

This time I flew after him, with his tin-trunk possessions huddled awkwardly in my arms. Crying like the baby he had carted on Bihar Colony's streets, I begged him to take them back.

Abdul relented. But if he ever smoked in the kitchen again, I have no memory of it.

I went back to Boston, took my oral exam, wrote my dissertation and defended it. I married Alex, the love I had tried to flee. I didn't return to Karachi for almost three years, and when I did, it was to see Amma, my grandmother, in the last week of her life. She died as she had lived, afloat on a memory of home, of mother and siblings left behind in Bihar, India.

A year after Amma's death, while Phupijan and her family were visiting from Nigeria, Abdul took ill. He had lost control of his bowels but refused to be cleaned or fed. Phupijan's daughters, Shazia and Saima, both medical students, tried to medicate and keep him hydrated with fruit juice, but Abdul had an intractable will. His body, already frail, had whittled down to a matchstick figure. Despairing, my father considered handing Abdul over to Abdul Sattar Edhi's shelter, internationally known for its generous care. But my mother, whose second marriage had ended after ten years, and who now lived a few miles away with her third, much younger husband, whom she had met at the hospital where Amma was admitted, asked Abbu if she might take Abdul to stay in their apartment for a while. Abdul had neither the strength nor the desire to get up from his charpai, so Ammi's husband, Shahzad, had to bundle him up in his soiled sheets and carry him down from the balcony into their car. In the apartment, he nursed and bathed Abdul back to health and restored him to my father a month later, ready for tea and beeri again.

I saw Abdul for the last time in 1998, a year before his death. I had used the excuse of a conference at Srinakharinwirot University in Bangkok to make a detour to Karachi with my still-new husband. A fleeting visit, its most salient memory is not my own goodbye to Abdul, but Alex's. After our bags had been carried downstairs to the car, all friends and family embraced and thanked, Alex turned back to the kitchen in search of Abdul, and to everyone's surprise—especially Abdul's—hugged his bony frame, showered or not.

And while I flapped my professional wings as an adjunct professor in Massachusetts, Abdul began to cough incessantly. Troubled, my father took him for medical tests at Civil Hospital. Abdul was diagnosed with tuberculosis, the disease that had swooped down on my father's ancestral village in Bihar in 1940 and claimed the lives of his young mother, his aunt, his grandfather, and his ten-year-old sister, Akhtari. Now my father took Abdul to the Ojha sanatorium in Karachi. Civil Hospital had refused to let Abdul stay in the ward for fear of his infecting other patients.

Though Abbu had been able to get Abdul a place at Ojha sanatorium thanks to his contacts, he was unable to keep him there. At first, the nurses complained that Abdul refused medication. My mother, once the new bride whom Abdul had shooed from his Bihar Colony kitchen, offered to care for him as an attendant, but she was told that women couldn't stay in the men's ward. Then my father hired a personal attendant for him, but the man, terrified of TB, avoided Abdul and spent his time outside on the grass. Eventually, the administrator declared that since Abdul's tuberculosis was at an incurable stage anyway, his bed would be better occupied by a patient whom they had some hope of saving.

Abdul could last for weeks or months in this condition, he said, and offered to write a letter recommending his admission to Edhi's shelter.

Where was my father to take Abdul now? He didn't have the physical strength to take care of him in protracted illness, my siblings and I couldn't extricate ourselves from our American lives long enough to come and help, and nobody would nurse an obstinate patient like Abdul for money. Abbu knew that instead of bringing him back to the home, he would have to deliver him to Edhi's. The Edhi office accepted Ojha sanatorium's recommendation but said that they would find a place for Abdul, not at the shelter close to our house in Gulshan, but at Edhi Home, their larger facility for charitable long-term care. Ammi wanted to check the place out before Abdul was sent there, so together my parents—failed spouses, but the most dependable of friends—made the excursion to the outskirts of Karachi on the Super Highway. Edhi Home struck them as a beautiful space—far from the urban fray, green and open. The long hall held a line of real mattresses, covered in clean linen. My parents spoke to one of the residents, an older man, who turned out to be garrulous in both Urdu and English.

"My daughters-in-law wouldn't have me, so I live here," he said. "Where else do you get a free half-pao of mutton to eat every day?"

In a voice knifed with pain, my father tells of the morning he went to discharge Abdul from Ojha sanatorium and help him into the ambulance that would take him to Edhi's. The moment Abdul saw that my father had come to get him out of the sanatorium, his eyes shone with the prospect of home. With sudden energy, and a smile that displayed only gums, Abdul sprang from the hospital bed, gathered his meager belongings, and with a child's trusting joy, got into the ambulance.

The ambulance drove away, and my father wept.

Nobody could have known that Abdul would die within four days—that the first two of those days, Abdul would lie in a transitional space, crowded and impersonal, waiting for Edhi Home to make room for him. By all accounts, he died on one of the comfortable floor-mattresses in the serene and bright hall, a garden beckoning from the window.

When Edhi officials called to inform my father of Abdul's death, he went to identify Abdul's body at the mortuary, accompanied by his closest friend—Taqi Uncle, for whom Abdul had made many a cup of tea—and by my mother's husband, Shahzad. The three men walked together through the giant deep-freeze, bodies laid out on the floor as well as on shelves built into the walls. They peered into one lifeless face after another until they found Abdul's. Then a kindly official told my father that Abdul's body had been washed and shrouded, and asked him whether he would like Edhi Home to take care of the burial. Abbu conferred with his friends, who advised that in light of his own frail health and Abdul's solitary life, it would be best to let the shelter arrange the burial.

"What time will you schedule Abdul's Janaza prayer?" my father asked the Edhi official. "I would like to be there for his last rites."

He was told that the burial would take place not in Karachi but in Hub, on the road to the Baluchi capital, Quetta. Their policy, the official said, was to wait a few days until they had accumulated enough bodies for a collective funeral. The prospect of a delayed and less-than-individualized tajheez takfeen appalled my father. Though he worried that few people would show up for Abdul's funeral, he chose to bring him home.

Since Edhi's practice—reasonable but unorthodox—was to bathe the dead using a garden hose, my father redid the entire ritual of the final ablution at home, in accordance with Muslim custom. Masjid-e-Noor provided the low wooden bed, or takht, for the purpose, as it had for my grandmother, and for Rubina before her.

In the backyard of our house, near Abdul's bedroom, my father, Ammi's husband, and two neighbors rest Abdul's body on the takht. They warm the water and scent it with leaves of the purifying neem tree. Then they proceed to bathe the body, each gesture sacred. Strong, gentle hands wrap Abdul in a spotless white sheet and set him down in the living room, cleaner than he had cared to be most days of his life. When my mother views him, his eyes are slightly open as though suspended in a private dream. Then the men shoulder the cloud-light takht and carry it to Masjid-e-Noor, my father at the head as Abdul's next of kin.

And so, on a temperate day in February 1999, Abdul left our home for the last time, some fifty years after he first arrived in the family. The Imam led the janaza service within sight of Abdul's balcony. Shopkeepers in Kamran Market had pulled their shutters down to join in the communal prayer for Abdul's final journey. In fact, the neighborhood had turned out in such numbers that the bus hired for the cemetery had no space to spare.

My father, with the busload of neighbors, carried Abdul's body to Haseenabad Cemetery, the same place where he and other men from our family had taken Amma three years earlier. Abdul lies somewhere near my grandmother, in a traditionally unmarked grave like hers, layers of Karachi earth smoothed over their Bihari dusts.

Blind Date

At twenty-one, my mother has striking eyebrows—expansive, dark, and gently converging. Lush like Lalmonirhat's hills that cradle the white colonial building she calls home. My father sees her for the first time during the wedding ceremony, reflected in a mirror. His heart beats easier at the sight of her light-skinned face, her downcast eyes, and still lips that have never been painted before this night. But the fine hair that rims the upper lip, and especially those eyebrows—so bold, so black, and sharply angled—make him unsure of his ability to keep her. Throughout their 23-year-old marriage, my father will have a recurring nightmare in which another man carries his wife away. (Until one does.) His howls will awaken his sleeping children.

A good Pakistani bride in 1962, my mother doesn't open her eyes to look upon her groom's face until the throng of geet-singing women in brilliantly hued, silk Benarsi saris have ushered her to the bridal chamber. They sit her down on a bed strewn with roses and gardenia, scooping the emerald silk of her flamboyantly flared paijama after her. A paisley print woven from threads of solid silver splashes across both the paijama and red tunic in provincial Bihari fashion—much to the bride's dismay, who had hoped for something trendier from the stores of the big city where, she hears, the groom and his sister live together. She sits inert as a still life, seeing and saying nothing, the ideal of chaste and pliable femininity.

The singing women help her cross her left leg and bend the right one, resting her chin upon her knee. They place her hennaed hands in a clasp around the knee—artfully, so that the bejeweled fingers of her right hand cover the shriveled left one that doesn't open. Adjusting her vermilion-and-gold dupatta over her head one last time, they exit, still singing of maiden temptresses and the fast-beating hearts of their suitors, satisfied to have staged just the right degree of bridal modesty and mystery.

When the groom and bride are finally alone, he lifts her veil of garlands as gently as he can. A teeka with a single ruby at its center glimmers on her forehead, its tiny white pearls brushing against those startling eyebrows. A fine hoop of gold, the bridal nose-ring she will never wear again. The groom's shapely hand reaches for her chin and tips it up from the knee, ever so slightly. As if on cue, the bride opens her eyes. She sees the slim, dark man her parents have chosen for her, an assistant professor of physics in faraway Karachi. Her eyes take in the crisp white shervani collar that encircles his neck, the wedding turban he will never wear again. The severe, pencil-thin mustache that restrains the generosity of his full lips. She looks into his big, dark eyes and wonders at their melancholy. And what she feels for him is not the heady passion of the romances she has secretly been writing, but the chill of alienation.

The man seems kind, if remote, as virginal as she is, and they spend the night telling the stories on which their forevers will depend. At twenty-nine, he already feels his life ebbing. In time she will discover the little boy he used to be, who lost his mother at eight, his father at eighteen. But on this night she sees the face of her future and recoils.

In the bathroom, the bride prays. Allah Mian, plant love in my heart for this man. She prays and prays, as if for summer rain in predicted drought.

Greenford's Gift

First memory of Greenford, Middlesex:

September, 1967, the beginning of a new school year. I'm a four-year-old in Mrs. Lord's class. She's a kind woman with a gentle voice and frequent smile, a dark "fringe" bordering her white forehead, and the rest of her short hair pulled back into a little ponytail. She has gathered us in a sitting circle around her chair as we share our "News." I have not shared any news yet—but once I begin sharing, it will always be the same news: that I have an older sister in Pakistan (my aunt Anjum's daughter, Naghmi). I am a quiet child, still feeling my way around the contours of the English language. But I understand well enough when the freckled girl with strawberry-blond hair sitting next to me scrunches her nose in a grimace and hisses: "Blackie. You're wearing boys' shoes."

In 1967 Ilyas and Talat Najmi, my Chotepapa and Khalammi, bought a small, semi-detached house on 13 Long Drive, and all seven of us—Chotepapa, Khalammi, and their baby daughter Rubina, as well as my parents, my younger brother Amir, and I—moved into it from urban Shepherd's Bush. (Within five years we'd be joined by Rubina's little brother, Azfar, and my baby sister, Sadia.) Eleven miles northwest of London, Greenford wasn't quite Surrey or Richmond, but it was considered a posh enough suburb that various commercial vans parked themselves on Long Drive every week, bringing their groceries to our neighborhood to sell. To the northeast, Long Drive hiccupped into Hill Rise, making its undulating way towards Oldfield Lane North, where the red double-decker buses parked outside the Greenford tube station. Across the street from the tube station was our "Post-Office Park," with its rocket-shaped ride and a spinner we called a merry-go-round. A little beyond the park stood the J. Lyons and Co. factory, a giant of the British food industry, about to begin its precipitous decline. To the east of Long Drive lay Birkbeck Avenue, which led to our schools, Oldfield and Coston, at the southern end of Oldfield Lane North. We Najmis were the first "coloreds" to move into the Long Drive-Hill Rise neighborhood.

If you stood facing 13 Long Drive, you'd see the stucco exterior, a brown that goes out of its way to be gloomy. In later years Chotepapa painted it a turquoise that buoyed the spirits of all the houses on Long Drive, though it probably raised eyebrows, too. To the left you'd see the drawing room's rectangular bay window, divided into narrow panels, and each panel descending from a square; Chotepapa and Khalammi's bedroom window above it, and the smaller window of the box room that Amir and I shared parallel to it, on the right. My parents' bedroom, also located upstairs, wouldn't be visible because it looked out onto the backyard, as did our one bathroom (separate from our one toilet) adjacent to it. All our windows had the same slate blue trim as the front door, and all the front doors on the odd-numbered side of Long Drive shared the same design: vertical panels topped with nine little frames of opaque glass, and those glass squares softened with a curvy line in the wood above them. (The even-numbered houses of Long Drive had front doors outlined in red triangles.) It's a door that is at once idiosyncratic and the suburban norm. The slate blue of our front door has a brassy "13" affixed to it, right above the slot through which the postman slips the longed-for blue aerogrammes from Pakistan.

You'd see, if you looked, that Long Drive dwellers all

inherited the same basic front yard: a concrete square with patches of planter beds in each corner and one in the center. (During our second Greenford stint, John the Scotsman enlivened number 13's ground with pink-toned crazy paving while we children surrounded him with our chatter.) If you lingered until the spring, you'd witness our front yard's precious period of beauty, when pansies and pastel roses filled it with color and fragrance, the meticulously crafted white snowbells looking as though they were about to tinkle out a tune. And here, the children's biggest favorite: snapdragons in vivid color combinations! We called them our rabbit flowers and pressed our little thumbs and index fingers strategically on either side of the rabbit's jaw to make it open and close in conversation.

If you entered through the front door of 13 Long Drive, you'd find the white banister and carpeted staircase to your right, both of which often served as our playgrounds. To your left would be the drawing and dining rooms. The bay window of the drawing room beckoned— you could sit on the ledge if you were small enough and observe the world going by. In our family album there's a photograph of five Najmi children sitting on the couch in front of that window, the silhouetted trees on the rust-colored curtains forming the backdrop. We're celebrating Sadia's second birthday in 1973, none of us having arrived at double digits yet. Everyone looks cheerily focused on the cake or the camera—except for Rubina and me, perched at opposite ends on the wooden arms of the couch, sticking our tongues out at each other, eyes shut. We had been quarreling over ownership of the decorations, though in this picture Rubina has acquired the coveted paper lace circling the cake and tied it stylishly around her face with a little bow on the top of her head, while I have transported a big, red, plastic flower from one of Sadia's gift boxes to my own head.

Straight across from the front door, at the opposite end of the narrow hallway, lay the kitchen. It was small, like all the other rooms, but white and bright and warm. The mothers made curries on the stove and used the door of the pantry, which opened vertically, as a space to roll out their chapatis. Against the kitchen's left wall was a narrow, white counter with stools underneath it for the children. In our rushed mornings before school, Chotepapa served us Weetabix, or 8-till-1 muesli, or—Rubina's untiring favorite—Ready Brek, the porridge that made us all feel like Goldilocks. In later years, Amir and I would be walking home from Coston on an October day, the light already dimming as we kicked our way through the rustling leaves on the pavement. By the time we got home we'd be cold and ravenous, but we could already smell the warm, buttered toast that Khalammi, the only parent at home to greet us, would have ready on the stove's overhead toasting tray.

The kitchen door led to the backyard, and as you stepped out, immediately to your right you would see another door, part of the dark, wooden fence which opened into the alley that separated us from number 15. On days when the rubbish was collected, one of our grownups would take the big dustbins out through that door. The backyard was two long strips of lawn with a narrow concrete path running down the middle and leading to the garage in the back. I loved its symmetry. For Rubina's third birthday we all acquired a swing on the left lawn, adjacent to Mr. and Mrs. Brown's backyard. The garage looked like a little house itself: a brick building with a front door and two little windows on either side of the door, edged in that same slate blue. It opened into the alley, but since Chotepapa parked his Morris Minor on the street, the garage served as a tool-haven instead. For us children it afforded a good shelter when we played hide-and-seek, and it was a place dark and undefined enough to be molded according to the needs of our imagination.

We exchanged few words with the Browns, a couple with two invisible teenage sons. Our parents worried that we were too noisy for the staid English couple, but there was nothing to be done about that. I was fascinated when, on summer days, Mrs. Brown, a youthful forty-something, chose to sunbathe in her backyard. She'd lie perfectly still on her stomach, dead to the world, like a blond Sleeping Beauty in a bikini, whose smooth bronze back had been released from its bra strap while she awaited her prince. Mrs. Brown struck me as the most glamorous woman in Greenford. I tried to get a peek at her breasts from this angle and that, wondering if I'd grow a couple of those some day. My mother and aunt weren't likely to oblige by lying outdoors in bra and underwear.

Nextdoor to the Browns, towards Birkbeck Avenue, lived the MacNamaras with their five children. They were a lively Irish family and seemed more like us than anyone else we knew on Long Drive. The father had a regular job and sometimes also cleaned his neighbors' windows on Long Drive. The mother worked the night shift in a factory. Ammi and Khalammi exchanged greetings with her from their backyards. Sometimes while Khalammi was hanging the washing out to dry, Mrs. MacNamara shared her anticolonialist, anti-English sentiments across the pointy red hats of Mrs. Brown's ceramic gnomes. Three of her children—Christine, Sean, and Denise—were young enough to be our playmates, but we didn't see them every day because they went to a Roman Catholic school. They seemed to accept the fact that whenever their dad drank, there would be trouble at home. Though our parents didn't allow us to go over to their house, they welcomed the MacNamara children to come and play with us, especially in the summer. On those summer days we sometimes threw a sheet over the swing to make a "wigwam" and used the seat as a table around which to gather for our powwow. Linda, who lived across the street in the apartments bordering Hill Rise—oh, how I envied her the communal building with its black, wrought-iron stairways on either side!—often joined us.

We didn't know any children to the south of our house. Ron's corner shop was our big attraction there, the only commercial entity in our residential area. The small store with its essentials and chocolate treats was part of Ron's home. When I returned to visit Greenford a lifetime later as an eighteen-year-old, Ron was still there, and from his corner shop I was able to buy the perfect card for Sadia's tenth birthday: one with a picture of the Swedish pop group ABBA on the cover.

What Khalammi remembers about the southern end of Long Drive is a neighbor a couple of doors down from us. She was an elderly woman, whose daughter would position her in the bay window of the living room before leaving for work, and there the woman would stay until her daughter returned at the end of the day. When Khalammi worked at Oakshots, she would pass by the woman's window, look into it, and wave. Sometimes the woman waved at Khalammi first. It was a small, essential ritual. Then one day the elderly neighbor no longer appeared in the bay window, and the milk bottles delivered to her door each morning accumulated.

For decades J. Lyons and Co. had been Greenford's biggest employer and, at its height, also the biggest food empire in the world. After World War I, when the company chose Greenford for its expansion, it gave the town's population, which had dwindled since the late nineteenth century, a lifeline. Its location on the

Grand Union Canal was strategic, with easy connections to and from the London docks. Already in the early 1920s Greenford afforded access to central London and to the West Midlands on the Great Western Railway. The development of Western Avenue had begun, and even the Underground was inching its way towards Greenford, having reached Acton, four miles away. (As it turned out, Greenford tube station didn't open until June 1947, a couple of months before the British Partition of India and the creation of Pakistan.) The strategic expansion proved immensely successful for J. Lyons and Co. In the 1920s, the Greenford factory's industrial preeminence was such that King George V and Queen Mary visited it on multiple occasions.

Before Lyons came to Greenford in 1921, it had already had a vibrant existence for over thirty years, catering such events as the Buckingham Palace garden tea parties and the Wimbledon tennis championships. Its white and gold tea houses promised quality at a reasonable price throughout London and its suburbs and would thrive for almost ninety years, until 1981.

With the Greenford expansion, the company diversified into tea and coffee processing, and the manufacture of all kinds of foods, including confectionery, baked goods, ice-cream, and cereal. Rubina's Ready Brek was invented right here in Greenford. After World War II, J. Lyons and Co. diversified the British palate with frozen foods. It licensed the American Wimpy hamburger brand-name for use in Britain, establishing a hugely successful fast-food chain, the first of its kind in the country. In 1973, Lyons acquired the booming American ice-cream chain Baskin-Robbins. Even as late as 1990, after the company's merger with Allied Breweries, Allied-Lyons bought the world's largest doughnut and coffee chain, the US-based Dunkin' Donuts. It seems that Britain and the US, outgoing and incoming world powers of the twentieth century, still angled for dominance in the food industry long after the British empire had crumbled.

Breadth of food production aside, J. Lyons and Co. employed state-of-the-art technology in its manufacturing process. It built, operated, and sold the world's first office computer: LEO, or Lyons Electronic Office. And one more highlight on the company's postwar pages: Margaret Thatcher, after graduating from Oxford with a degree in chemistry, worked in a Lyons food laboratory, researching ways to make ice-cream airier and easier to scoop. (Then while I was at Coston, as Education Secretary she took the free one-third pint of milk away from schoolchildren over seven years old, inspiring the nationwide chant: "Thatcher, Thatcher, milk snatcher!")

As I write this, I am gazing at the black-and-white stills of a video posted on the webpage of British Pathé. The images depict a cold day in 1928 when the Prince of Wales—later Edward VIII, who abdicated for the love of an American woman—visited the Lyons factory in Greenford. The incongruities occlude my sense of reality. Those roads and pavements on which a crowd awaits to greet the Prince are *Greenford*, where my first consciousness is grounded. The overcoats in which the men, including Edward VIII, are bundled up, look just like my father's dark gray winter coat, the one I never saw him wear outside of his English life. Yet the cars and vans are from another time, as are the Girl Guides with whom the Prince shakes hands, and the workers, mainly women, waving goodbye with eager, open faces as the royal car leaves the factory. They wear long gowns and white caps. I imagine them returning to this day in 1928 ever after, for the memory and the story: a day when a true-blue prince came into their lives, curious about what they did on their feet, how they spent their long hours every day, how they processed and packaged tea—his royal fingers even touching some of the packages and helping them along. "Some housewives will buy packets of tea which the Prince of Wales has helped to make," one title card comments.

It's always about the tea. After all, tea is the world's most-consumed drink, after water. Chai: South Asia's elixir. Many a student on the Indian subcontinent has relied on it to fuel those all-nighters during exam season. Even class divisions blur a little where love of tea converges, the separate and unequal cups notwithstanding. Ammi and Khalammi's side of the family, the Balkhis, especially, loved their tea. Strong, black chai, creamy and sweetened, heightened that mystic strain which in family lore began with the 8th-century Sufi saint Ibrahim bin Adham. In 1838 this Balkhi ancestor was introduced to readers of English literature by the Romantic poet Leigh Hunt—and Hunt must have identified with "Abou Ben Adhem" enough to have a line from the poem serve as his epitaph. The Balkhis' Sufi strain emerges again in the 13th-century Persian poet Rumi and, apparently, still runs like an unworldly current through his descendants in South Asia. What tea could do for their imaginations and memory! I imagine my still-young grandfather and his teenaged daughter Talat lifting teacups to their lips while ghazals pour out of them in their Saidpur garden. My grandmother, Amma, an honorary Balkhi by virtue of her wifely devotion to my grandfather, who learned to live with so little, permitted herself this one indulgence besides memoir-writing.

You see why South Asians are perceived as garrulous; it's the chai that makes us so. Chai has an intimate relationship to words. It unwinds our tightest emotional coils, coaxes us out of our bundled-up individualities into the shared, open spaces of the communal. Fired with memory and imagination, this chai-inspired propensity for words yields poems and stories. (And yes, a cup of hot tea with cardamom keeps me company as I write this.) Let it be said: South Asians measure the quality of human exchanges, the quality of creation, by the teacup.

That the story of chai should be so inextricably linked to South Asia's colonization, then, might be one of history's wryest ironies. At first the British East India Company, fortified by an army of its own, grew opium on Indian lands—at the cost of food and cotton—in order to trade with China for tea. But by the nineteenth century, tea cultivation in India's Assam province and in Ceylon (Sri Lanka) had become a staple of full-fledged empire. So when I look at the stills of Prince Edward's visit to the Lyons factory in 1928, I am seeing tea leaves from India and other British colonies (including Nyasaland/Malawi, where Khalammi and Chotepapa's family spent three years before returning to Karachi in 1978) arrive in Greenford for processing. Space, time, and histories converge. The barges that carry the tea have sailed from the London docks to the factory's Custom House on the Grand Union Canal. At Lyons the tea is inspected, blended, packaged, and distributed. But many brown hands, mostly women's, have picked the tea leaves with deft fingers before Prince Edward ever touched a package in Greenford.

As I click on the Lyons factory stills one after the other, another incongruity: my eyes search among the workers for an image of my mother. But she hasn't even been born yet. In another forty years, she'll be there at Lyons, a woman in her mid-twenties, wearing the yellow factory gown, a white muslin kerchief tied over her head in such a way that it resembles a princess's crown. She'll be the only one-handed worker in the coffee packing department, her left hand having shriveled up long ago, before Pakistan's birth, when as a toddler she dipped her fist into a pot of steaming tea—yes, tea—in Patna, India.

In 1967 Ammi stands among other women in the Lyons assembly line, eight hours a day, focusing all her mental energy on grabbing the glass jars full of coffee beans as fast as she can, pulling them off the conveyor belt and into cardboard boxes for another group of women to wrap in plastic. One false move and the glass jars will smash. She'll be responsible for the waste and the mess, and worse yet, for disrupting her coworkers' similarly focused missions. The forewoman issues her a warning during her first week: one hand or two, if she isn't able to keep up with the other women, she'll have to go. My mother, equipped with a master's degree in political science from Karachi University but with few options in this alien land, challenges her one good hand beyond its known physical limits. And she keeps her job.

Between eight o'clock in the morning and five in the evening, my mother had forty-five minutes for lunch. Instead of getting off her feet, Ammi ran all the way home in her white kerchief—past the tube station on Oldfield Lane North, up Hill Rise, down to 13 Long Drive. Her two-year-old son, Amir, would already be sitting in the bay window, waiting impatiently for the fifteen minutes they will spend together before she runs again, all the way back to the Lyons factory, before her forty-five minutes are up.

During this time, my father and aunt were at home with Amir and Rubina, while I was at Oldfield Infants' School, in Mrs. Lord's class. My father was writing his master's thesis in physics, though he would have liked to be working on a doctorate. He already had a Master of Science degree from Karachi University—

in fact, he had a teaching position at Urdu Science College in Karachi and was officially on a four-year leave from there—but with a family to support, a Ph.D. would require at least six years to complete. Abbu let the doctorate dream go and opted for a second master's degree instead; after all, a British M.Sc. carried more prestige than a Pakistani one and would serve him well upon his return to Urdu Science College. So he enrolled in Chelsea College of Science and Technology (now part of King's College), whose degrees were awarded by London University. Until the thesis-writing, he took classes in the evenings and worked during the day. That is, once he found work.

"Two things go against you, Mr. Najmi," a sympathetic official at the employment agency told Abbu. "One is that you're highly qualified. The other is that you're colored."

A memory that still prickles Abbu, now eighty years old, centers on his application for a position in the state-owned telephone department. He knew he had scored 100% on the math test and that his grammar was solid enough to have served him well on the English test as well. There remained only the reading test. Abbu read aloud the full page given to him. At the end of the application process, the woman who appeared to be the chief evaluator told him:

"We're sorry to have to reject your application for the job. You see, there was one word on the page you read for us that you pronounced in such a way that we couldn't understand."

I'm on the phone with Abbu, my Sunday morning call from California to Karachi. He mulls over the word, pronounced or mispronounced almost a half-century ago.

"That word was 'river,'" he tells me. "Maybe I said 'reever';

or maybe I pronounced the final 'r' instead of saying 'rivuh.' But how incoherent could I have been?" he asks, his voice crackling with the memory of the humiliation.

On that day my thirty-something father, dignified and restrained, fired back: "Your prejudice is so pronounced that nobody can miss it. I'm very sure that no other applicant did as well on those tests, and yet you deny me the job based on this one-word excuse."

The woman seemed sorry. "I apologize on my own behalf as well as the Telephone Department's," she said. And so saying, she walked him out of the office, all the way to the elevator.

Eventually, Abbu found a job as a file clerk in an insurance company. It paid about ten pounds a week, of which two or three pounds went towards the tube fare from Greenford to Holborn.

"I might as well have sat at home and collected unemployment," he says. "It would have been as much as six or seven pounds a week. And I would have qualified because I had a family to support."

"Why didn't you apply for it, Abbu? You could have studied full-time for a while and maybe gotten that Ph.D."

"And eat for *free*?" he asks, incredulous.

After his regular work day was over, my father would do overtime until it was time for his evening class at Chelsea College or for the Spoken English Course for Overseas Graduates he was now taking, sponsored by the Inner London Education Authority. He enjoyed the Spoken English class. At the end of it, he was one of only two students out of fifteen or sixteen to be appointed as supply (or substitute) teacher by ILEA.

"The truth is that most of us who arrived in England from India, Pakistan, or the West Indies needed time to tone down our accents," Abbu tells me. "It's one thing to teach at the college level. But we were applying to teach at high schools in the inner city. How could we have engaged those young people with our thick accents?"

Abbu's Pakistani accent seems not to have mattered to his high school students. On the phone with me, he recalls in vivid detail the moments that made his supply teaching a gratifying experience.

"Hurlingham Girls' School—that was my best teaching time in England," says my father.

Hurlingham Girls' was a comprehensive school, with about 2500 students and a hundred or so teachers. Every day some number of teachers wouldn't show up to take attendance, and the Deputy Headmistress, Mrs. Gascoign, would have to be in several places at once. Luckily, my father was always there early to help her out.

"You know what she told me one day?" Abbu says on the phone. "She said: 'Mr. Najmi, I don't know what I would do without you!'" His voice is beaming.

He recalls that the class with a reputation for out-of-control behavior was Form 4S. They hardly had a permanent class-teacher because nobody wanted that job. But names and events from that class, small and fleeting, have stayed with my father across decades and continents.

"Millicent, whose parents came from the West Indies, spoke deep and loud—it was like a roar from the belly. One day, I was supervising preparations for Open House in Form 4S when another teacher—a white South African woman—came by to offer her help. The moment Millicent saw her at the door, she bellowed: "We don't want you! Mr. Najmi's here to help us."

"Millicent," my father said to her later, "think about the meaning of your name. How big can a milli-cent be? So much sound out of something so tiny!"

A white student named Barbara in Form 6 once asked my father how old he was.

"Oh, you missed by just one year, Sir! What a pity you're younger than my mum," she laments. "I would have proposed you for her."

By 1970, Abbu had proved his mettle at a variety of Inner London high schools. Ammi had gone from Lyons factory to office job, to ILEA's Teachers' Induction Course, and supply teaching in primary schools. But my father's four-year leave from Urdu Science College was up. Rather than apply to stay, my parents decided to return to Karachi, shortly after my seventh birthday. The fracturing of family as we had known it so overwhelmed Chotepapa and Khalammi that within a couple of months they followed suit, renting 13 Long Drive out to strangers.

Two years later, the process would reverse itself: my parents would follow Khalammi and Chotepapa back to England. By August 1972, we were all at Long Drive again, now numbering nine Najmis. In another two-and-a-half years my parents would return to Karachi for good. My father would rise through the ranks and eventually retire in 1994 as principal of Urdu Science College. My mother would found a preschool in our living room, which would grow one year at a time until it became Meadow Secondary School on its own grounds. But for a couple of years Greenford was my home again and would remain so until I was almost twelve years old.

Blackie. You're wearing boys' shoes.

How do four-year-olds know to be so canny and so cutting? In one fell swoop the girl had flung me out of both her race and gender communities, a pariah. Though I made no reply, and though Helen and I eventually became good friends, her comment had planted itself in me, a seed that grew independently of my personal relationships, throwing down roots like tentacles, whose grip I could weaken with time and education, but from which I would never free myself entirely. It grew green and thick and strong, flourishing on the casual, everyday racism of Greenford's schoolchildren. And it fostered layers of unbelonging, of wanting to be good enough, which would thrive long after Greenford itself had become an abstraction, past tense.

But you love the first landscape of your consciousness, even if it's a complicated love, and you identify with its culture on many subliminal levels. However nondescript it may appear to an outsider—with its row upon row of semi-detached houses, its small, green patches of park, its tube station like any other on the Central line, and the habitual opaqueness of its skies—you invest it with your first awareness of being, and it claims you thereafter with a tender tyranny.

Returning to Greenford as a nine-year-old in 1972 and staying until I was almost twelve meant that I recovered several of my former Oldfield friends in Miss Betty Cox's class at Coston Junior Girls' School—including Helen, whose face turned a beetroot red when she recognized me. It also meant that I was more keenly aware than ever of the "Pakis Out!" graffiti on buildings, in parks, and at the tube station. It meant wincing in silent shame when older English girls walked past me in the Glaxo's field remarking, "Funny smell!" as if to each other, and pinching their noses for emphasis. It meant that to walk the mile home from school was to contrive to walk with English girlfriends, for fear that some of the Coston boys being released from school at the same time might choose to kick my behind again or spit on me as I made my way home. I don't remember how often this actually happened; what matters is that I expected it to happen. (Amir, on the other hand, would get beaten up in his schoolyard at playtime by a couple of Sikh boys who wore their long hair in cotton-wrapped buns, and who had a score to settle about the Partition of Punjab.) It meant the heart's thumping terror at the sight of any group of white teenage boys approaching, because they might well be aligned with the neofascist National Front skinheads, who, on two occasions beat up my uncle Shahid, Noshaba Phuppi's husband, as he returned home from teaching high school. They had a verb for it: *Paki bashing*, which became the noun *Paki Bashee* to refer to the white supremacist vigilantes. At the very least, it meant that if Pakistan seemed to be defeating England in a cricket match at Lord's or the Oval, the low wall under construction around the front yard of 13 Long Drive would be torn down in vengeance overnight. Not that either Amir or I thought of sharing our terrors with our parents. At our age it just seemed the natural order of things.

But there was another, long-ago Greenford. If I had known of it as a child, Greenford might have served as a richer crucible for me. I might have forged a relationship with it that transcended the hungers and hurtings of my own little historical moment.

Greenford—or Grenan Forda, to go back to its ninth century name—was already a substantial suburb in the early 1970s when I was growing up there. Its history didn't concern me then, nor was it taught at either Oldfield or Coston schools, but it's a quaint history nonetheless, of an ancient parish in the ancient county of Middlesex. (In the seventies Middlesex was still an essential part of our postal address.) Entirely agricultural until the mid-nineteenth century, Greenford finds mention in the *Domesday Book*, that mother of all surveys compiled in 1086 so that William the Conqueror would have lands, livestock, landowners, and property taxes at his fingertips. The *Ealing Times* of August 24, 2012, drawing on the *Domesday Book*, tells us without a hint of satire that in 1086 Greenford's population consisted of "27 people and a Frenchman."

Fast-forward through eight centuries of bucolic pace: in 1856 an eighteen-year-old named William Henry Perkin discovers the world's first aniline dye—Tyrian purple, which he calls Mauveine—and the following year he establishes a chemical factory on the banks of the Grand Union Canal, west side of Oldfield Lane. It becomes the foundation of the coal-tar industry: aniline from coal-tar and dye from the aniline. So it is that Greenford finds itself the epicenter of the global chemical industry's phenomenal eruption. Perkin goes on to show the world how to affordably manufacture alzarin, the brilliant red, which until that point could be obtained only organically from the madder root. Greenford legend has it that the Grand Union Canal changed color like a chameleon, depending on the dye of the week. In short, as *British History Online* will tell you, for a good seventeen years after his first aniline dye discovery, Perkin's Greenford dyes dominated the British market. Perkin was knighted in 1906, on the fiftieth anniversary of the aniline color purple.

Though he had business acumen, Perkin the chemist was in it for the thrill of the research rather than for commerce. By 1874 he had sold his business and devoted himself to his laboratory, located across from the factory. Here, among other things, he synthesized coumarin, applying a process which came to be known as the Perkin Reaction. Coumarin launched the perfume industry as we know it.

The closure, in 1885, of the factory Perkin had founded thirty years earlier was responsible in great part for Greenford's diminished population at the end of the nineteenth century. The site of Perkin's laboratory is now a distribution center for untold loaves of Hovis bread. Nothing remains in Greenford of either the factory or the laboratory; their last vestiges vanished in 1976.

But looking out at the unorthodox palms of my backyard in Fresno, California, a professor of English unmoved by the sciences as a schoolgirl, I think of William Henry Perkin. What is it about him, about my recent discovery of him that quickens the pulse and tightens the throat? What sends me flying to husband and children with each new detail of his life? With triumph tinged with sadness?

I tell my two children that most schools in Perkin's day didn't give much space to such frivolous pursuits as the sciences. His own father had hoped to make an architect of his youngest son. But at the City of London School William had a teacher who conducted chemical experiments during lunch break. The boy gave up his lunches to observe. At fifteen he persuaded his father to let him enroll at the Royal College of Science. Three years later, as a laboratory assistant looking for a way to synthesize quinine to combat malaria, he made the breakthrough discovery of aniline in his home laboratory and patented it.

Perkin "retired" at thirty-six, with the means to support his love of research and the values to prioritize it over the seductions of commercial glory. Let Germany go on to build a chemical empire. For Perkin, it was about the inquiry, about venturing beyond the known frontiers of knowledge, seeking new horizons, Odysseus-like. It was about not settling. Not selling out. The man showed us that we could keep our feet firmly rooted in the earth without withdrawing our heads from the clouds.

Perkin has given me the memory of another Greenford. Thirty-seven years after leaving the west London suburb—a psychic terrain as much as a geographical one—I can look back on it with something other than an anguished mix of tenderness and terror. Today I can go to Google Satellite, insert myself at Long Drive, where the low wall rebuilt one cricket season still encloses number 13. I can make a right onto Birkbeck Avenue, past Stanley and Jeymer Drives, which signaled the proximity of home on our long walks back from school; past 14 Birkbeck Way where my friend Carolyn Waller lived. I make another right and walk the little yellow figure that is me onto Oldfield Lane North, past my elementary school on the left. I can linger there for a moment or dash across the street, the way I did at the age of five, so excited to see my mother that I pulled away from Inge, our babysitter, and let the oncoming car bounce me toward Ammi instead. I keep walking southward then, across Western Avenue (part of the now roaring A40), to where Coston Middle (now Primary) School stands, on my right. It's all eerily, incredibly there. But it's the buildings I can't see on Google Satellite, can't touch with the little cursor-figure, that tug at my heart and urge my footsteps in electronic wanderings around Oldfield Lane North.

It came from somewhere here—Greenford's glorious purpling of the world. For the first time ordinary people, and not just royalty, could afford to dress in purples and reds. I try to wrap my head around what this means. Greenford's synthetic dyes, far more economically manufactured than colors obtained organically from plants, insects, and mollusks, turn a black-and-white picture of the world into a carnival of colors. The teenaged William searches for a cure and finds beauty instead. Beauty by accident. Beauty made available to you and me, straight out of this factory on Oldfield Lane North. And as if that isn't earthshaking enough, from the laboratory across the street, Greenford gives us the gift of fragrance.

I can live with this Greenford. The Greenford of scented rainbows. I can love it, revere it, take pride in it. I can trump the seventies and their National Front skinheads with the nineteenth-century history of one man's intellectual pursuits. I can look beyond a childhood of unbelonging, to the scholar, the researcher, the writer of some eighty articles. The scientist—the artist—who painted the world in brilliant hues and perfumed it.

And all of a sudden Greenford emerges from decades of historical amnesia to share this epiphanous moment with me: the summer of 2012 sees the announcement in a local paper of a new, £90 million high school in Greenford, to open in autumn 2013. Its name: William Perkin Church of England High School. Specializing in science, it will serve twelve hundred students, providing them with an ample library and laboratories that look out on green, open spaces. But that's not the first thing you'll notice on this campus. William Perkin Church of England High School will stand out among English high schools because everywhere you turn, you'll be reminded of Greenford's gift to the world. Twelve hundred blazers and twelve hundred ties in Perkin's purple—the rich, regal purple of the people.

fragment 2

Toddling in Greenford, you liked to eat dirt.
Small fistfuls of earth, an appetite for life.
Bad child, bad child.

I envied you all your toys, especially the bride doll,
eyes opening and closing behind the white veil.
And your father, the fun parent, who unlocked the world for us.
Greenford's princess, lucky Rubina.

How is it you don't smile in our childhood photographs?
Darkest of the five of us, how dark
the brooding eyes.
Odd one out.

And there we are sticking our tongues out at each other
from opposite ends of the couch.
Both wanted the cake decorations for our hair,
so you pulled out a fistful of mine.
Bad Rubina.

Fireworks, or the Bombing of Karachi

It's the sounds that terrify. First, the dreaded siren, menacing in its ascending scale and filling the air as it swoops down, reaches into my body and hollows out my stomach. Coming from where, exactly—Masjid-e-Noor? Or from vans equipped with loudspeakers keeping vigil in Gulshan's lanes? It's part wail, part nagging, but there's no mistaking the threatening tone. Drop all play, grab the ball of cotton wool some grownup gives me, stuff it in my ears so I don't go deaf from a blast in the vicinity, between my teeth so I don't bite my tongue off. Run to shelter, under tables, under chairs, and hope that my mother, clutching my baby sister—so new to the world—will make it, too. Brace myself for the deafening thuds with which bombs will hit the earth, shaking the ground. It might be the FEE FI FO FUM of an ogre except that this is no leisurely giant's pace. If an explosion doesn't deafen me, my own heart's pounding will. I am eight years old. I don't want to die.

The siren means instant blackout, so here I am, hunched in the darkness, trembling. Thinking *but I'm with my siblings, my cousins, my friends, and we were just playing*. How did the game get so deadly?

Time stretches while I crouch, disoriented in the darkness, tasting the cotton wool between my teeth and praying that if we have to go, one mighty bomb-blast takes us all together, leaving no-one behind to sorrow.

We don't know it yet, but this will prove to be a temporary stay in Karachi, sandwiched by life in suburban London for another few years. Our family of five have joined Khalammi, Chotepapa, Rubina and Azfar in their newly built home, 465-A/1 in Gulshan, a five-minute walk away from where our house, 379-A/1, awaits finishing touches and electricity. Since war broke out between Pakistan and India, 465-A/1 camouflages itself in a layer of cheap, mud-colored paint, as do all neighboring homes. Roadsides are dug up to form trenches, should people be caught out of doors during an air raid. Indoors, the adults observe such safety measures as they can: they paper the windows for blackouts, taping them at the edges as though that will keep the glass intact, the tape itself a gesture of agency in the face of absolute powerlessness.

Nine of us live in the two-bedroom home at 465-A/1, plus a domestic worker whose Bengali ancestry renders him mildly suspect for a couple of weeks. *Does he really take a flashlight up to the rooftop during blackouts to invite Indian warplanes to bomb us?* Since war broke out, Abbu and Chotepapa's youngest sister, Noshaba, is staying with us along with relatives from Bihar Colony whom Chotepapa has invited to Gulshan because their neighborhood has been heavily bombed. They include my elderly and incapacitated great-aunt, to whom the blackouts make no difference because she cannot see. Ammi and Khalammi's mother, my Amma, is also staying with us. At night, most of us occupy floor space. To accommodate everyone at meal times, Khalammi and Ammi spread a big, white bedsheet on the living room floor, dot it with dinner plates along the edges, and plant the curries, veggies, or daal in the center with rice and chapatis. The women may worry about rationings and hoardings, but we children who border the bedsheet with crossed legs and holiday appetites never go hungry. The guest family from Bihar Colony includes two girls my age, Kauser and Kishwer, who infuse the wartime winter with giggly warmth.

Kishwer is particularly fun to frighten because the slightest "boo!" startles her.

A second siren signals that we have survived the bombings for now and can go back to the patriotic songs on the radio—the lyrics of which I will remember forever because they sing a simple world of good and evil, victory and defeat, enemies and martyrs. Some are sweet love songs to Pakistan, like two of Sohail Rana's compositions, "Sohni Dharti Allah Rakhay" and the jaunty favorite of children, "Jeevay, Jeevay Pakistan." Both are sung by twenty-year-old Bengali singer Shahnaz Begum. In this fraught time when the Bengali people seek their independence from Pakistan, Shahnaz Begum appears on our black-and-white television screen with her earnest and perfectly chiseled face, her big, kohled eyes, dimples at the ready, and her hair bobbed, with two carefully curled locks by each cheek that look particularly lovely in profile.

But the patriotic songs on radio and television elide the reality of my many relatives in India. Abbu's beautiful sister Masooma, the Innocent, tucked away in some Bihari village where the love of six Pakistani brothers and sisters can't reach her. Amma's mother, my great-grandmother in Patna, whom I will never meet, but whose love leaps across the Wagah border between India and Pakistan whenever that border isn't sealed, and materializes on our palates as succulent layers of dried mango or crunchy sesame-seed candy, and in our hands as little plastic hens that lay sugar eggs. India is home to all of Ammi and Khalammi's aunts and uncles and their offspring; cousins of all ages, including mine. So many invisible loved ones who had stayed put in Patna after Partition that I don't know which side to sing for, though I know I want to live.

The 1971 war with India, which will decide the fate of

majority ethnic Bengalis in East Pakistan, lasts only thirteen days, from December 3 to 16. Pakistan's supposed preemptive strike results in India's Operation Trident, targeting Karachi's naval vessels and oil tanks. Among Pakistan's devastating losses are the lives of all 222 sailors aboard the PNS *Khaibar*, known in its colonial incarnation as HMS *Cadiz*. Another thirty-three men are aboard the minesweeper PNS *Muhafiz*, built for Pakistan in Bellingham, Washington, in the early years of the Cold War when the United States and the Soviet Union were lining up their proxies in South Asia. The PNS *Muhafiz* sinks before its sailors can send a distress signal, no time to bid their breaths goodbye. Karachi harbor burns for days, the Arabian Sea bearing witness.

The architect of the attack, Admiral Nanda, was born in Karachi. Against the quiet tug of birthplace, the noise of nationhood.

Years later, in America, I read about India's Navy Day. During the weeklong celebrations, various competitions are held for schoolchildren, who are also invited to visit the Indian Navy's vessels. While Navy Day has its roots in the Royal Navy of the colonial era, its dates have shifted to December 4 to commemorate Operation Trident. On the occasion of its fiftieth anniversary in 2021, there's much gloating in the Indian press about the destruction wreaked on Karachi that long-ago night. I'm sure, had the winners and losers of that war been reversed, the gloating would have been no different. But it's hard to stomach, all the same.

I will miss Kausar and Kishwer when the war ends and they return to their neighborhood of Bihar Colony. Life will take us on divergent trails, and though we will have dodged the bloodthirsty bombs of our childhoods, we'll never see one another again.

The border with India will remain closed for years, my grandmother on one side of it, my great-grandmother on the other.

Shahnaz Begum will return to her birthplace, Dhaka, in newly independent Bangladesh and sing patriotic and filmee songs in Bangla for her country. When she dies in 2019, at 67 years of age, Bangladeshis and Pakistanis alike will mourn her. Shahnaz Begum will breathe her last on March 23, Pakistan Resolution Day.

After graduate school in Boston, I'll devote my scholarly energies to war narratives, mostly those written by Asian American women. Someday in faraway Fresno I will have to explain to my children why I love and fear balloons—love the sight of their whimsical bounce in the air, but grow anxious and watchful at the mere thought of their popping. Why I have never joined them and their dad to see Fourth of July fireworks except on television, where I can lower the volume.

Someday when the children have grown up and gone, and I have only myself and my cats to think of on Fourth of July, beloved Palestinian American poet Naomi Shihab Nye will gift the world the words I fumbled for:

> To enjoy
> fireworks
> you would have
> to have lived
> a different kind
> of life.

Who can soften the sound of smashing glass? There's something terribly final about its shattering, about the emptiness that reverberates in the wake of the smash. The moment demands our mourning. Something fragile, broken beyond repair, something that might have been beautiful. Perhaps that's how our hearts would sound if we could hear them breaking, or the hope of a better world if we could hear it fall apart.

Suraiya's Schools

As I go through what I have of family letters and photographs in Fresno, California, I come across a clipping from Pakistan's oldest English-language newspaper, *Dawn*. The date isn't visible, but the content suggests that the article, written by Saadat Rizvi, was published in late 1975, when my mother was a young woman in her early thirties. Titled "The Playhouse—Where Children Look and Learn," the article appears in the "Women's Corner" of the widely circulated newspaper. The male author begins in a well-intentioned, if patronizing, tone, referring to Suraiya Najmi as an ambitious and "overzealous" woman out to make her mark in this world, a woman who proves how much can be achieved with "a fair degree of dedication and sincerity, the sex notwithstanding." The article goes on to describe her work at English Playhouse as a revolutionary experiment that she is conducting in the "quiet and serene suburb of Gulshan-e-Iqbal."

English Playhouse was founded on March 3, 1975, in the living room of our home at 379-A/1. Having moved back to Karachi from Greenford just two months prior, Ammi intended it to be a home-school of sorts for my sister, Sadia, who turned four years old just ten days after the Playhouse was born. It grew year by year with Sadia until eventually Ammi established Meadow Secondary School to see the young graduates of English Playhouse through secondary school.

English Playhouse was so named, first, to signal the school's emphasis on English as the medium of instruction; second, to underscore the significance of learning through play, and third, to suggest a less formal, homier environment. In my mother's mind, all three concepts were crucial to the aspiring middle class she served. Proficiency in English, that old colonial imperative, was the known golden key that could open up worlds of future success for the children of ambitious parents who may have struggled to acquire the language themselves. Learning through play, on the other hand, was a novel idea for those same parents, and many initially questioned the apparent waste of time when their children could be engaged in more visibly academic endeavors. The related idea of a relaxed environment that permitted freedom of movement and prohibited corporal punishment—even the tiniest tap of the ruler on little palms—as counterproductive to learning was also new for Gulshan-e-Iqbal's parents when the preschool first opened. Many parents worried that Ammi's philosophy was too lax and indulgent. But the Playhouse proved its credibility over its thirty-three-year lifespan.

Ammi had set our living room up in such a way that the preschool had seven "corners," or designated stations for math, language arts, science, etc., so the children could move from one to the next, depending on what inspired them. Some educational toys were bought for Sadia before we left Greenford; she had dedicated an entire suitcase to them for fear that in Karachi her youngest would not have access to the creative learning tools that Amir and I had benefited from. Others she obtained locally with her twenty-year-old brother, Anwar, who had taken her about town, riding side-saddle on his motorbike to purchase such things as beads and buttons to serve as math tools. A white, wrought-iron bookshelf offered a small library, and my mother had even managed to create space for a Wendy House, as child-sized doll houses were called in England, where children acquired social skills through domestic play. Colorful pictures and learning posters adorned the walls, some of which were captioned in my father's calligraphic hand. On the bright rug at one end, the children would sit around my mother, sharing their daily "News." The class that English Playhouse alumni, including my cousin Sheba, recall most fondly is "Music and Movement"—a challenge to middle-class conventions, as this was an unstructured dance class in which children learned the joy of moving to popular Western music from a tape-recorder. The Playhouse had a humble beginning but a bold and imaginative one.

Before long, the twin grandchildren of Karachi University's Vice-Chancellor were commuting some distance to attend English Playhouse. One pregnant mother moved from wealthy Defence to Gulshan-e-Iqbal in order to enroll her unborn daughter in English Playhouse. Apparently, it was a good move. Her daughter Ambreen, now in her thirties and raising her own children in Toronto, says in a Facebook post: "I loved going to Playhouse and Meadow. I was allowed to be myself, there was a safe space provided to be who I was and encouraged to spread my wings. Outside the walls of Meadow, the world was dark and confusing. Meadow was a heaven on earth for me."

Within two years of starting English Playhouse in our living room, my mother was looking for a larger space to rent. But the deposits and advance payments required were so staggering that by 1977 my parents had decided to build another level upstairs and move the family there, leaving all of the downstairs to English Playhouse. Ammi would rent the space from Abbu, whose sole property 379-A/1 remained—an astonishing injustice on Abbu's part, and one that Ammi didn't contest at the time. That summer, while a military coup toppled Prime Minister Zulfiqar Ali Bhutto's government and brought General Zia-ul-Haq to power, contractors built another story above us. The red and white signage of the preschool would flourish on the ground level for twenty-five of its thirty-three years before merging with Meadow Secondary in Gulshan-e-Iqbal's Block 10A. During this quarter-century our nameless street was popularly referred to as the "Playhouse-Vali lane."

Today the blurring of residential and commercial zones has become integral to the character of the area, as several small businesses thrive on both ends of our residential lane: a tailor, a greengrocer, an IT service. The owner of the corner house facing Kamran Market has rented all of his downstairs space to commercial enterprises such as a pharmacy and a houseware store. Municipal authorities tend not to be finicky about such zoning particulars, though you might have to pay them off occasionally to keep them at bay.

In 1975, however, English Playhouse was the only commercial entity inhabiting our lane. I wonder again at the patience of our neighbors, though at the time I took their support for granted. True, many sent their children to the Playhouse, but many others did not have preschoolers to benefit from its proximity. To awake five days a week to a hundred little voices saying a communal prayer, then singing an abbreviated version of Pakistan's national anthem, followed by a string of English nursery rhymes like the Rainbow Song or Swallowed Peanut—surely, such rituals lost their novelty quickly. But even now my conversations with former neighbors suggest that they believed in what my mother was doing for the community and applauded her endeavors, whatever the inconvenience to themselves.

Old-timers will say that English Playhouse contributed much to this earnest, aspiring neighborhood. Not only did parents find an affordable preschool for their children at a time when private schools had become big business, but over the years scores of adults found employment there—as teachers, aides, and janitors—and many women, like my aunt Anjum, discovered their own potential in working with my mother. Among them was Mrs. Ghaffar, Tausif's mother, one of the original Playhouse parents, whom Ammi had hired as a teacher. A small-statured, maternal, and quietly smiling woman, she showed up for work one day without her customary burqa on. Though nobody pried, it was clear that Mrs. Ghaffar's inner world had undergone a revolution. Many young single women, too, learned to assert themselves through their work at English Playhouse and at Meadow (and at least one—dimpled Miss Roshan—was "discovered" by a parent who then orchestrated Miss Roshan's marriage to her brother). Among the most memorable of Ammi's employees was Meadow's long-serving custodian, Majeed. Like Dolly, who later kept house for Abbu, Majeed was from Bangladesh, working in Karachi and sending money home to support his wife and son. Besides being energetic, efficient, and utterly reliable at the school, Majeed was also a drag artist, often invited to perform his dances at weddings in Gulshan-e-Iqbal's Bangladeshi community.

Meadow Secondary School, including English Playhouse, in Gulshan-e-Iqbal's Block 10A, graduated its last class in 2008. But you can still hear its children's voices on Meadow's Facebook page, strong, bold, and brimming with love and memories, some of which go back forty years. On those sad occasions when one among them has died too soon, the page also serves as a space for collective grieving. Created by alumni Sundus Sohail and Arsalan Mansoor, Meadow's Facebook page transcends spatial and temporal distances; it represents a global connection, with alumni posting from Karachi,

Dubai, Toronto, and Sydney, as well as diverse regions of the US. As with human beings, so sometimes with the life of a school: though it may cease to exist as a physical entity, it endures in the lives and memories of all who ever looked upon it with love.

    The story of Meadow and English Playhouse is a story of one woman's ingenuity, audacity, and heart. It finds its center of gravity in 379-A/1 and is inextricably linked with my family's history. But it is also the story of a small community in the urban sprawl of a poor country, reaching deep within itself to find its own resources and endeavoring to raise its children on them. The story tells of a vision acquired across the seas, brought back and adapted to the home environment, and from home released outward into the world again in the thousands of bright-eyed students who embraced it over the course of thirty-three years, and who now, as adults in varied patches of the globe, embody its humanistic values and pass them on to their children. One such Meadow alum, Fawwad Masood, writing in 2017 from Kentucky, describes Meadow as an ecosystem that fought against "educational apartheid" in Karachi. "Even though the minds have forgotten the knowledge learnt through books, the hearts remember every lesson of love," Fawwad writes. "The souls that burn with the fire of love and compassion can't help but kindle other souls. And hence the message and purpose of Meadow lives on, in each and every one of us."

    Forty-five years after its founding in our living room, as I read the *Dawn* journalist's report on English Playhouse—his tone curious, at times tentative, but always awed—it strikes me how much of Ammi's educational philosophy centered on the vital necessity of freedom: physical, emotional, intellectual, and imaginative. At one point she is even quoted as comparing traditional preschools to concentration camps where children are forced to sit and suffer whatever is imposed upon them. The overstatement sounds like my mother, as does the laser-sharp apprehension of a larger truth and strong advocacy for the young. That she has been brave, defiant, innovative, and counterculture, I have always known. But it's the first time that I see English Playhouse as a dimension of her quest for freedom from tradition that will manifest in her personal life in just a few years.

Saadat Rizvi concludes his article: "It is still to be seen how an alien idea can make an impact in a country like ours. But given Surraiya's [sic] dedication and sincerity, it appears it will, in not too distant a future." He is writing about English Playhouse, but it occurs to me that the statement also applies to the founder herself. Intellectually hungry Suraiya Jabeen, who was denied school for most of her childhood because the only schools around her were co-ed, followed no script. She is nothing if not an alien idea to many who have observed her trajectory from a distance—with an approach that is, like Rizvi's, curious, often tentative, but always awed.

Apa

An icon of English Playhouse was my aunt Anjum, whom we children—Amir, Rubina, Azfar, Sadia, Sheba, and I—called Bari Khalammi, or Big Auntie, because she was our mothers' older sister. Bari Khalammi served English Playhouse for twenty-seven years, from the day it first opened its doors, on March 3, 1975, until 2002, shortly before uterine cancer claimed her life at the age of sixty-one. A slow learner as a child, Anjum Ara was kept out of school to avoid the embarrassment of falling behind her talented younger sister, Suraiya (though Suraiya didn't get much formal schooling either). At twenty-one she was divorced from the abusive man to whom she had been married briefly, and thereafter raised her daughter, Naghmi, with her mother, our Amma, with the modest but reliable financial support of her two brothers overseas.

The world might have passed Anjum Ara by but for English Playhouse, which gave her purpose, a reason to get up in the morning, make a cup of chai for herself and for Amma to have with Papay rusk biscuits, and brush her thick, wavy, and stubborn hair. More than that, English Playhouse gave Anjum an identity. My mother called her Apa for the respect owed to an older sister, and Apa is who she became to the generations of students and teachers who went through English Playhouse, and to the parents and grandparents who dropped their children off and picked them up. Into Apa's arms they would entrust their two- to five-year-olds, the new children screaming and contorting, and from her arms they would gather them five hours later. Some of the youngest children might emerge from the folds of Apa's sari as from the skirts of a Pakistani Mother Ginger. In the words of a

Playhouse alumna, Gloria, now in her thirties: "It was a white gate that Apa used to pull open, and more than that she would open her eyes wider behind her glasses and greet everyone with her bright smile." Another student, Hena, recalls the sari wrapped around Apa's girth and the keys dangling from her waist. She was their keeper, and they knew it. She would keep watch at the gate during recess while they went down the red and silver slide or spun on the little merry-go-round, or while they chased after one another in a game of chor-sipahee (thief-police), or hopskotched at langri pala. Usually gentle and soft-spoken, Apa was fierce when it came to her duty. She knew each child's guardians and wouldn't release the children to any number of other relatives who might endeavor to pick them up, no matter how long they had been waiting under the gulmohar tree. When the preschool's popularity grew and school vans began to ferry children between English Playhouse and distant neighborhoods, Apa held their drivers similarly accountable. Indeed, she could be quite intimidating when she hollered. But Playhouse children loved her unquestioningly, as only children can.

My mother says that English Playhouse began with her Apa and lived its best life while she was alive. Anjum Ara had been living independently in her Maymar apartment near 379-A/1 for six years after Amma's death. Looking back, I marvel at the example she set for other women in the family, including me. A woman in her fifties, without formal education, living by herself in a time and place where women were not seen as capable of, much less entitled to, living with their own company and finding it enough. But Anjum Ara had what so many people yearn for: meaningful work among colleagues and students who cherished her, and no-one to boss her around at home. She watched Indian movies on her VCR, indulged her Balkhi taste for chai, and doted on Naghmi's three daughters, Naureen, Aafreen, and Mahnoor. When cancer took hold, my mother took charge; she hired a 24-hour caregiver for her Apa and remained her anchor in this life. Some months before Apa's death in October 2002, my mother suffered a severe case of shingles and had to stay away from her sister. But Apa couldn't help herself; whatever the risk to her own immune system, she walked to her sister's home across the street from 379-A/1 where my father lived, and stood at the threshold for a glimpse of her.

I visited Karachi briefly with my toddler and my baby two months before Bari Khalammi died. Azfar was flying from San Diego, and his offer to stop in Boston in order to help me travel with the two children made my visit possible. We didn't know then that Azfar's father, my Chotepapa, would die first. But we knew that Bari Khalammi's cancer had gotten to the marrow of her bones.

In her short-short hair that she no longer colored, Bari Khalammi was as sweet as she had ever been. Photographs show her holding baby Cyrus in her arms the night we took her to Sea-View beach, and cupping two-year-old Maya's face in both her hands as though to commit the shape and feel of it to memory.

In the last weeks of her life, when she could no longer tend to her duties at English Playhouse, Anjum Ara found a new love. And for this new love she stitched little cotton frocks.

"You know," she told me in a conspiratorial tone, her eyes bright as any Playhouse child's, and head cocked to one side, "even though I can't leave my home, I can see Naureen's flat from mine. If I look up, I can see those little baby clothes drying on the line in her balcony. I can imagine my great-granddaughter inside, cooing."

Anjum Ara never got to sing her great-granddaughter a lullaby. But I imagine the thread of wonder that connected her to this newborn. Perhaps the baby embodied all the children she had ever loved, all who loved her back as Apa. But this baby also embodied *her*. Did Anjum Ara's own life flash before her as a sweep of moments, big and small, that had gone into the making of this baby girl? All of her yesterdays concentrated into a single circle of light, a flesh-and-blood miracle, three generations down. A vision of the future beyond her present, finite pain.

Sky-dying

One terribly early morning in October of 1980, my siblings and I awoke to my father's loud sobs, mingled with the voices of other adults, wafting in from the living room of our two-bedroom home in Karachi. We ran to the living room, where we learned that our uncle, Abbu's older brother, Idris, had died. He was only fifty-two.

We had never seen my father shake with sorrow, give in to grief like a leaf swept up by a rushing river. Did his shoulders heave like that as an eight-year-old boy in long-ago Bihar being told that his mother and gentle older sister were dead?

"There's no-one left to watch over me!" my father sobbed.

At seventeen, it had never occurred to me that my father needed watching over, much less that his brother held the place of a guardian for him. My uncle Idris, or "Baray Abbu" as we called him, was only four years older than my father. After the Partition of British India in 1947 Idris Najmi had led the way to Pakistan, still a youth of twenty. He fled the Hindu-Muslim riots in Delhi, hopping the hopeful train to Pakistan. My uncle made it across the border safely. But the train before his and the train after his arrived in Lahore chock-full of corpses, bodies mangled and throats slit with machetes.

Not that I knew this while Baray Abbu was alive. It took my father sixty years to tell me his terror.

What he did tell us, time and again, and always with the same hiccup in his voice, was that when he had offered to drop out of college to help support the siblings in their new homeland, his older brother told him: "I'll sell my own hide if I have to, but you'll stay in college."

Baray Abbu seemed pleasant to us, if reserved and distant, but my mother and aunt Talat spoke of their brother-in-law as a handsome man with a warm, poetic temperament. I have a hard time envisioning a personal conversation between the brothers, but apparently when he had visited us in the London suburb of Greenford, Baray Abbu had remarked to my father that he should cherish the wife he had. And he had let my aunt, his younger sister-in-law—for whom he brought guavas from Pakistan because she craved that flavor of home in her pregnancy—color his hair.

In Karachi we looked forward to Baray Abbu's occasional visits from Islamabad (where we understood him to be an important person in the Ministry of Labor) because they showed my father in an unusual light: deferential, solicitous, and obedient. If my uncle said, "Haroon, bring me a pair of slippers"—and he always asked Abbu rather than us—my father would spring up immediately and return with slippers to place at his brother's feet. If my uncle walked into my father's room while he lay on his bed, Abbu would sit up hurriedly, at attention. He'd speak only when spoken to. We thought Abbu was afraid of his older brother, and this amused us. But my father insisted that what he felt for his brother was not fear, but the kind of reverence you have for someone you love deeply. Baray Abbu seemed not to notice. Certainly, he never said thank-you when Abbu jumped to do his bidding. But his son Farrukh would tell us how his father spoke of his younger brother at home: as exemplary in his conduct, a model of love and respect for his three sons to emulate.

Baray Abbu had been attending a conference in the U.S. He visited Farrukh and Adeel there, two sons still in their teens. Before returning to Islamabad, where his five-year-old daughter

Ayesha awaited him, he was to perform the Hajj in Makkah that would cleanse him of his sins. So he boarded his connecting flight from London, draped in the pilgrim's white ehraam. But somewhere between London and Jeddah, Idris Najmi's heart stopped beating. So quietly that the passengers sitting next to him didn't realize he had slipped across the silk-thin line between breath and death.

The flight returned to London to disembark my uncle's body. The Pakistan Embassy oversaw his last rites, his namaz-e-janaza, at East London Mosque. Old Pakistani friends of my father's near Greenford heard the news of Idris Najmi's death and flocked to East London Mosque to attend his janaaza prayer. Then Baray Abbu's body was flown back to Islamabad, to his wife and daughter.

Sometimes, looking up at the pointed cypresses of my California home, I think about the manner of Baray Abbu's death. Of the soul unanchored in the sky. On the way from one continent to another to another. From professional to spiritual to familial callings. Sons here and daughter there. And so much ocean in between. Did he like what he saw of his sons' lives in their newly adopted land? Did they remind him of himself, the youth who left Bihar to be all that he could be in a new homeland for Muslims? Did the thousands of miles between his sons' new country and his own sadden him?

I like to think that Idris Najmi wanted to go that way: suspended above earth and ocean, straddling the loves that preoccupied him—not having to choose among them.

The Little Room on the Roof

Before construction began upstairs in 1977, ours was a single-story, two-bedroom home. Stairs led to the hospitably flat rooftop, girded by a low wall on three sides and a metal rail in front that had a geometric design—blue, triangular outlines, connected to one another with opaque circles, pale yellow in color, like so many full moons. Single-story or double, the roof was a haven on summer evenings when you could emerge from the heat and humidity trapped inside the house to catch the sea breeze upstairs. When we returned to Karachi from Greenford, the roof was a space at once open enough and private enough that I could take my five-year-old sister, Sadia, there for our singing time together. High up above our daily lives, I taught her the songs I knew, perhaps to ensure that even though she'd be growing up in Karachi, she would carry the tunes, if not the bittersweet memories, of my own Greenford childhood. Songs like "Sunshine Bright," "Oh Dear, What Can the Matter Be?" and "Glad That I Live Am I." Then in later years, the roof became the place where I'd walk with my mother, for exercise and woman-to-woman conversations.

But at twelve or thirteen years of age, I considered the most fascinating aspect of the roof to be the solitary little room perched on it. Measuring only 8' 6" x 9' 6", it stood oddly in the middle of the north side of the roof. Tiny as the room was, it had the same detailed flooring as the other rooms downstairs: an unpretentious matte marble surface, cast with a mosaic of little white and gray stones. It was one of Al Azam Builders' signature aesthetic flourishes in the identical homes of our street. The original plan gave the room only one window, but my parents had a second, much smaller one carved out of the opposite wall, high up, for cross-ventilation. The roshandaan—literally, "box of brightness" in Urdu—flooded the little room with sunshine. Perhaps Al Azam had envisioned the room as "servant's quarters." But for us the little box of a room served other purposes.

For a year or so after we returned from Greenford in the final days of 1974, the Little Room on the Roof was my father's tutoring space. He had returned to the Physics Department of Urdu Science College with a master's degree from England, but the college had yet to decide on his seniority status—he had taken two leaves of absence totaling six-and-a-half years—and on a salary that was commensurate with his qualifications. My mother's preschool, English Playhouse, had launched in our living room within three months of our return to Karachi, but my father supplemented the family's precarious income by tutoring students in physics. He refused to offer private tuitions to his own students at Urdu Science College, not wanting to be counted among professors who milked a cash cow, but despite this self-imposed ban he found himself a much sought-after physics tutor. So for a while a small, wooden table with stray chairs occupied the center of the Little Room on the Roof, and here Abbu would sit with a student or two in the late afternoons or early evenings after his workday at Urdu Science College was done. A cooling breeze flowed between window and box-of-brightness, and on long summer days a portable fan propelled its blades defiantly from atop the Burma teakwood bookshelf against the wall.

My father's books overflowed from the clean-cut lines of this bookshelf. He and his siblings had purchased it secondhand when they migrated to a Karachi neighborhood ironically named Bihar Colony after the Indian province they had left behind. The

Burma teakwood bookshelf was among the first acquisitions of the four oldest siblings, still in their teens and early twenties, who had opted out of Bihar by 1950 to begin new lives in the recently created state of Pakistan. As with my grandmother Amma's furniture, the teakwood had most likely been reincarnated from a former life as planks that held down the colonial railway's metal tracks. When the wood lost its usefulness in the train tracks, it was ripped out and auctioned, and found its way into the tender hands of carpenters. The bookshelf had traveled from who knows which part of the Indian subcontinent, bridging pre- and post-Partition history to become the centerpiece of our Little Room on the Roof. We knew it had survived the great Bihar Colony flood of 1958 that left sediment a foot high and swept away my father's prized black-and-white photographs—my young father so pained at the loss that he gave up photography after that. The bookshelf, which stood on short and angled mid-century modern legs, was four feet tall and some five feet wide, its shelves protected from Karachi's ubiquitous dust by sliding glass. Where the four shelves ended on the right, a teakwood door opened to accommodate Abbu's oversized physics books.

Not that my father read only physics books. When I became an English major at Karachi University, I was amazed to hear Abbu recall in affectionate detail the bleakness of overpowered lives in Thomas Hardy's novels, the wry colonial realism of Somerset Maugham's short stories, and, especially, the stark beauty of the aging fisherman's endurance in Ernest Hemingway's *The Old Man and the Sea*. But I never found evidence of Abbu's love of English literature, as I did of Urdu poetry and prose, in the Burma teakwood bookshelf. Those books had been borrowings from Greenford Library—like the lost photographs, not his to keep.

But literature or physics, the Little Room on the Roof bubbled over with books: inside the bookshelf, on top and beside it, strewn in heaps and piles of all sizes against the four walls. A deliciously dusty, musty place.

For us children this solitary room represented all the possibilities of unsupervised play, especially when our Zia cousins visited from Nigeria. But alone or in a group, our "playing" here was hardly physical. Even after the tutoring table and chairs disappeared, books compressed the already tiny quarters and circumscribed our movements. But oh, the imaginative space of that little room! The moment you entered, you knew you had walked into another world—or rather, into multiple other worlds. You could reach for a book with gold or silver letters on the spine, blow your magic breath over the hardcover, and crack it open to see the year and place of its birth. Then you could imagine a life for the book and wonder at the events it had lived through: World War II perhaps, or the year of your own birth, or, if the book was relatively new, the violent independence of Bangladesh, which your parents still spoke of in whispers. You could try to understand the science on the page and marvel that it had anything at all to do with you. When you tired of English you could reach for a physics book written in Urdu, the front cover opening like the back of an English book, your eyes following the curvy script from right to left. Though Urdu is your first language and you're fluent in conversation, your lessons in reading and writing began only after your return from Greenford. So it's frustrating that the words are printed so close together, the sentences separated by dashes instead of periods, question marks facing east instead of west, and the comma inverted and dangling in mid-air like the opening of single quotation marks. Urdu poetry, on the other hand, widens your eyes. You like the arrangement of the lines on the page: the two-line stanzas of ghazals, each shayr or couplet complete in itself and coexisting with other shayrs, similarly self-contained. Flip the page to other shapes of Urdu poetry: to the block appearance of the nazm, for instance, a genre more single-minded in focus. You offer up a loud and appreciative "Vaah!" at the end of a mellifluous line, whether or not you really get what it's saying, because you like the ritual. You are the granddaughter of Urdu poets on both sides, after all, and you have heard it said that your aunt Talat, your Khalammi, is a poet, too.

The Burma teakwood bookshelf harbored secrets. It breathed the mystery of past lives, which my brother Amir, two years my junior, was particularly adept at illuminating. One day he uncovered an astonishing dimension of our Khalammi when he found three books awarded to her at Central Women's College in Dhaka, in 1964: first prize for debates in three different languages: Urdu, English, and Bengali. (One of the prizes was William Golding's *Lord of the Flies*, a curious choice for a young East Pakistani woman just discovering her word power.) And on another occasion Amir found, tucked away behind the opaque wooden door, at a hard-to-reach angle, an illustrated book on sexology that showed no signs of wear. This, we learned later, had been a gift from Dr. Hai, the neighbor kitty-corner to us, and my mortified father had quickly tucked it away in the recesses of the Burma teakwood bookshelf.

But you don't have to open any book at all. You can just find a spot on the floor to situate your bottom and look out the window at the crows in the sky. If it's spring, you can watch the sparrows weave their nest in the window ledge of the Little Room and wonder at their faith in the fragile. Or you can gaze up at the milk-white clouds and imagine your schoolgirl's World Atlas mirrored there—all the places you'd go if you could just untether yourself. If it's early evening, when neighborhood boys have been released from siesta time, you might see the whimsical beauty of a solitary paper kite against the clouds. More than one kite, and you'll dash outside the Little Room for more sky than its nesting window lets in. Patung, our word for "kite," the ung lingering against the palate as though your foot holds the note on a piano pedal. Patung-flying on the roof is a boy's pastime, like pigeon-calling, or playing cricket in the street. But kites are the gift of ancient Chinese philosophers, a meditation on the human spirit. You look up at the sky, and there they are one minute—flutterings in turquoise, amber, and magenta—and the next minute they are gone, overpowered by the wind or devoured by bigger, stronger kites that have cut or snagged them. But while they soared, they lifted your spirits on their paper wings, beyond the confines of geography and time. So audacious in their bamboo spines; such cherished ephemera.

    The summer I turned fourteen, we lost our Little Room on the Roof. That July, as General Zia-ul-Haq's military coup overpowered Zulfiqar Ali Bhutto's government and bequeathed us a doubly long summer vacation, day laborers unloaded piles of cement bricks on our rooftop. By the time I returned to Khatoon-e-Pakistan for my tenth and final year of secondary education, our family of five had moved upstairs, leaving the 240 square yards of the lower level to English Playhouse. The second story mirrored the downstairs so precisely that living in it felt surreal. Even now it muddles the mind, daring memory to separate the years of my growing up into two distinct phases, downstairs and up. Still the same two bedrooms, one of which we three siblings shared. Ours still the middle room, with a door opening into our parents' bedroom. Identical mosaic floors that had crept up the outdoor stairway and settled into the rooms upstairs. There were only a few new touches: built-in closets from floor to ceiling, smoothed over by maple-colored formica doors; two roshandaans instead of one to brighten our days, and a balcony with the same mosaic flooring as the rooms and stairway and wide enough to accommodate, some years later, a bed and an old tin trunk.

But for all the sameness upstairs, a revolution had occurred in the Little Room. It was not demolished but reincarnated as our kitchen. The same 8' 6"x 9' 6" space acquired cabinets the color of clementines, countertops, stove, and refrigerator. To the left of its window, the Little Room now had built-in cement shelves painted white, with dark, plexiglas doors sliding over them. An aluminum sink found itself installed perpendicular to the window, with more clementine cabinets beneath it. Our upstairs home was brighter and airier, which meant that the summer sun fired it up like a tandoor oven, and the hottest spot was the Little Room-turned-kitchen. Aside from the usual demands of desi cooking—frying onions on high heat for just about every dish, pressure-cooking meats and lentils, and leisurely simmering rice and curries—a huge pot of Karachi water would have to be kept at a rolling boil for twenty minutes before it became potable. Box-of-brightness notwithstanding, there wasn't enough ventilation to exorcise the steam, and on summer afternoons the sweat would river down your face and neck, and soak up your spine.

As my parents found their feet financially, an array of part-time cooks, or those aspiring to the title, worked in that space: Laal Mai, who spoke Saraiki and returned to her village on the

Sindh-Punjab border for the holidays; Hasina from Bangladesh, who worked full-time at Khalammi's but came to our house for a couple of hours in the afternoon to cook enough food for lunch and dinner; whose years with us rekindled the Bengali language and girlhoods for my mother and aunt, and gave Rubina an emotional anchor in her own home. And then there was Abdul, the only "real" cook, who knew the Bihari palate, but who himself preferred to live on heaps of brown rice and spicy mango pickles, downed by gallons of tea. Abdul would be our only live-in cook. For most of his thirteen or so years upstairs at 379-A/1, the balcony would be his home, and the Little Room-turned-kitchen his professional territory.

The Burma teakwood bookshelf moved out of the Little Room. It became part of the surreal new middle room on the second floor that Amir, Sadia, and I would share until, one by one, we left for schools and separate lives in the United States. By that time, the door connecting us to our parents' bedroom opened into a stark, masculine space, my mother having moved out two years after Amir left. When we lost the Little Room on the Roof that summer of 1977, Abbu gave his overflow of books away, mostly to the library of Urdu Science College. But the Burma teakwood bookshelf stood its ground—situated in our bedroom, a few feet away from where our three heads lay on their pillows, within breathing distance of our dreams.

The original mosaic floor of the Little Room on the Roof remains. Sparrows still nest in its window ledge.

fragment 3

That Ramzaan in Gulshan when I kept my first roza,
you wanted to fast, too.
Who ever heard of a five-year-old fasting
Sunrise to sunset,
without food or water?
But defiant and determined, you showed us your mettle,
what steely strength
and fierce physical resolve could do.
What you could put your body through.

What you could put others through, too.
Remember when you pushed your little brother, Azfar,
and his head hit something sharp?
I emerged from the bathroom just in time to see the blood,
to call for help,
to join in the chorus of blame.
I saw your violence,
your jealousy,
but not your pain.

He was so easy to love, your brother.
Sweet sunshine, gentleness, and joy.
Beloved of our mothers,
beloved of me.

No wonder you threw a glass bottle at him once.
Before you came to love him, too.

So easy to love,
so unlike you.

fragment 4

You with your staccato volleys,
your blurtings, your ragings,
your rebellion.
Impetuous, impatient.
Always arguing,
questioning,
provoking.
Irreverent. Iconoclast.
Why did you make it so hard for us to like you?
Bad Rubina.
Odd one out.

Burglar in Braids

I awake with a start. The Karachi sun beams through the window of the second-story bedroom I share with my two siblings. I know it's a Saturday—the day of the week that can't come soon enough for me. But it never begins with the sound of my father's voice, so uncharacteristically loud and abrupt this morning.

On Saturdays, our home turns into a mini-salon where Ammi talks to us about things that matter to a teenaged girl like me—relationships, desires and dreams, and, increasingly, the oppressive policies of the dictatorship that has governed since 1977 and smothers us even in the cosmopolitan city of Karachi. In a minor but symbolically significant move, General Zia-ul-Haq has declared Friday, the Muslim sabbath, as the official weekend, to signal the country's alignment with Islam and with oil-rich Saudi Arabia. So our neighborhood Kamran Market shuts down on Fridays. I miss the usually bustling scenes: women choosing from vibrantly colored reams of fabric, flirting with the handsome shopkeeper as they challenge his asking price; wrinkled men lined up for rice, lentils, and sugar at the grocery store; popular Urdu and Punjabi songs blaring from the barber's radio. On Fridays, children do not throng Mr. Book's to eye the pretty, pastel stationery in the glass display, nor do the butcher's caged hens cackle. Even the so-called Irani hotel, frequented by the shopkeepers and day laborers, closes down, at least during Friday prayers at the market's Masjid-e-Noor.

But, ah, Saturday! Now the first day of the week, Saturday brings the market back to life. The street vendors call out their wares in varying degrees of tunefulness; our metal letterbox with the diamond-shaped peephole looks forward to the approach of the postman's bicycle, and Mehtiyar, the Christian cleaning woman with one seeing eye, and Laal Mai, the Saraiki woman who cooks lunch and dinner in the same two-hour spell, arrive at their accustomed hours to do their jobs unobtrusively. Abbu leaves for Urdu Science College as usual, where he serves as physics professor to four thousand, hotly politicized undergraduates. On Saturdays, it is just Ammi and us three siblings at home. On Saturdays, we are free to be ourselves, to imagine, to reflect—to dare to think our own thoughts.

    Then, to awake to this. The voices come from the direction of my parents' bedroom. I leap out of bed but pause cautiously at the threshold of the open door. My mother is sitting up in bed, her eyes wide with curiosity, while my father—my father, dressed for work, complete with sunglasses on, stands by the window, holding a woman captive by the hair. She appears to be about thirty, wears a faded, pale-blue, cotton qameez with a baggy shalvar of the same color. Her slim, dark legs show through the shalvar's fabric, grown translucent with age, and a once-white dupatta drapes her shoulders. The woman's long, black braid fills my father's fist. She grimaces but makes no sound, her narrow-framed body, the color of bittersweet chocolate, both rebellious and resigned in its stillness. She is unarmed.

    Abbu tells us the breathless story: he had stepped out of the house as usual, but instead of heading straight to work, he stopped by Kamran Market's Faisal Bakery to buy eggs and bread for our eventual Saturday breakfast. He returned home within minutes and noticed two slender young men hovering outside our house, their faces turned up towards the balcony. As Abbu approached the gate, they shuffled away, towards the marketplace. But coming up the stairs, Abbu found the entrance to the second floor wide open. Though he hadn't locked the door when he left the house, he knew he had closed it behind him. So he set his bakery purchases down and entered his own home like a thief. Down the narrow hallway, towards his bedroom. There lay Ammi still asleep, oblivious to the woman who had entered the house and was now rummaging through the steel armoire where Ammi kept her clothes and personal belongings, including her jewelry. The woman's back was turned. My father sneaked up from behind and grabbed her by her dangling braid. He pulled her away from Ammi's armoire. "What do you think you're doing here?" he demanded, his voice hoarse from its unaccustomed volume.

Ammi discovers that most of her jewelry has already vanished, though there is no sign of it on the woman. While Abbu immobilizes the intruder by her braid, Ammi calls her journalist friend, Zaheda Hina, who knows a trustworthy police officer—one who will not come seeking bribes from all parties. Only then, while we wait for justice, do I see that the woman is visibly pregnant. For a fleeting moment, something about the swell of the woman's stomach bends my straightforward sense of right and wrong. I see a habitually mild-mannered man clutching a pregnant woman by the hair while his wife looks on. Then my parents' faces come into focus; they reflect the shock of the violation, of the woman's brazen daring, and the sheer luck of my father's return to the house this morning. Abbu's staccato breath hints at the fear he does not put into words: what if this woman works for a gang that means to return with a surer plan? My murky moment passes. Abbu has caught a burglar in the act.

Still wincing, the woman says nothing. And neither do I.

The police officer who appears is a stout, middle-aged man in khaki uniform and wields a baton for effect. With him enters a younger officer, subordinate in his manner, tall and sleek, with a mustache that covers most of his upper lip. A couple of inquisitive neighbors slither into the house after them, observing the action from the threshold of my parents' bedroom. My mother has donned a shawl and sits alert now on the only chair in the room. The older officer asks for my father's account of the incident and then my mother's, taking notes as they speak. Then he turns to the woman. Using the informal second-person "tum," which in Urdu marks a child or social inferior, he interrogates her:

"What were you doing here?"

Silence.

"Do you confess to the burglary?"

Silence.

"What did you do with the jewelry? Did you throw it over the balcony to your accomplices?"

The woman is whimpering now but will not say anything. The younger officer grabs her by the wrist and marches her through the hallway to the dining room that leads to the balcony. The two young men whom Abbu had seen lurking outside have disappeared. The officer begins to strike the woman—his big brown hands, left and right, come down on her, smash against her face, the side of her head, her bony shoulders. A cry escapes the woman. Ammi rushes to the dining room, asks the officer again and again to stop.

The woman's pee trickles down her thin cotton shalvar and forms a little pool on our dining room rug. She sobs but says nothing as the two policemen take her away.

The next day, our local paper reported the event with a

sensationalist flourish. It attributed to Ammi immense, endangered riches that she didn't possess. The article portrayed her as a woman who, hysterical from the loss of her wealth, ran into the streets exclaiming: "I've been looted! I've been looted!" According to Mehtiyar, who cleans our home, neighbors believed that Ammi's known generosity to the poor would always shield her from harm. Sure enough, within days the police had recovered my mother's stolen pendants and earrings, and returned them to her without so much as a hint at expecting compensation for their efforts. My father took to locking the door behind him on Saturday mornings.

Nobody asked what became of the pregnant woman.

Monsoon Muse

May and June are cruel months in Karachi. When I look online at the city's average temperatures and average humidity for these months, I'm inclined not to believe them. Too tame. The figures don't tell you how ferociously the sun glares down at you, as if intent on boring a hole through your body with an invisible magnifying glass; how its laser rays blight the land and wither the faces of its defeated citizens. Week after week there is no respite, except at night when the cooling sea-breeze blows its balm over the coastal city. Worst of all are the Loo winds, their hot, dry breath straight out of a blast furnace. When the Loo strikes, Karachi's children descend from their school buses at three o'clock in the afternoon to fall prostrate on their beds, too limp to eat. The only positive aspect of the Loo winds is that they provide a reprieve from the customary high humidity. Stand in the sun for five minutes and your clothes stick to you as though you've just emerged from the waves of the Arabian Sea. If you have money—and electricity—you'll want to spend most of May and June in your air-conditioned bedroom. If not, you'll want to take three showers a day, as we used to do as children. Assuming you have ample water supply, of course.

Just when you think you could burst a blood vessel from the mounting heat in your brain, the skies darken. And with a suddenness that stops your heart, the clouds crack open and let out a downpour as fierce as the sun's rays had been earlier. A collective shout reverberates in the dramatically cooler air—relief, elation, the exhilaration of the crazed! You run to your rooftop like all your neighbors and inhale the aroma of newly moistened earth for the trippiest of highs. You're soaked through within minutes, and your parents warn of exposure, but even they know that it's worth it. Pretty soon you can hear romantic filmee songs floating through windows and doors flung open in the lane, and giddy jokes and laughter from the direction of Kamran Market. Time for something hot and spicy to go with the rain—pakoras, maybe, or chickpea cholay, or samosas with mint and cilantro chutney. If you're lucky you might even partake of my father's favorite: corn-on-the-cob roasted over charcoal and purchased from a street vendor who has doused it in lime juice and red chili pepper. Let's hope you don't have to drive anywhere because Karachi will soon resemble Venice without the gondolas.

Abbu, cautious and risk-averse, was especially wary of wading about in our very first car, acquired when I was fourteen: a white Volkswagen Beetle like Herbie (before those cars became neon-trendy Slug Bugs), already ten years old before we owned it. But during one monsoon downpour we heard someone banging on our front gate—someone smart enough not to risk electrocution by ringing the door-bell. It was my mother's friend, the fearless Urdu journalist, editor, and fiction writer Zaheda Hina, whose illustrious career would go on to win her both fame and notoriety in South Asia, and multiple awards and honors. We don't know it yet, but in 2006 Zaheda Hina will be nominated for Pakistan's highest civilian award, the Presidential Pride of Performance, which she will turn down in protest against the military government of General Pervez Musharraf. When we first met her, Zaheda Hina was married to the gifted Urdu poet John Alia, a wispy man whose long hair she had to shampoo from time to time. Together, they were a power couple in the literary world. John Alia, already a familiar name in Pakistan, would achieve posthumous recognition in the 21st century as one of South Asia's preeminent poets.

My mother had come to know Zaheda Hina through her daughter Fanny, a classmate of Sadia's at English Playhouse and Meadow. Ammi credits this friendship—and Bertrand Russell's *Marriage and Morals*—with shaping her feminist consciousness in her late thirties. Zaheda Hina, herself ethnically Bihari, will also be the one to identify the genius of my grandmother's family memoir, written in Bihari Urdu.

Zaheda Auntie had a dark and sultry beauty. She was tall, slim, and imposing, with short hair and metal-rimmed glasses. She was the first "real" writer and the first avowed atheist I had ever encountered. To her I owe my knowledge of many European writers and my still-treasured copy of *The Complete Works of Oscar Wilde*. Zaheda Auntie, with her unique synthesis of urbanity and irreverence, struck me as a marvel of a woman.

Now, during the monsoon downpour, her daughters, Fanny and Sohaina, sat in the backseat of their car, engine running while their mother stood at our gate.

"What are you doing, lounging around at home in this gorgeous weather?" she hollered at me. Her laughter rang out loud and melodic, revealing the chipped front tooth she had acquired some years earlier when she fell out of bed, pregnant with Sohaina. "Grab that mother of yours and whoever else wants to come, and let's go for a ride!"

So we all piled into her car and plowed through a foot of muddy water, our windows rolled down so that the diagonal downpour could hit our faces. Many a car lay broken down and abandoned, brake and clutch having surrendered to the deluge. Only the yellow mini buses raged on, splattering smaller cars that dared to swim alongside them in the roads. As usual the Yellow

Killer carried a human overload, but today the young men hanging from its steps and perched on its rooftop serenaded the passersby at top volume, casting lovelorn looks to make any teenage girl feel like the star of a romantic Bollywood movie.

One night in the summer of 2007, the monsoons went beyond the usual flooding of streets and broken power and telephone lines. I was visiting Karachi again with Maya and Cyrus, now seven and five years old. My cousin Naveen Balkhi was getting married in Malir that night, and Khalammi had taken us to Gulshan's busy Rashid Minhas Road in the afternoon to buy appropriate sandals for Maya and Cyrus. It had been a too-bright summer day when we walked into the Bata store, but we emerged from it a half-hour later to find the skies an opaque and sickly yellow—not just a promising pre-monsoon gray. In the minute or two it took for Khalammi's driver to bring the car to us, the wind had whipped up.

"Mama, the billboard just ripped," Maya announced. Sure enough, on the billboard across the street a gigantic hole had formed where, just seconds ago, the face of a voluptuous, pink-skinned and red-lipped woman had been. The billboard, advertising some brand of talcum powder, was already tearing up at the edges like an 8 x 11 sheet of paper.

"Looks like a dust-storm approaching!" Khalammi said. "We need to hurry home."

It turned out to be much worse than the dust-storms that sometimes twirl through the city, usually leaving no trail other than a thick film on every object in your house. No, this turned out to be a cyclone approaching the Karachi coast from the Indian Ocean. For the next few hours we tracked its passage nervously on TV, as the winds howled around us. Then, miraculously, the cyclone changed direction, validating the legend that no cyclone can destroy Karachi because Abdullah Shah Ghazi, the eighth-century Sufi saint, lies buried in its coastal earth. But the cyclone changed course only after its accompanying winds and rain had caused massive destruction all over the city. Some two hundred Karachiites lost their lives that night, either from electrocution or from debris that struck with the force of deadly projectiles.

There was no way to make it to Malir that evening. We missed Naveen's wedding.

That was the last time I visited Karachi in monsoon season. With each year, the monsoons, kind or cruel, recede further and further into the distance of time. What endures is the image of a bold brown woman at the gate, a writer-woman calling me to step out into a fleeting moment and abandon myself to a fearless, reckless love of beauty.

The Najmi Creation Story

One of the best things about moving to Karachi as a child was that nobody made fun of my name there. Back in Greenford, I didn't mind the occasional "Semolina" from classmates at Oldfield or Coston, but the relentless "Nudge-me"—or, following *Monty Python*: "nudge-nudge, wink-wink, say no more!" made me chafe. It was a constant reminder of my alienness among English children. And British comedies were often blatantly alienating anyway. If I wanted to punish myself for being a Paki child, all I had to do was turn on the telly and watch something crass and inane that passed for humor in great swaths of English society at the time. No surprise that "Nudge-me" would be leveled at me not only with the poke of an elbow in my side, but with the backslapping glee of creative genius every time. Throughout my childhood in Greenford, I looked forward to the day I would marry out of Najmi.

Historically, the Indian subcontinent has never set great store by the convention of grouping human beings by last name. You knew your lineage, your every cousin multiple times removed; you knew who married whom, of what family, and how closely or tenuously you were related. That's what mattered: the memory space devoted to these connections, reverently passed down to your children through regular visits and, with the widening world, reinforced by narrative. The names you gave your children had nothing to do with your sense of familial cohesion. They were complete in themselves, without patriarchal tags attached. Even well-known families used surnames inconsistently. My Balkhi grandfather didn't think of assigning his Sufi-literary family name to his daughters. He gave Ammi the Farsi name "Suraiya Jabeen," alluding to the brightest star of the Pleiades cluster, and named Khalammi "Mah Talat," or "beauteous face of the moon." But this cavalier attitude towards surnames irked our British rulers and confounded their sense of a bureaucratic world order. Under the British, South Asians slowly began to adopt Western modes of nomenclature, though in Pakistan the process is far from complete; even though a married woman undergoes a name change, she often opts for the husband's first name as her new surname—a phenomenon Ammi once explained to us as motivated by the feeling of "total grab" over said husband. Total ownership of husband though it might be, the practice has subverted the British Raj's vision of nominal orderliness in the Subcontinent.

"Najmi" is an invented name for us. Once when I asked Abbu what our real surname was, he replied that it might be "'Siddiqui' or something." It hardly mattered. Because growing up in Karachi, I came to love the Najmi creation story. My paternal grandfather Ibrahim served as the Deputy Director of Islamic Education in the Indian province of Bihar, but like my maternal grandfather, Izhaq Balkhi (the railway doctor), he was also a poet. In fact, he was a published poet of some stature, who used "Najam," the Arabic for "star," as his pen name. To this he added "Nadvi," a convention among the graduates of the theological school Nadwatul Ulama, or Nadva, in Lucknow. From "Najam" my grandfather derived "Najmi"—meaning "of Najam," though it also translates as "my star" in Arabic—and appended it to the names of all his children. That wasn't all. Grandfather Ibrahim Najam Nadvi's identity as a poet was so important to him that, following tradition, he added "Najmi" to the names of all his shaagird, his apprentices in poetry. Although they were not his flesh and blood, he claimed them as his poetical descendants. Today "Najmi" is the surname or middle name of the poet's great-grandchildren in parts of the earth he probably never imagined—places as far away from Bihar as Texas, Massachusetts, and California. And much as I balked at the name during my childhood, two marriages later I choose to remain a Najmi.

What I never anticipated was how, one day in the distant future, my biracial, Fresno-grown children would relate to my family name. For simplicity's sake, Alex and I caved to convention and gave them his last name, "Vannini." My cousin Farrukh's wife, Nancy, asked me to picture them trying to spell out "Najmi-Vannini" in kindergarten, and I felt for them. In hindsight, I need not have sympathized so much. By the time he was in high school, Cyrus was hyphenating his middle and last names as Najmi-Vannini. I waited for him to tire of it, which didn't happen, so a couple of years later I finally coughed up the $600 it cost to add the hyphen, and made the name-change legal.

That same year, the summer before she left for college and as soon as she turned eighteen, Maya asked me to write "Najmi" in Urdu on a slip of paper. Then she entered the studio of a tattoo artist on Fresno's busy Blackstone Avenue. When she ties her hair up in a ponytail, you can see it on the back of her neck: *Najmi* in curvy, right-to-left Urdu script, inscribed on her skin in her mother's handwriting.

Story of a Storyteller

One July afternoon in 1982, my friend Lubna and I are still sitting in our English Department classroom at Karachi University, long after Professor Rafat Karim's lecture on Shakespeare has ended and students have dispersed. Lubna's father, who works in the consular services, has been appointed to Paris, and I am more heartbroken than envious that Lubna is leaving. In the back and forth between Karachi and Greenford, I hadn't been able to hold on to friendships, and later I'd learned to seek out books rather than people. My friend Misbah from St. Joseph's College had quite rightly called me a snail who comes out of her shell periodically to sniff the air, only to go back in, oblivious of all around her.

So Lubna is the kind of saheli I have never had until now: the one you hang out with every day, who will worry if you're absent from class, and with whom you visit the library, or walk over to the Refresho or the Samosa Vala on campus, or catch The Point—that idiosyncratic University bus about which I've written a humorous essay, published in the *Dawn*, though it will be three decades before I realize that the essay is my creative nonfiction debut. It's a given that you and your saheli appear together. It has taken me eighteen years to find such a bestie, and I can't believe our togetherness is to end in just a year. The gift of an overcast day in July and the pre-monsoon breeze that flutters through the palm trees of Karachi University, making them look like tall, skinny models with out-of-control hair, deepen my melancholy.

Suddenly a young man, obviously a foreigner, pokes his head through the classroom door and asks where the Chair Dr. Kalimur Rahman's office is located. I can tell from his accent that he is Arab, which is to say, probably Palestinian. While Palestinian women students are deemed to live piously and studiously on campus, Palestinian men, who far outnumber their women compatriots in enrollment, rightly or wrongly have acquired a reputation as drinkers, smokers, and playboys. In any case, most girls at the university have been raised not to address male students, Palestinian or Pakistani, unless necessary. Lubna and I give this fellow the information he seeks, but gloom makes me reckless. Just as he is turning to leave, I toss a question at him:

"Shouldn't you be in Lebanon?"

I intend this to be cutting. The subtext is: Israeli Defence Forces have just invaded southern Lebanon in an attempt to drive your Palestinian Liberation Organization out of the country; images of the people's suffering abound in our newspapers and on television, and you who should be ministering to their needs at this terrible time are idling around here?

It's a moment fraught with implications. In asking the question, I have pounced mid-river on the cub pilot of my life's steamboat, grabbed the helm and hat from him, and set myself on a wild, uncharted course.

The young man leaves the threshold and limps into the classroom in response, sits down with us, and embarks on an hour-long story. He *has* been fighting; he just returned from Beirut in fact. He waves a bullet at us, strung from a keychain, and explains his limp as a bullet injury. He tells us about his refugee family, his father who died four years ago. His words sketch vivid scenes of suffering and survival. For the first time, the Palestinians, that anonymous group of whom we have been hearing almost daily on the news for years, become individuals—fighting, loving, sorrowing. Never mind that the young man forgets to limp on his way out of the classroom.

Over the next few days, weeks, and months, I will sift fact from fiction in his narrative. Early on I will realize that parts of his story were not factual—his father was very much alive, for instance, though his stepfather was killed—but were woven from the fabric of a communal and political reality. A composite of many true stories, it strikes me now as a particularly artful narrative, true if you heard it holistically, but not faithful to the facts, and told with a savvy sense of audience. Kind of like Filipino American writer Carlos Bulosan's 1943 narrative, *America Is In the Heart*. In August, the PLO will withdraw under the supervision of the Multinational Force, and on September 11, the Multinational Force, which was expected to protect the civilians, will leave Beirut. I will read with a new kind of investment about the right-wing Lebanese Christian Phalange's savage rapes and mass slaughter of Palestinians and Lebanese Shias in the IDF-occupied Sabra and Shatila camps. Eventually, I will learn of the Palestinian student's personal tragedies—the way he lost a baby brother in the stampede that ensued when Israel occupied the Gaza Strip at the end of the Six Days War in 1967. But almost immediately, that July of 1982, I will fall in love with this hazel-eyed and curly-lashed 21-year-old student in the Journalism Department. And I will not be the first young woman or the last, in life or in literature, to fall for a storyteller, one who places glimmering or ghastly worlds at our feet with wit and dramatic flair.

But in my Gulshan world there's no such thing as dating, no space for romance or for getting to know someone before deciding on marriage. Too many Pakistani women and men have sacrificed a youthful love on the altar of this oppressive tradition. The argument is that love marriages are often foolish and don't last anyway. Two love marriages later, I can say that the point is not the success or failure of a relationship, however we define it; the point is to have some agency in the matter. For two years, I will somehow brave the leers and snickers behind my back, my father's anger and sorrow. When the young man graduates, returns from the refugee camp of Khan Younis in the Gaza Strip with his parents' blessings, and suggests a life for us in Abu Dhabi, I am still an undergraduate. But I choose to marry rather than give him up.

    We celebrate our Nikah at the Sheraton in Rubina's lifetime, my prudent father giving in, against his better judgment, to the young groom's desire for an expensive venue. The idea is to be officially married in order to begin the paperwork for Abu Dhabi, but to wait for the actual wedding until my education is complete and his job is secure. But a year later, Rubina dead at her own hands and my nights wracked with grief and horror, I will ask my young man—officially my husband—to move into 379-A/1 with Abbu, Sadia, and me, into the home that Amir and Ammi have left behind. We plan to be there for a few months, until that elusive job in Abu Dhabi that he believes awaits him materializes. But his is a nation of youths with no country and no passport. Unlike his gentle family, who host me in Khan Younis the following summer, he is an angry man, prone to smashing things around him when he isn't getting his way. He will remain in our lane for three years, fond of my parents and kind to my grandmother, but unable to keep a job or his temper. He'll check out the women visible from our rooftop and get into sometimes farcical, and sometimes dangerous altercations with the men in Kamran Market. Only my parents' standing in the community will protect him. Finally, it will be my funded admission to Tufts University that will get us both out of Gulshan.

And yes, the storyteller will break my heart. He will be funny and warm, but in a fit of wrath he will gather my books from the shelf in our second-floor apartment in Somerville, Massachusetts, and throw them in the kitchen trash. He will decree that my all-but-brother Azfar, who is an undergraduate at nearby Harvard, should keep to the living room when he visits instead of walking into the kitchen with me. And when I try to escape the storyteller's latest smashing spree, he will bolt the door and obstruct my exit.

But at Tufts I will be reading other stories. A seminar in 20th-Century American Women Writers will introduce me to women of color whose writings, even when couched as fiction, spring from deeply personal experiences that resonate with me—Maxine Hong Kingston, Leslie Marmon Silko, and Louise Erdrich among them. We are a composite of all our readings, ourselves texts that may or may not be legible to others, but today if I had to identify one book that altered my personal, professional, and political trajectories, it would be African American author Paule Marshall's 1958 novel *Brown Girl, Brownstones*. Even in my twenties, in contrast to most of my peers, I identify not with the young, US-born protagonist Selina Boyce, but with her middle-aged mother, Silla, who comes to the US from Barbados as a young woman. She's not a self-aware character, or even a sympathetic one for many readers, but her immigration story interlocks with the story of her beguilement in love. Paule Marshall's clear-sighted and lyrical prose will articulate for me "the slow blurring of the self" that happens in a marriage that demands more compromise than it is worth.

The day the Gulf War breaks out—January 16, 1991, the angry young man leaves for work. As he goes, giving me a kiss goodbye, he says, half-joking, "I have decided to be nice to you from now on." And once he's gone—after almost six years of living together, on two continents—I will sneak out of our Somerville home, into a room on Medford Hillside.

I'll be gathering my few belongings quietly when the sadness of the morning will be alleviated by two surprising phone calls. One comes from the young man's boss and friend, Alex, who says with gentle voice, "Something told me to call you." To this day, I don't know what made me trust him with my secret. Six years later I'll be married to him and in time we'll raise two children together. But that's another story.

The other surprise phone call is the one I make to my cousin Farrukh's wife, Nancy, in Reading, twelve miles north of Somerville. I have hardly told anyone what I'm about to do—not even Azfar because I know he's in the middle of finals—figuring I'll make the short distance to Medford Hillside in a cab. But at the last minute I need a friend to help me through this ending. Nancy will ask no questions, just get in her car at once and drive the twenty minutes to Somerville. She will be there in staunch, silent support to help me take my belongings to the Medford apartment I'll share with three undergraduate Tufts women.

In California, Sadia and Amir will keep my confidence. Sadia, so young, so steadfast in her love. Amir will have wired the money that will make possible my new life, freed from fear of the curly-lashed storyteller's own dark story.

My father will never say *I told you so.*

fragment 5

Was that all there was between us, then?
All there was to you?

Surely that wasn't all.

There's the photograph I took of you by the Arabian Sea.
You stand alone in the sands, black waves of hair
sweeping across your face.
The trace of a smile, intended for me.

That winter's day on your Gulshan patio, I interrupted your reading
with my camera.
Do something interesting, I said.
And you obliged with a sudden high kick.
Foot in air, book in hand,
your laughing eyes
caught on camera.

Another photo of four girls arm in arm,
sisters together,
shortly before my foolish first marriage.
"What are you worried about, Baaj?" you had said.
"You're the kind of person who'll marry, have two kids,
and live happily ever after."

At seventeen, you did not think you would live happily ever after.

fragment 6

How beautiful you are at my wedding,
all white and golden grace!
Your classmate Nasreen, and Hasina, the Bangladeshi cook
beside you.
Hasina, whom you loved,
kicking down the class walls that enclosed us.
I see you standing beside her by the gate
until we make space in the caravan of cars
How worried you were she'd be forgotten,
left behind, less important.

Your gift of lacquered lapis trays, with peacocks
spread in splendor.
They outlived the marriage,

outlive you.

Part 2

Amma

I called her Amma. It's an old-fashioned word for "Ammi," mother, but I called her Amma because that's what my mother called her. Before she shrank, Amma was five feet tall. She had long, black hair which she pulled into a single braid down her back, eyes that glistened, and teeth so precisely formed, they looked like two rows of pearls when she smiled. I loved her girth, her mellow edges. Amma's flesh circled her midriff like the clasp of a lover, and when she lay on her side, you could see her stomach in profile, lying next to her.

Amma sits. Even in my earliest memory, she does not walk. Sometimes she hobbles, and later she rests all of her body's weight on a walk-aid in order to get to the bathroom. But mostly Amma sits—on her bed and on her rattan stool. Sitting, she peels potatoes; sitting, she showers. Sitting, she embroiders and stitches—a collage of vibrant triangles on a small silk purse, placemats that look like magnified grape leaves, a whimsical tea-cozy in the shape of a swan.

Amma is a woman of few words. But sitting, she tells stories that captivate my younger brother, Amir, though I take them for granted at the time. Fables and fairytales, of peasants who stand up to their village lords, orphan girls who come to reign as beloved queens, and jackals who outwit their prey. Amma also had a repertoire of farcical stories centered on simple-minded characters like the bungling religious figure, Mullah Nasruddeen—stories that made you laugh, but which championed the simple-minded in the end. Most stories had intricate plots, erupting in scatological humor of the kind you don't expect from your grandmother. Amma did the telling in her at once gritty and lilting Bihari dialect, fully focused on each moment of the story, her facial expressions reflecting how she felt about a character's actions, or indicating a twist in the plot, or anticipating her audience's surprise or pleasure. She told the story with great patience, always willing to return to subtleties that we might have missed.

My favorite fairytale, however, was the one about Amma's early life. She was the first surviving child of the Imam family, landowners in Patna, in the Indian province of Bihar. Her father's estate, Kashana, was built to accommodate a large, multigenerational family, friends and relatives who stayed for months, students and scholars, tutors for the children—his offspring totaled eight in number once Amma had set a good example by surviving—horse-and-carriage, motor car, and even an elephant. Amma was born in Kashana in 1920, a sickly child whose parents indulged and coaxed her into living. Though her name was Kaneez Fatima, she went through life as Baby. Younger cousins referred to her respectfully as "Baby Baji," nieces and nephews as "Baby Khala," grand-nephews and grand-nieces as "Baby Naani." Her husband wouldn't have referred to her by name publicly—it would have been indecorous to suggest the intimacy of the relationship so openly—but I can hear the soft tones of the handsome young poet as he calls her "Baby" in private.

It was a legendary marriage. Amma, the petite, pretty, and pliable seventeen-year-old, who had remained soft-spoken and good-tempered despite her sickliness, and Izhaq Balkhi, the 24-year-old physician, raised by a single mother after his father's untimely death. Luckily, his father had left lands behind in the village of Sain near Patna for his four children to grow up on, and Mariam, his sharp-witted and well-read young widow, administered these lands. But Izhaq Balkhi had the Sufi strain in him. Literary, principled, otherworldly, my grandfather would never be rich, even as a railway doctor in what became East Pakistan in 1947. But in their 28-year marriage, he would leave Amma with gossamer memories that she would have to subsist on for over thirty years after his untimely death.

The estate of Kashana was large enough to accommodate Amma's new groom in 1937 and six of their seven children who were born there over the next decade. But after the Partition of the Indian subcontinent in 1947 my grandfather, frightened by the religious killings in Bihar, decided to migrate to the eastern wing of newly created Pakistan. It was unknown territory, but it promised a utopian Land of the Pure, where Muslims could be all that they aspired to be, in a humane and principled society, as the impassioned rhetoric proclaimed. Amma was the only one in her family to leave India, to leave behind her parents and six siblings, to clutch at her heart as Kashana receded far into her past. There would be train journeys home from time to time, courtesy of my grandfather's employment in Pakistan Railway, and vast, arid patches of longing in between.

Nobody was prepared for my grandfather's death from esophageal cancer in 1965, least of all his forty-five-year-old wife. Of her children, my mother, Suraiya, and my aunt Talat were safely married to two Najmi brothers—sons of Ibrahim, the poet—and soon my parents would take Amir and me to join Khalammi and Chotepapa in England. But there remained my older aunt, Anjum Ara (who would one day become the Apa of English Playhouse), cognitively slower than her siblings and desperately retrieved from a violent husband, and her four-year-old daughter, named Naghma-e-Mussarat for the beauty of song, though everyone called her Naghmi. Also two uncles, bookends in the sibling birth-order:

Raza, the eldest (engaged and in love), and Anwar, only ten years old. Amma had already buried two of her seven children: Ashfaq, who was born with cerebral palsy and never grew up, and Ishrat, who died in a mental institution in Ranchi, Bihar, within three years of being admitted there. She had lived to be seventeen.

Amma's days in the green hills of Chittagong and Lalmonirhaat came to an abrupt end. After her husband's death she found herself a thousand miles away in my parents' home, in West Pakistan's largest city, Karachi, an industrial desert by comparison. Another displacement followed when she, Anjum, Anwar, and Naghmi moved to the small, rural town of Mirpurkhas, about 150 miles away from Karachi, and back then a sparse, isolated community where horse-driven tongas served as cabs and school buses. They had moved there with Raza, who, as the eldest son, was now responsible for his mother and younger siblings. He assumed this responsibility dutifully for several years. But ultimately the arrangement proved to be untenable. My family lived mostly in Greenford at the time, but in the summer of 1974 my mother traveled to Mirpurkhas to help relocate Amma back to Karachi, along with Amma's two adult but dependent children, Anwar and Anjum, and her granddaughter Naghmi.

Having witnessed their circumstances, my mother no longer wanted to live an ocean away from her family, especially from her troubled teenage brother. Abbu was only too glad to have the decision made easier for him. By the time we packed up from Greenford and returned to Karachi six months later, Amma—along with my aunt Anjum, my nineteen-year-old uncle Anwar, and 13-year-old cousin Naghmi—had learned to live with even less than they had had in Mirpurkhas. To my eleven-year-old eyes it was evident that the eggs and butter on the breakfast table—or rather, the breakfast sheet spread out on the floor—in their modest Federal B Area home were loving gifts that extended their hospitality budget as far as it could go. Within five years Anwar and Naghmi would leave the nest, and Amma and her eldest daughter would live out the rest of their lives in one small, rented apartment after another, whatever the sons and brothers were willing or able to pay for. Thanks to them, they were not homeless. Because Amma's sons now lived overseas with their families—my uncle Raza in Malawi and Saudi Arabia, my uncle Anwar in the U.S.—and because my mother now had her own school and her own money, my mother assumed day-to-day responsibility for Amma and aunt Anjum—her Apa—until their deaths, six years apart.

Nobody would have predicted that role for my mother. Growing up, Suraiya had been her father's favorite and emphatically not her mother's. Amma's middle daughter had been much too mouthy as a girl, her words sometimes propelling her invalid mother out of bed and into a spanking and slapping frenzy that left Suraiya's face swollen. But after my grandfather's death, mother and daughter began to grope toward each other in the darkness of their grief, and in time Suraiya became the child Amma most relied upon, the one who understood her needs before she articulated them.

So the fairytale of Amma's early life brimmed with an irony that I could see only when I had grown up myself, read a lot of literature and taught it. At one point, Amma and my aunt Anjum rented a two-bedroom apartment in a gray building, stark and spare. Like their other flats, it provided essentials but did without the aesthetic touches that would have raised the rent. The apartment building was a lower-tier enterprise of another Indian immigrant, a fellow Bihari, who named his building projects after landmarks in Patna. This unlavish apartment complex with bare, concrete floors, wrought iron windows that begrudged the sun, and a balcony from which my aunt Anjum let down her basket on a rope with money for the vegetable-seller and pulled it up again with okra or eggplant—this apartment complex that Amma lived in was named after the home in which she was born, her father's estate, Kashana.

But I never heard Amma speak nostalgically of the material things she used to have growing up. I never heard her draw such comparisons between her past and her present. Instead, she saw her life as divided into two discrete, hardbound volumes: the first marked by my grandfather's presence, the second by his absence. I imagine the first volume as being in full color; the second as black and white, more white than black—like the white saris Amma wore, by choice, all the days of her widowhood. Naghmi Baji and I tried to get her to wear the tiniest touch of pastel sometimes, asked her to do it for our sakes, and, when that didn't work, teased her about following an obsolete Hindu custom for widows when she wasn't even Hindu. But Amma would look at the lemon or lilac fabric in our hands and shake her head.

"That's not how I feel," she said simply.

Nothing connected the hardbound volumes of Amma's past and present except the yearnings that flowed from one to the other—yearnings for faces she loved and lived without. That was the continuity in Amma's two-volume life, that flow and overflow of absence.

When I was twelve or thirteen years old, Amma started writing. Not just the long letters to her mother and siblings in Patna, but the story of her life. "Samina and Naghmi have nagged me into writing my past," she'd say, beaming. She wrote in long, lined notebooks that reminded me of our teachers' attendance registers. Now when we visited her flat, we always found her sitting with pen in hand. She would put her pen down when she saw us and offer to read from her "diary." We often said yes, sometimes to humor her and sometimes because we really wanted to hear what she had written. But just as often, we were merely touching base on our way to someplace else, my mother standing on the threshold, her car keys jingling on the keychain. *Maybe next time*, we'd say.

Over the next two decades, Amma would sit and write and rewrite. We were happy that she kept busy, though it wasn't until an author friend of my mother's, Zaheda Hina, made us aware of the fact that we understood Amma's work to be an important contribution to Urdu letters—a literary history, in Bihari dialect, of the landowning class in pre-Partition Bihar; of displacements in the wake of political events, and of flux that follows the arc of time. After Zaheda Hina's pronouncement, we dangled the promise of publication before Amma, and Amma kept writing.

When I boarded the plane from Boston to Karachi in early 1996, I didn't know if Amma would still be alive at the other end of my 22-hour flight. I stumbled into the hospital room with my parents and Chotepapa, who had come to pick me up from the airport as the day dawned, and there she sat, looking not only alive but radiant.

"She who loved me came tripping all over herself to see me," Amma said.

I gave her the wedge of Kraft cheese-spread that I had saved for her from the plane, the little white rectangle filled with raspberry jam. She had always liked the dainty packaging of airline food. That was the last food she showed any interest in, if only because I had brought them.

Amma lived for a week, and during that week she released all the words she had kept packaged up inside her. The day after my arrival she insisted on being discharged from the hospital and taken back to her home in Maymar Apartments—to the rented space she shared with my aunt Anjum, in the same complex where my mother now lived. Against everyone's advice, Ammi honored her wishes. Gradually, Amma would refuse medication, oxygen, food, and water, and Ammi asked us all to honor those wishes, too. But until the last thirty-six hours of her life, Amma gave us the words we never thought she had. I stayed by her side, not wanting to sleep at night because I would miss something.

At one point she awoke from a few minutes of sleep and turned her head towards me.

"I dreamed I was lost in a jungle," she said. "But then you appeared."

That week Amma's stories hit all the highs and lows of her seventy-six years. Revealed to us in the lightning flash of her ebbing life were the memory, the vision, the heartache beneath the placid surface. She quoted Urdu poetry, including my grandfather's ghazals. She called out to her husband in a wail I had never heard before, asking how he could have forsaken her in her youth, condemned her to a lifetime without him. She cried out for her mother, her own Amma. And she, who had sorrowed for her two mentally handicapped children, asked me to bear witness that her mind never lost its moorings, even at the end.

As news of her physical agony spread—the gasping lungs, the failing kidneys, the slow collapse of the overburdened heart—relatives I hadn't seen in years came to visit their Baby Baji, Baby Khala, Baby Naani. And however painfully the breath came, however many sores flecked the inside of her mouth and throat from scouring medication, for each of her guests Amma had a story—about their births, about their parents and grandparents—a story that gave them context, that tied them to her, and to something bigger and beyond them both. As Khalammi and Chotepapa's 17-year-old daughter, Sheba, cupped her palm against Amma's chin to catch what her grandmother's stomach rejected—a gesture as generous as it was self-effacing—Amma recalled the collision with the yellow minibus, when she had sat in the passenger seat with baby Sheba, how her head and arm had leapt to intervene between the baby and the impact, taking the blows that would leave her arm and forehead blue for weeks. Amma paid the heart's every debt in stories that week, recalled every gesture that had made her feel a tad less powerless during three decades of dependent widowhood. She startled us, too, with her knowledge of us, assigning to family members quirky name tags that compressed their stories: her daughter Talat became "Mullani" for her piety; her son-in-law Ilyas's innocence rendered him "Bholay Mian"; for me, a graduate student in Boston, she had coined "Professariya," pronounced like a sing-song Bihari endearment, and her youngest sister in India, Iffat, was affectionately typecast as "In-Law Worshipper," straight out of Bollywood. Once or twice Amma claimed mischievously that her illness was intended to test her daughter Suraiya's mettle. It turned out that this quiet and passive invalid, well-versed in Farsi and Arabic classics but lacking a formal education, the woman we saw sitting, had spent the years reading us closely between the lines.

  Amma's transformation from reticence to sudden and forthright volubility shocked, amused, and awed us. She spoke her mind that week, her words at once incisive and kind, and often crackling with wit. Still at the hospital against her will, when the doctor asked what she had been eating, Amma retorted, "I've been eating my heart out in this place." And when I emerged from the shower in an unflattering shalvar-qameez suit that was many times my size, she asked why I was covered in elephant-cloth. Once home, and cajoled into sleep by our relentless wills, she awoke a few minutes later and told us with a grimace of revulsion that she had dreamed of a woman whose head was infested with lice—lice crawling on every inch of her scalp.

"And that was the benefit of sleep," she added wryly.

The afternoon that Naghmi Baji, Sheba, and I conspired in kitchen whispers to smuggle medication into her cereal, Amma's voice floated towards us: "You girls had better not be up to any 420-ing." And hearing that uniquely South Asian use of the term (from Section 420 of the colonial Penal Code) applied to us, we girls dissolved into laughter. After that we gave up trying to pull the wool over her eyes, trying to keep our grandmother with us against her will.

By the time my uncle Anwar and his daughter, Soubia, arrived from Delaware, Amma had lost her sight, though there was nothing physically wrong with her eyes. One visitor, flustered to find Amma's vision gone, thought to compensate by speaking to her in a loud voice. Eyes closed, Amma observed with gentle matter-of-factness: "I'm not deaf."

The night before Amma stopped talking, her bedroom was packed with relatives. Like a blind Tiresias, Kaneez Fatima sat on the bed that her husband had special-ordered for her forty years earlier, recycled from Burma teak wood that had once served in railway tracks, and which Pakistan Railway subsequently auctioned off to its employees. Never one to inhabit the spotlight, on this night Amma gave instructions for her funeral and injunctions for us to live by, and named again the kindnesses of people long gone. She reminded us to leave her in an unmarked grave—no arrogant, egotistical tombstones—so that when Qiamat came and Allah raised her on the Day of Judgment, she could rise with humility. Again and again, she told us to cherish those we loved, whatever the world's opinion. She spoke of my mother's years of caring—"like a son, really"—the visits back to Kashana she had made possible. And though her interactions with my aunt Anjum had been fraught with the pressures of their limited lives under one roof, she now publicly affirmed her faith in her eldest daughter's strength, her ability to endure alone in their shared apartment.

"Speak up for yourself, Anjum! Don't let the world treat you as a fool. We're alike, the two of us; the only difference is that I benefited from having a kind husband. The world thought me a simpleton, too."

Then, without warning, her words focused on me:

"I have given Samina permission to marry her friend," Amma declared.

Amma and I had never had the kind of relationship in which I would need to seek her formal permission for anything. She had met Alex when my uncle Anwar had flown her out to Delaware on a visit visa and taken her on daunting road trips that included wheeling her around Plimoth Plantation and Niagara Falls. Amma approved of Alex implicitly, as she had approved of the Palestinian student I insisted on marrying years ago while still an undergraduate at Karachi University. The only question she had asked me then stemmed from her curiosity about this species of marriage that bypassed all the rituals of form and arrangement.

"What excitement can there be about the marriage when you've already met your groom?" she had asked, her eyes keen with a genuine wonder. "Where's the suspense in it?"

This time around she hadn't asked even that. "Love marriages" yielded plenty of surprises, as it turned out. Nor would it occur to Amma to point to my failed first marriage as evidence that the new-fangled didn't work. Her daughter Suraiya had opted out of her arranged marriage after twenty-three years, to say nothing of the sorrow that Anjum's beautiful, by-the-book wedding had wrought. Hadn't the cruelties of that marriage hastened her own husband's death? No, it wasn't about arranged marriage or love marriage; it was about what you made of it. When Amma pondered the prospect of Alex entering the family, she wondered if I would wear white for the wedding, like the English memsahibs in pre-Partition India.

"I've always liked brides in white," she said. "How different from the vibrant reds and fuschias our dulhans wear!"

In Amma's bedroom now, eyes dart toward me. That I have a "friend" in Boston rather than a marriage proposal mediated by my elders breaks the rules of middle-class propriety enough; the fact that he is, as they suspect, a white American of Christian background extends wildly beyond the pale. But the very next instant, all eyes return to focus on Amma's face. She had made her point and moved on. I may not have been prepared for a wedding announcement, but Amma had seized the moment. Her dying breath had wrapped itself around me like a protective sheath. Her public blessing had sanctioned my unorthodox course. It didn't matter whether I cared what my relatives thought. What mattered was that my grandmother had embraced the totality of me before the eyes of the community to which she belonged—a community that sought her out as the family elder, a reminder of where they came from and who they used to be. A reminder, too, in the uncertain present, of their connection to one another, whatever the nature of their becomings in this tumultuous megacity, 1700 miles and a lifetime away from Patna. What mattered was that Amma claimed me that night. And in that public embrace, Amma gave me everything she had to give.

While Amma was alive, her manuscript didn't get beyond the proofs of the first volume, six hundred pages long. Sons and grandsons had shared the printing cost with my mother, but the publishers had dragged their feet; the demands of our daily lives, the disruptions in our civic lives, our collective inefficiencies and muddled priorities stole the years away. During that last week of Amma's life, Zaheda Hina, the author and journalist who had validated Amma's writing of twenty years, finally brought the proofs to her. By that time, Amma could no longer see. Surrounded by us, her daughters and granddaughters, she held the loose pages in her hands, her fingers caressing the cool, smooth surface of her memories. I like to think that in that moment Amma imagined those pages as a book. I want to believe she envisioned her memoir among the rare Arabic and Farsi manuscripts of Patna's Khuda Bakhsh Library. I want to believe she saw the book as it sits today on a shelf in my office in the English Department at California State University, Fresno. Sitting on my shelf, a hardbound copy of *Memories of Days Gone By*, Part One of Amma's two-volume life, Part Two still awaiting print.

Sweet-and-Twenty

"Are you two homos?" my mother asks her nephew and the light-skinned Parsi boy sitting beside him.

Azfar and Meherwan burst out laughing. It's 1987; they are seventeen in the Islamic Republic of Pakistan, where, by law, they can be lashed and stoned.

We don't know it yet, but theirs will be the longest-running love of our generation.

Soon they will be in New England, taking the Greyhound bus between Harvard and Brown. Then will come the move to the West Coast for their master's degrees in electrical engineering at UC Davis before the two make a home for themselves in San Diego, in 1993. We don't know it yet, but their throwing down roots in San Diego will make them the pioneers around whom many family members will cluster in the course of a generation—to work, to raise children, to go to college, to heal, to retire, and, for our aging mothers, to make one last migration across the oceans. Azfar will design the logo for San Diego's 2006 Pride Parade. The torch, lit with rainbow flames that arch back as though pushing forward against the wind with strength and grace, will remain a beloved symbol of San Diego Pride. In 2018, it will still be in use when my aunt, Azfar's believing, practicing Muslim mother, attends the Pride Parade for the second year in a row. Her presence there on the sidelines, standing by herself and cheering, will say all that there is to say about holiness, faith, and love.

Apollo 11 landed on the moon four months before Azfar's birth at Perivale Hospital in west London. I have a six-year-old's memory of the televised event: both pairs of parents and the three children of our melded family huddled together in the small living room of our Greenford home, glued to the black-and-white television screen. But my world was transformed in 1969, not by Neil Armstrong's first footstep on the moon, but by the arrival of the baby boy I had been praying for. He arrived ready to love and be loved. He would be my ideal baby brother—not like pesky Amir, who reveled in toppling my neat pile of books in the box room we shared on Long Drive. When I came home from school, I would run up the stairs to my aunt and uncle's bedroom, which they now shared with two children, Rubina and baby Azfar, in order to give my parents the other bedroom and let Amir and me occupy the small but separate box room. I'd find my happy baby with round cheeks and ready smile. If he seemed restless, I rocked the pram and sang "Puff, the Magic Dragon" until he quieted. He was everyone's "Attu," as my mother had nicknamed him, but only I was his "Apa." As a toddler, he cried many a morning when I left for school. "A-pa-a-aa-a-aa"—I'd hear the long, tragic wails as I shut the door behind me, and my little-girl heart sank and soared to be loved like that.

  We lived in Greenford until Azfar was five years old and I was eleven. There followed a period of time when we were wrenched from each other to live on different continents, as Chotepapa and Khalammi moved their family to Malawi for three years. But by 1978 we had all returned to Karachi, to 379-A/1 and 465-A/1, to come to young adulthood within walking distance of one another in Gulshan.

  1989, on another continent: I am nearing the end of my first year as a graduate student at Tufts University in Boston and only now beginning to think of people as "gay" or "lesbian." It's not that concepts of sexuality and gender that lie beyond the heteronormative are absent among mainstream Pakistanis. But throughout South Asia's history, they have had a paradoxical presence in the social consciousness, being at once visible and invisible, though always relegated to the margins. On one hand, the transgender community—commonly referred to as Hijras, though Khwaja Sira is the more dignified term—have had a time-honored visibility in South Asia. Until the British penal code of 1860 targeted them, they had a self-sustaining social and economic infrastructure. Their position in the mainstream was by no means equal, but—perhaps because in the popular imagination they were associated with Mughal courts, or because their prayers and curses were believed to be powerful, or simply because they embodied the mysteries of human life—they'd be invited to dance and perform on festive occasions such as weddings and births. In the Karachi of the late-twentieth century, Hijras were a fairly common sight, if by that we mean transgender women, in particular. I usually saw them at Bahadurabad Chowrangi, where, after buying books at Universal Bookstore, we would be sitting in our parked car outside an eatery, waiting to be served our plates of spicy chaat. If a Hijra person approached the car window, it was usually to ask for alms. I'd watch from the backseat with a mix of fascination and fear, their garish makeup, women's clothing, and deep male voices jarring to my eye and ear.

But they were there—and they are very much there now. Still marginalized and stigmatized, often ostracized by their families, and vulnerable to violence, trans people are nevertheless asserting their rights as citizens. High-profile trans Pakistanis like news anchor Marvia Malik, and models Kami Sid and Rimal

Ali, have helped spread awareness of the issues they confront. So while Pakistan's Christians and Hindus have been terrorized by blasphemy laws, and even Muslims of minority sects have been under violent attack, surprising news about the Pakistani trans community reaches me in California. In 2009, Pakistan became one of the first countries in the world to give legal recognition to a third gender, and three years later, its Supreme Court affirmed the community's fundamental right to education and employment. In 2016, while Target stores in the U.S. had to put up a fight for all-gender bathrooms, Pakistani clerics issued a fatwa pronouncing marriage between trans individuals legal, as long as the couple comprised of a man and a woman. (Intersexed people are still not allowed to marry anyone.) The clerics also called for compassion for trans people because, as they put it, their plight was not a choice. Then in 2018, Pakistan's Transgender Person (Protection of Rights) Act came into being after a unanimous vote in the Senate and the National Assembly. The law allows Pakistanis to identify as male, female, both, or neither, and it protects the civil rights of trans citizens, including the right to run for office. Five trans people ran for office in the country's general election in July 2018.

But there are no laws to protect Pakistanis against discrimination or harassment based on sexual orientation per se. In fact, homosexuality remains illegal in the country. Most people who might identify as gay or lesbian in the West remain closeted in Pakistan. The Hudood Ordinances—laws that General Zia-ul-Haq implemented in 1979 as part of his theocratization of the country—are harsh against homosexuality; if caught in the act, a person may not only be imprisoned for up to ten years, but flogged or stoned to death. It's true that these punishments are not likely to be enforced, and that powerful but ill-paid police officers would rather use the knowledge to blackmail. But there are extrajudicial punishments to fear, meted out by mobs. In 2014, three gay men in Lahore were the victims of a serial killer who lured them on Facebook.

In middle-class Karachi, people may acknowledge romantic or sexual interest in persons of the same sex but still balk at the Western labels. Men walking hand in hand might be a common enough sight, but that homoeroticism remains unnamed or else it's dismissed as a phase boys go through. Many men and women who are Westernized enough to think of themselves as gay, lesbian, or bisexual will nevertheless maintain the facade of a heterosexual marriage.

At Tufts University, I hear for the first time such course titles as "Gay and Lesbian Literature." Stories I have never heard before beckon. Only now is it dawning on me that Azfar and Meherwan love each other as more than friends.

And I'm devastated. The thought alienates and repulses. My sister, Sadia, talks to me on the phone from Hamilton College; she says the unfamiliar often feels that way. But she is sad. Her concern is that life will be harder for her Azfar Bhaiya than for the rest of us. I think Sadia is the better of us two. I am not religious, but I can't shake off my own discomfort and sorrow.

The next time Meherwan takes the bus to Boston to see Azfar, the two of them visit me in my third-floor apartment in Somerville. Theirs is a generous mission: to help me past my limited ways of seeing so that I am not hurting anymore. When they enter my home, the flesh-and-blood reality of them begins to gnaw at the granite abstractions that have been occluding them from my view. In the doorway, Azfar's big, beautiful eyes focus on me with a tender frankness, his smile all sunshine, warming the world around him. Meherwan walks behind me and greets me with a gentle "Hi, Sam." I realize with a pang that he's nervous. Then they are both sitting before me, the same individuals they have always been, my love for Azfar reflected back at me in his eyes.

"Well, you don't look any different," I say, and Meherwan's face relaxes a little.

I worry that I may have had something to do with Azfar turning out this way, since I'd often dress him up as a Pakistani bride when we were children. He would sit still and close his eyes while I did his makeup, our sisters helping. We put rings on his fingers and beads around his neck, saving the prized tear-shaped pendant as a teeka for his forehead. Then came the dramatic part: a glamorous red and gold dupatta pulled over the bride's bent head. Said bride sat compliantly on the floor or bed in traditional bridal pose, with one leg crossed and the other one bent so the chin could rest on the knee, as we had seen in the square black-and-white photos of our parents' weddings. Hands clasped around the bent knee, showing off the rings. The bride sat mute, with eyes closed, because we all knew the perfect bride must barely be conscious of, let alone enjoy, her own wedding.

Azfar and Meherwan talk me through my conceptual wilderness with a patience and compassion that exceed their twenty years.

"But think about it, Apa. Would you ever have thought of dressing Amir Bhaiya up as a dulhan?" Azfar asks. "Obviously, I *wanted* to dress up. I was different. Remember how I'd scribble 'I love Starsky, I love Hutch' all over my notebook?"

I tell Meherwan I'm glad he's not some older man who seduced my baby brother—like the Ancient Greeks, you know? I'm glad he's someone I have known and liked. The two sit next to each other on the couch a foot or so apart, public displays of affection a luxury they have seldom had. Meherwan is more reticent than Azfar, but the earnestness in their voices is the same. In the course of our conversation, their two faces come into sharper and sharper focus, until the unexamined layers of mangled belief and bigotry, which had seemed so natural until this moment, come unraveled. I see them for who they are: two young people who have found love and companionship and joy in each other. Why begrudge them? It's more than I have with the angry young man I will leave within two years, and I find it in me to be happy for them.

But still.

"It's just that I've always seen Azfar as the most perfect man in the world—in every way. Handsome, brilliant, warm, and wise. A gift! I always thought how lucky that woman would be whom he'd fall in love with someday. And now . . . what an enormous loss for womankind!"

It's not an argument, but it's the truth of a deep and benighted sisterly love.

Meherwan's eyes search my face. Then he speaks the words that clear the film from my eyes.

"But Sam," he says, his voice soft as dew in springtime. "Why not think of it as a gain for *man*kind?"

fragment 7

And what of the jokes and books we shared,
the movies seen on rented VCRs?
Your passion for The Fountainhead, for Anthony and Cleopatra
above all of Shakespeare's plays.
"They died nobly," you said.
Death as a choice
Among limited options.
And Chariots of Fire—how you watched that film
not just with your eyes
but with your whole body.
Olympic runners,
running from what?
Towards what?
Runners who make it to the finish line,
who endure.
Who win against all odds.

fragment 8

Unlike me, you finished at St. Joseph's,
Blazed a trail for Sadia and Sheba,
Blazed a trail for me.

Rubina Najmi: first girl in the family to win a scholarship to America.
Against all odds.
Smith College, class of 1989,
your way out.
Against all odds.

Trailblazer. Black sheep.

Quarantine Song

Hammersmith Hospital, London, 1967:

    A wordless child. I have no English.
    I lie in a hospital bed in a big room. I'm the only one in it and it's getting darker. The voices of children float through, but the door is shut and I cannot see them. I'm not one of them.
    Everybody has left. Even my mother. Hospital rules.
    And the bed is cold.
    Women in white caps walk in during the day, but they never stay.
    Men in white coats come in groups. They stare and prod and write things down on paper. They talk among themselves and I don't know what they say. Nobody smiles.
    One man in a white coat has a brown face. He looks like my Chotepapa.
    We came on a plane. Karachi is far away, where the sun is. Phuppijan is there. Naghmi Baji is there. Phuppijan can't hold me anymore and Naghmi Baji can't play with me because the plane isn't going back.
    I am all alone.
    But I don't cry out. And I don't try to run away. I am the eldest. I will be four years old soon.
    The memory is amber, the color of dusk. My first memory.

    Chotepapa will bring me home from the hospital for my birthday. To Shepherd's Bush, where my parents and brother and I share his flat and a bathroom that's common to all who live in the building. There are seven of us in Chotepapa's two-bedroom space, including his wife (my Khalammi) and their baby girl, Rubina. When Chotepapa brings me home, my mother will dress me up in a lemon frock she has sewn with her one good hand, with dark-blue, diamond-shaped patches down the middle that shimmer like moonlight. She will put a matching lemon ribbon in my hair and a dab of red on my lips. She'll outline my big eyes with a pointy kohl flourish. There will be color photographs, lots of them, for me to remember the day by: here I am standing by my small, golden-haired doll in a red dress, pretty packages visible on the dresser behind me; and here are images of me amid orange and yellow balloons, my eyes half-closed in sleep, as now my father, now mother, and now my aunt hold me against blue and gray floral wallpaper. One photograph catches me with my arms flung around Chotepapa's neck, his smile beaming. It's the same smile his son, Azfar, will flash at us in years to come. Chotepapa, so called because he is more than an uncle to my brother and me; he is our Little Papa, even though he has a baby daughter of his own now.

Chotepapa has brought us to live with him in London. Enough of Karachi, enough of Pakistan, he said.

Now he wants to move us all from Shepherd's Bush to the cleaner suburbs.

"My little niece got sick here. Who ever heard of malaria in London? Enough of the dirt and the damp. Enough of sharing a bathroom with other tenants. We're moving into a semi-detached. A home of our own in Greenford!"

Greenford, 1967-1975:

And throughout our childhoods in Greenford, until our return to Karachi, Chotepapa will be the sunshine parent for my brother and me, and for my little sister when she arrives. He will be boat rides in Ruislip Lido, swings in Ravenor Park, late-night dinners with family friends in Walthamstow. He'll give us summer days in Wales, that summer we actually went on vacation to Cardiff and Swansea. And when we squeeze into his car for long drives—as many as nine of us in a matter of a few years—he will be laughter and song. Danish songs, German songs, English songs he has taught us, which we sing together, just the children and he.

> *My bonnie lies over the ocean,*
> *My bonnie lies over the sea,*
> *My bonnie lies over the ocean,*
> *Oh, bring back my bonnie to me.*

He has made something of himself from Copenhagen to London, this boy who lost his mother at six, and his father at sixteen in newly independent India. But it will never be enough for him, the lone splendor. He will always want to plant other stars in the sky. His older brother's family is just the beginning.

Taunton, Massachusetts, 2002:

When Chotepapa died, I couldn't grieve.

I had a baby at my breast, a toddler at my knee. I had the upturned, expectant faces of new students at a new college, an hour's drive from our southeastern Massachusetts home.

At Agha Khan Hospital in Karachi, Azfar and Sheba had to make a decision. The decision to take life-loving Chotepapa off the ventilator. But as they searched each other's faces, Chotepapa's heart gave out. His last gift to his children, who held each other and cried.

All the cousins gathered in Karachi except me.

I get up at five, nurse the baby in his sleep. I lead the tearful toddler back to her Daddy. I put on my teaching clothes, pack lunch and breast-pump into my teaching bag, and begin the long commute on Routes 495, I-95, and 128.

In the classroom I open my mouth to speak, but no words form.

A wordless professor of English.

Because the mouth creaks with cankers. More cankers than teeth. Every canker a sprouting childhood memory.

Bring back,
Bring back,
Oh bring back my bonnie
To me.

The Cat Connection

One early winter's morning in Boston, in the last days of 1998, my husband, Alex, opened the back door of our house to find his gray tabby, MoeMoe, stretched in an arc at the top of the porch steps. MoeMoe's front paws lay within touching distance of our door.

Alex rushed indoors to get a towel, folded MoeMoe in it, and cradled him in his arms. Rigor mortis had already set in.

I grieved for a cat I had never touched in all the years I had known him. I'd pour the Alpo dry food from a big Garfield-shaped container, place the bowl on the kitchen floor, and back away as soon as he approached. Just as dutifully, I made sure MoeMoe always had clean water to the brim. But if, while I was opening a can of shredded turkey for him, his tail caressed my ankle, I'd jump and move away. MoeMoe was a gentle cat, but I, who had grown up without pets and still had recurring nightmares about cats that clawed me, could appreciate him only from a distance. I was the observer who documented the love between Alex and MoeMoe with my camera.

My relationship with animals has been fraught. I had very little interaction with them growing up, either in our immigrant lives in England, or in Pakistan. Dogs may be marginalized as unsanitary in Muslim cultures, but I don't know that cats fare much better even though Prophet Muhammad is said to have been fond of them. The stray cats in our Karachi neighborhood kept me up some nights with their howlings, which entered my dreams. During the day they trod the low walls that separated our neighbors' patios from our own—scrawny, unkempt, and terrifying in their vulnerability.

Perhaps the distance between animals and humans has never been great in my mind. Perhaps as a child I could imagine the desperation if I were cast aside and left to fend for myself. Fear erased pity, upsetting the delicate balance of the two that Aristotle considered vital for catharsis in Greek tragedy. The growls may have been just brawls or mating calls, but they frightened me. Like a Greek chorus, they haunted and held me accountable. For what, though? For the boys who perfected their aims by hurling stones? Or for the dearth of food and shelter and compassion in the world?

My barely acknowledged ambivalence about animals would crystallize around the big Muslim holiday of Baqr Eid, as we call it in Pakistan—meaning the second Eid, which occurs ten days after Hajj in Makkah, in accordance with the lunar calendar. For those who didn't grow up celebrating Baqr Eid, I should say that it commemorates Prophet Ibrahim's near-sacrifice of his son (believed to be Ismail rather than Izhak), and so in his honor Muslims sacrifice cows and goats at Baqr Eid as a gesture of unquestioning love and obedience to Allah. The flesh of the sacrificial animal is then divided into three equal parts: for consumption in one's own home and family, for one's neighbors and friends, and for distribution among the poor. You're encouraged to do the qurbani slaughter yourself, but most people rely on a professional qasai. My father, who could normally not stand the sight of blood, and whose vasovagal tendencies my son Cyrus and I inherited, could—amazingly—do the qurbani with his own bare hands at Baqr Eid. It's faith. It's also hard labor to clean up after the sacrifice because you have to separate the edible parts of the carcass from those that must be discarded, and because your veranda is now a mess of blood and entrails. That's why most of our neighbors, like most Karachiites, preferred to slaughter their animals in the street rather than in their own yards.

I had no problem with this when I was a child. In fact we children of the neighborhood would dress up in our festive new regalia and head out excitedly to watch the entire process: the lovingly fattened cow or goat led by a rope to the qasai's butcher knife; the panic in the animal's eyes; its thrashings as multiple hands hold it down; the red fountain spurting from its throat, its will to live still thrumming in the quiver of a leg. But as I grew older, Baqr Eid had me in a quandary. I didn't want to offend Abbu or spoil the festivities for anyone, but at times under some pretext or other, I had to shut myself up in the bedroom I shared with my siblings. I'd raise the volume on my cassette player high enough—Boney M's "Rasputin" or Neil Diamond's "Forever in Blue Jeans," perhaps—to drown out the distorted gasps from sliced windpipes, the bleatings and mooings, the sounds of dying in the lane.

The annual spectacle should have immunized me to lesser agonies. Or strengthened my faith. Shown me that the end ennobles the means. That loyalty to principle and purpose trumps the heart's rebellion. Or taught me to privilege the symbolic over the literal. Instead, at thirty-five I turned vegetarian.

It happened a few days after Alex found MoeMoe dead outside our door. There were no visible marks of violence on him, either by another animal or by a car. Somehow MoeMoe had hauled himself home to die. Somehow he had made it up the red brick steps of the porch and laid down on his side, his front paws extended toward the door in a frozen gesture of belonging that claimed us ever after.

Less than a week later, Alex and I were sitting at the kitchen table. Even as he cut into his steak, he remarked, "It's odd that I'm mourning one animal and eating another." He had uttered the precise thought that had been looming in my consciousness since MoeMoe died. Two years married, we were very different people whose ideas sometimes converged in momentous ways. We stopped eating meat after that.

When I visited Karachi in early 2006 with my children, Maya, who was not quite six years old, and four-year-old Cyrus, I had neglected to check the Muslim lunar calendar beforehand. So I arrived at my father's home in Gulshan where I had grown up and, after all these years, was faced with the prospect of street sacrifices again. I was especially concerned for my tender-hearted, Vegetarian American children. Luckily, Khalammi (my aunt Talat) lived in richer, more Western, and more sanitized Clifton, so without explaining my motives to Maya and Cyrus, we fled to her seventh-floor apartment for three days while Karachiites emulated the Abrahamic patriarch. High up there, we were safe from the sounds and even from most of the sights, but when we ventured outside, the children would see the occasional gut lying by the roadside and wonder. Then in the empty compound at some distance beneath our seventh heaven appeared unmistakable blotches of redness and fleshiness. It was time to level with my kids about this particular holiday in the city they had come to love.

"It's sacrifice," I say.

"What's that?"

"It's when you give up something valuable to please your Creator."

"Why does that please your Creator?"

"I guess because you've passed the test of love."

"I don't like tests"—this from Maya's experienced kindergartener perspective.

I try a different route.

"For many poor people in Pakistan it's the only time of the year that they get to eat meat."

"Why would they want to?" Cyrus asks.

Um. For the protein?

"I don't like petting dead animals," he adds decisively.

"Look, honey, Baqr Eid is a holiday—like Thanksgiving. You know how most people in America celebrate Thanksgiving by eating turkey? Well, in Pakistan you celebrate Baqr Eid by eating beef and mutton." Then, with a deep breath: "The difference is that in America you don't see all the turkeys being killed for the holiday. In Pakistan the animals are killed in the open."

I refrain from adding that in Pakistan children don't come home from school with brightly colored artwork and hand-prints depicting cows and goats cheerily anticipating the holiday that will massacre them. Thank goodness for small mercies.

We left Khalammi's Clifton apartment and returned to my father's home in Gulshan when Abbu indicated that the coast was clear. No sign of carnage left, though a toneless voice on a traveling loudspeaker still urged us to donate our hides to the orthodox political party, Jamaat-e-Islami. Otherwise, the neighborhood's cleanup was complete. All but that metallic smell that dallied in the air, haunting our street for days.

Alex buried MoeMoe in our backyard, near the blue Siberian squills he had planted earlier that spring. He had lived to be eight years old. Many well-meaning pet-owners suggested that we get another cat, but it offended me that they thought MoeMoe was replaceable. Eight months after he died, we sold the house. I didn't want to live there anymore, and Alex was easily persuaded.

For the next thirteen years, during which we moved again—this time across the country to Fresno, California—we had no pets, though our children often asked for them.

Then in the summer of 2012 Winnie found his way to us.

We came home that June day to discover three kittens huddled together in the junipers of our front yard. Someone had left them there in a box. They seemed about three months old. My children, who were ten and twelve at the time, saw their chance.

"Honey, I'm not comfortable with pets in the house," I objected.

"They can be yard cats, Mama! And they can come to the garage for shelter when they need it."

I didn't say that there's enough heartbreak in life without attaching yourself to four-legged beings you will one day have to bury.

The winning argument came from Maya. "You don't want us to grow up to be like you, do you, Mama?"

In the end, I said yes because I didn't want my children to grow up like me, skittish around animals, incapable of experiencing the joy of holding them.

So my children named the three kittens Tigger, Winnie, and Piglet. Tigger looked almost exactly like MoeMoe and had his serenity, too. He appeared to be the natural leader. not because he sought the position but because he had a quiet confidence that made the other two cats, and the rest of us, look up to him. Piglet had a beautiful slate-gray coat. She and Tigger would snuggle in their sleep. She didn't much care for any humans except Cyrus. For him she would emerge from her various hiding places and allow herself to be petted. And then there was Winnie, a motley white and black in color—a cow print, as Cyrus calls it. He got along with his siblings but spent much of his time doing his own thing. The three became our yard-and-garage cats.

At about the same time, a limping feral cat we called Molly discovered our neighborhood on San Jose Avenue. Before we knew it, kittens were birthed in our backyard every few months and it became our job to find homes for them. We did keep one kitten from Molly's first litter, a blue-eyed, fawn-furred beauty with a raccoon tale, whom Maya and Cyrus named Snickers. We would also have kept Millie, who was born later—an affectionate and lively little one with black, white, and ginger markings, but she disappeared. We like to think she found a friendly home somewhere else. Alex managed to trap Molly, finally, and get her neutered before releasing her into the neighborhood again. For weeks after, he had the battle scars to show for it. But even after Molly was no longer procreating, cats kept multiplying on San Jose Avenue—apparently, there was the proverbial Cat Lady who didn't neuter her cats. Other kindly neighbors who loved cats fed them, too, so more kept coming for food that was readily available in the scarcity of life. By the time we moved out of that home—four years after we became cat owners, and a year after Alex and I divorced—first Tigger and then Piglet had disappeared on us. Only Winnie and Snickers moved with my kids and me into the condo on Calimyrna Avenue.

Tigger was the first of our Fresno cats to vanish. Maya and Cyrus looked for him everywhere. They made a flyer with Alex that had an image of Tigger on it—a photograph I had taken in the driveway one afternoon when Cyrus came home from school, threw his backpack on the ground, and as usual, before anything else, petted his cats, who had come to greet him the moment they heard him. In the image, you can see my now twelve-year-old's blue sneakers and his hand on Tigger's back. He and his sister went door to door with the flyers. I posted on Facebook, anxious about how my children would handle this loss just a year after their much-loved grandfather, my Abbu, had died in Karachi. Miracle stories about cats making it home months after they had been given up for lost kept hope alive. By the time my children understood that Tigger wasn't coming back, their sadness had lost its sharpest edge, and, to my relief, they showed no visible signs of grief. Two years later, when Piglet disappeared, it was a few weeks before our move to the condo, and my children were already savvier. Young teens, by now they had had to process death, disappearance, and divorce. On my part there was an element of relief because I knew Piglet would have had the hardest time with the move.

Not that moving was easy for Winnie or Snickers either. At first we tried to keep them safe in the condo's garage until they had acclimated to their new environment. But knowing that Winnie wasn't good at sharing, I had to get past my phobia and let Snickers into our home. I even moved her litter box inside, though I was still far from being able to pet her. At first she hid behind the bookshelf, but eventually she got comfortable, especially in Maya's room. After a week or two we thought the cats would be ready to venture outside. But while Snickers leapt from one rooftop to another and explored the courtyards and common grounds of all the condos in the cul de sac, Winnie refused to leave the garage. In fact, he became so neurotic that he would hide the whole day in a cardboard box half-filled with books, or else behind the water heater when the days got colder. We needed to intervene. Now that

Snickers wasn't confined to the indoors, we opened the pet-door between the garage and the kitchen and coaxed Winnie to come in. That's when we discovered that he's a dog-cat, as Cyrus puts it: zealous for human company, and not just for cuddles but for eye contact. If anyone should retire to their bedroom before the others, he'll follow them, meowing outside their door until they re-emerge. A quirky cat, he knocks the marble chess pieces around and chases his own tail until we're helpless with laughter. True, on Thursday mornings when the condo's landscaping crew comes by, I see traces of his post-move neurosis, as he hides behind the bookshelf for fear of the mowers and leaf blowers. But most of the time Winnie is very much at home in the condo.

So much so that as soon as we had let him indoors, Winnie booted Snickers out completely. That was the price we paid for Winnie's sanity, and it saddens me still. Sweet Snickers hasn't disappeared like Tigger, Millie, and Piglet before her; she comes inside to have her meals while we keep Winnie at bay. I've had a pet-door installed in our kitchen slider, which opens into the patio, so she can come and go as she pleases (or at least as Winnie will let her). And recently, after much research, I found a little cat-house online that Maya and Cyrus assembled over Thanksgiving break. I was eager for Snickers to have somewhere to go before the winter, which is also the time of year our arid San Joaquin Valley gets whatever rain it's going to get. Once my kids had assembled the handsome white structure with dark brown trim and two doorways, I placed it in the patio close to the kitchen slider. Reviews warned that you might never be able to get your cat to go in, and it seemed that they were right. I tried catnip as suggested, but that didn't work. I relocated the cat-house further away, and that didn't' work either, so I brought it back closer to the kitchen and under the eaves, and kept a close watch.

A month or so went by. The day Snickers began using her house for shelter from the rain I took photo after photo and sent them to Maya and Cyrus with a jubilant message saying I counted it among the greatest accomplishments of my life. All the more so as this year Fresno has seen more rains and storms than all the past thirteen winters that we've lived here.

When people hear that I'm a cat-phobic owner of two cats, they are incredulous. Some are impressed. I say it's not unlike a parent who loves their children but doesn't hug them. And it's a marvel to me that this is a comparison most people readily understand.

How far have I come? Some distance, to be sure. I don't jump as easily around cats, though I'm still very guarded. Once or twice, I have even touched their coats. I keep them well-fed and keep Winnie's litter box clean. But it's Maya, on her visits home from college, who replaces the collars that Snickers loses regularly, and Cyrus who administers the flea meds to both cats. I don't know what I'll do in a year's time when Cyrus, too, has left for college. What if Winnie or Snickers falls sick and needs to be carried to the vet? I'll have to enlist Alex or other cat-loving friends.

Sometimes I think that just as Winnie's irrational fear of the gardeners is mirrored in my irrational fear of cats, he and I will experience the empty nest as a shared loss. Maybe then, when it's just the two of us at home, our greater dependence on each other will give me access to a normal kind of love between pet and human. It's something I remain wistful about. Surely, I've been inching towards such a moment these twenty years?

In the meantime, I remain vegetarian. Through all the flux of the two decades since MoeMoe died, that has remained a constant.

And another thing. I don't know when it happened, but I became aware of it only recently: I no longer have nightmares about being clawed by cats.

Hiding Osama Bin Laden

"Mama," says eleven-year-old Maya one evening in May. "Some kids in my class asked me if my family had helped to hide Osama Bin Laden."

Hmmmm.

It's true that I'm from Pakistan and that my parents still live there in 2011—not way up north among the mountains in Abbottabad where Bin Laden has just been killed, but way down south by the Indian Ocean, in Karachi. And given the scant distinction that elementary school children make between public and personal conversation, my background and my parents' whereabouts must be common knowledge among Maya's classmates. But playing host to Osama Bin Laden—*really?*

Maya looks up from her social studies homework with tentative eyes. Ten years flash by me in one, indistinguishable moment. Maya was a toddler when the September 11 attacks happened. She had learned to walk the earth in Taunton, Massachusetts, barely three months before. I mourned the deaths and destruction on Ground Zero while she rummaged through the kitchen cupboards and built towers out of tupperware. Then I mourned the backlash against people of Muslim background like myself, while she closed her dark, pondering eyes to lullabies my grandmother once sang to me in Urdu. My childhood a spliced narrative of Pakistan and England, I thought I had finally found belonging in America. But the backlash told me that 9/11 was not my tragedy to grieve. It robbed me of rootedness in the world, even as Taunton gave Maya gravity, introduced her to the cloud shapes above and the fragrant woodbine below.

And while the world seemed to take leave of its senses, while we razed Afghanistan—the country next door to my parents, the country whose battered population had resurfaced from civil war and brutal Soviet occupation to find itself in the harsh grip of the Taliban—while we razed Afghanistan that October in order to kill one, Saudi man responsible for our national tragedy, I was about to bring an American boy-child into the world.

Cyrus was born five months after 9/11, when Maya was 21 months old. He learned to roll over on the rug, then crawl, and speak his own first words as the official rhetoric regarding Saddam Hussain's weapons of mass destruction gathered momentum and spread like a pernicious gas. The week Cyrus took his first independent steps in Taunton, we invaded Iraq. By August of that year, I had bowed out of adjunct teaching as an English professor, scooped up my two young children, and left for Pakistan. I don't know what I sought in Pakistan. It wasn't as though I had felt a complete sense of belonging there. But when the road ahead of you vanishes, you retrace your footsteps to where you began. I knew only that I wanted my children to live, for a time, near their grandparents and the web of relatives and friends who would mark their every developmental milestone with commentary and laughter. And perhaps Maya and Cyrus would begin to spout Urdu words just from being among them, since I had dropped the ball.

Five months later, we returned to Taunton, where my husband, Alex, had been waiting for us with quiet patience. I returned with the knowledge that the only text I could hold sacred was the US constitution—a contested turf, but one that I could trust in a way that I couldn't trust governments or public opinion anywhere. Even if we warred with two Muslim countries simultaneously, America would give me the space to raise my children as I wished: as secular Americans, invested in civil rights for all.

And secular they most certainly have been, for the most part. We began to celebrate the big Muslim holiday of Eid when we realized that we would be decorating Christmas trees and conducting Easter egg hunts because our children enjoyed them. That was when our secularity took the form of embracing a plurality of holidays. Other than that, my children's lack of religious indoctrination has taken even me by surprise. One year, shortly after our move to Fresno, California, Eid coincided with Rosh Hashanah, so a Jewish friend, Toni, and I made a joint presentation on the two holidays for the children in Maya and Cyrus's elementary school.

"Who knows the story of Adam and Eve?" Toni asked. All the children raised their hands—all except Maya and Cyrus. My children had never heard of Adam and Eve! That was the point at which Alex and I decided to include creation stories, religious beliefs, and diverse rituals of prayer and fasting in our repertoire of narratives aimed at raising our children as culturally literate Americans.

Yet, for all our attempts to provide our children with a multiplicity of narratives to grow up on, the post-9/11 decade has presented them with narrow choices that render our own parental philosophies irrelevant. Today I realize with a shock what I thought I knew: that Maya and Cyrus have no memory of America before 9/11. This means they have never lived in a world in which Muslims have not been hypervisible. They are growing up in an age that makes no distinction between "Muslim" (follower of a faith) and "Islamist" (adherent of a political ideology) but collapses orthodox, moderate, and secular Muslims into one, undifferentiated mass. Perhaps it is because Maya takes such a world for granted—as I who *do* have memory of a pre-9/11 America can not—that she appears so uncannily vigilant for her years. During the heady time of hope in Barack Obama's candidacy, my children had planted "Obama for President" signs among the cypress trees of our front yard in Fresno, alongside signs declaring "No on Prop 8" (a California proposition that refused the right of marriage to gay couples). But when, during a televised presidential debate with John McCain in early 2008, Obama asserted the need for greater military intervention in Afghanistan and Pakistan, Maya—not quite eight years old, and flitting within earshot—stormed out of the room, exclaiming: "He wants to terrorize Pakistan! I'm voting for McCain."

Fresno, where Maya has been living since she was six years old, forms a pocket of Christian conservatism smack-dab in the center of California. In 2010, at the beginning of fifth grade, the repeated attacks on a mosque in nearby Madera led to conversations in her classroom. Some explained the attacks as a reaction to the ill-advised plan to build a mosque two blocks from Ground Zero. Maya, finding herself a lone "representative Muslim" in class, asserted that the 9/11 terrorists were not really Muslims, only pretending to be. (She had heard my devout father say that the hijackers were not true Muslims and took that literally to mean that they were imposters.) Before the conversation could go any further, her teacher, a reasonable woman with brilliant blue eyes, extinguished it with: "I live in California, not New York, and school is not the place to discuss politics." And so the shiny gold coin of a potential learning moment, in which thirty-two young people might have pondered the sanctity of civil rights for all Americans, rolled away and disappeared into the chinks of a narrowly defined fifth-grade curriculum.

"So—how did you respond to their question about hiding Osama Bin Laden?" I asked my daughter.

Maya chewed on her pencil.

"I told them that just because Osama Bin Laden was found in Pakistan doesn't mean he was Pakistani," she said, her eyes soft with amusement.

Whew, I think. She doesn't seem ruffled. She isn't about to conflate her love of Pakistan, and of her grandparents' home, with religious affiliation. I imagine my parents rolling out the red carpet for Osama Bin Laden, on and on for five years—and chuckle.

A week later, I've read and sung and tucked Maya and Cyrus into bed, made myself a ritual cup of Ovaltine, and turned on the reading lamp by my night table when I notice Maya's slender body framed in the doorway to my room.

"Not sleepy, honey?" I ask.

Maya walks across the room and sits on the bed beside me. Her small hand rests on mine.

"Mama," she says, gentle as a baby bird. "I'd like to fast this Ramadan."

Membership Dues

At the kitchen table, I mull over the categories on the subscription form for the South Asian Review. In the early summer of 2011, I'm a newly tenured associate professor at California State University, Fresno, spending part of the congratulatory present Azfar has sent me. The categories on the form are obvious enough:

Student/Part-Timer
Instructor/Independent/Assistant/Retired
Associate Professor
Full Professor
Lifetime Membership

The form asks me to circle one and pay the corresponding amount for my journal subscription, which comes as a perk of being a South Asian Literary Association member. I know that both the organization and the journal have been around since the 1970s, publishing literature and critical discussions by authors from such countries as India, Pakistan, Bangladesh, and Sri Lanka, as well as writings of the South Asian diaspora. But this is the first time I have printed out the membership-cum-subscription form. A quick, oval stroke of the pen–that's all it requires. But I'm riveted to the pen's imagined circle, following it back in time.

I couldn't get out of Pakistan fast enough. My childhood fractured between two continents, I spent most of my Karachi years yearning for the nondescript London suburb of Greenford. Pakistan felt like the place that held me back—where, by the mores of my middle-class Muslim family, I couldn't wear a skirt or denim jeans but only shalwar-qameez, and though ours was not a hijab-wearing family, a dupatta was mandatory, even if it hung around our necks rather than covering our breasts. In my neighborhood, bikes and swimming lessons were off limits for an adolescent girl. I fancied myself at Riverdale High, hanging out with Archie, Betty, Veronica, and Jughead, my days infused with the glamor of their hamburgers, sodas, and high-school sweethearts. Later, poring over my French primer, I daydreamed myself into the Sorbonne and the streets of Paris. At Karachi University, I majored in English Literature and minored in French and International Relations—a curricular course intended as a runway to lift me off into other skies. My undergraduate years were a heady swirl of love, learning, and occasionally dodging the exchange of fire between rival political parties on campus. An exciting life, now that I look back on it, but at the time I felt shut out from the thick of the action. I could only gaze on the real world from continents away, my nose pressed white against the glass.

I smashed through that glass window with my fully funded admission to the graduate program in English at Tufts University. When I set foot on Boston's Logan Airport, I thought I had stepped into a movie—everyone spoke with that cool, casual American accent. I leaped into this American movie as a student, pouring my energies into discovering first African American writers, then Chinese and Filipino American authors. Sure, my dissertation ended up including a chapter on Bharati Mukherjee, but throughout my years at Tufts, it did not occur to me to take a course in South Asian American literature, if it had ever been offered.

Then in the fall of 2010—thirteen years after Tufts—I taught Bapsi Sidhwa's *Cracking India*. The Pakistani American novelist was to visit Fresno State, where I teach multiethnic U.S.

literature, and I wanted my undergraduate students to experience the thrill of meeting a writer they had just read in class. I took a risk, uncertain how my students, mostly white or Latinx, would relate to a novel in which a young Parsi girl experiences the 1947 British partition of India that birthed the Muslim nation of Pakistan. Why would they care about the bloody exchange of populations that ensued on all sides—Hindu, Sikh, and Muslim—in the wake of that Partition? But I needn't have worried. *Cracking India* reached my students across time, space, and political and cultural chasms. Its aesthetic appeal apart, the novel provided my students with context for Pakistan's hypervisibility in 2010—a visibility that does not result in sustained attention but registers in disconnected flashes in our sound-bite culture.

But for me the experience of teaching *Cracking India* struck terribly close to the bone. It asked that I not only grapple with the ideology behind Pakistan's creation as a home for Muslims (which I had certainly pondered before) but that I confront my Indian-born parents' and grandparents' history of migration from their native Patna, and my own place as an ethnic Muhajir immigrant, in Pakistan. Cracking India demanded that I acknowledge all the years of my grandmother's life spent longing for Kashana, the house her father built in Patna at the dawn of the twentieth century—the home in which she was born, which saw her a seventeen-year-old bride, and where she gave birth to all but one of her seven children, including my mother. My grandmother's lifelong yearning for her mother and her own seven siblings, all of whom she left behind when she migrated with her husband and children to Pakistan—I had to *see* it all as I taught *Cracking India*.

Wisps of family lore floated back to me, and I called my father in Pakistan to ask more questions as I prepped for classes.

As a fifteen-year-old, my father had taken part in rallies and processions in support of carving Pakistan out of India. "Our home in Patna became a shelter for the Muslims fleeing religious riots in the surrounding villages of Bihar province," he said on the phone. "I vacated my bedroom for a pregnant woman. She delivered her baby there." He didn't know what became of them.

My father's nineteen-year-old brother, Idris, escaped the Delhi riots and joined the trainloads of Muslims migrating helter-skelter to territories designated as Pakistan. "We didn't hear from him for a long time," Abbu told me on the phone. "Then we got word that his train had made it safely across the border to Pakistan." Silence. Then: "The train before his and the train after his arrived full of corpses." It had taken my father over sixty years to share this memory of terror for his older brother. And though Idris Najmi had died of natural causes by then, Abbu's voice trembled, remembering how his brother narrowly escaped a terrible fate during Partition.

An idealistic eighteen-year-old, impatient to live the dream, my father left Patna for Karachi, Pakistan, in 1950. He never saw his father again.

When Bapsi Sidhwa arrived at Fresno State in the fall of 2010, not only my students and colleagues, but much of the South Asian community of Fresno turned out to hear her read and introduce the screening of *Earth*, Deepa Mehta's film based on *Cracking India*. The auditorium crackled, the seats filled with South Asians of Sikh, Hindu, and Muslim backgrounds—and at least one Parsi, the author herself. Most had been born in India, Pakistan, or Bangladesh; others in the United States. As I looked around me, listening, I saw us offer up our bewildered shame and pain to one another, our secondary but persistent trauma. Our faces asked without asking how we might reconcile the historically bloody divisions among us with the here and now. In the landscape of America—site of yet another migration—the turban-targeting backlash since 9/11 had collapsed all of our imagined distinctions to reveal our oneness to ourselves with wrenching irony. Might we see an opportunity here to reconceptualize ourselves and read one another differently? To remain Muslim, Hindu, Sikh; speak Punjabi, Urdu, or Bengali, and at the same time to transcend these specificities as *South Asian Americans* in this time and place? Might we begin to tell a new story?

And so it was that Sidhwa's *Cracking India* grabbed me by both shoulders, whirled me around, and chucked my chin until I looked up, unblinking. *"What will you do with this legacy?"* it asked of me.

I didn't know. But I knew that it was time to make my way towards that expansive circle, the beginnings of an answer.

The slender, white ballpoint pen with *Fresno State* written across it in red letters has been lying alongside the form on my placemat. I pick it up and hold it between thumb and index finger with a pressure that turns my middle finger white. Firm and steady, I circle my subscription category in dark-blue ink: "Lifetime Membership," I choose.

Teaching as a Pakistani American Muslim Feminist

I am not given to retrospectives. At best, I have a tenuous truce with memory and history. But the tenth anniversary of 9/11 calls for an account of some kind—or, perhaps, accountability of some kind—and that narrative can only be personal.

Two months after September 11, 2001, I spoke on a panel at Wheaton College of being robbed of my right to grieve, of my feelings of homelessness in the backlash against the likes of me, a Muslim-bred Pakistani woman who called the US home. With the kind of visceral empathy that can sustain itself only in the moment, I realized then what it must be like to be Black in America and live with the daily reality of being disowned by your own country. I spoke of my fears of raising a biracial daughter in such a climate.

Today my concern is for my 11-year-old daughter and my 9-year-old son, as well as for Armaan, my "Blackistani" nephew (a term coined by my brother-in-law, Kip), and my part-Korean niece, Naïla, both just toddlers. I have wondered at my choice of "Suleiman," a recognizably Muslim middle name for my son, born five months after the 9/11 attacks. I have tried to temper my daughter's uncritical identification with all things Pakistani. Though I keep my children politically informed, I have not prioritized the teaching of Urdu. None of this comes from mindless assimilation. It reflects the simple fact of our constricting choices as parents of Pakistani American children in the decade after 9/11.

Shortly after the US invasion of Iraq, I scooped up my two children and left indefinitely for Karachi, Pakistan. After five months there, I returned to Massachusetts, having realized two things. First, that I, who held few texts sacred, trusted the US constitution, however contested a document; that governments might come and go, and public opinion might swing this way and that, but ultimately the constitution would hold America accountable. And second: my students wanted me back. The first conviction impels me to insist on my place in America, to claim "Muslim" not as a religious but as a political identity. And this claim in turn informs my identity as a teacher, as I am always aware of presenting an alternative to mainstream narratives of Muslim womanhood for my students.

My evolving sense of myself as a post-9/11 Pakistani American Muslim feminist professor has had to attenuate to the culture-shock of moving from Blue to Red zone within the U.S. When I left Massachusetts in 2006 to teach at a state university in California's agricultural San Joaquin Valley, I found myself on a heterogeneous campus with students who do not come from privilege, and who tend to espouse politically conservative values. Precisely because of their limited options, many enlist in the military, and many others have family and friends serving in Afghanistan and Iraq. Suddenly, with the appearance of the occasional student who attends class in fatigues, or the student whose fiancé is killed in Afghanistan a few weeks before her graduation, it has become impossible for me to think of the US military as implacably "other." These young people, whatever they may end up doing in Pakistan, Afghanistan, or Iraq, shape me within the walls of the classroom, as I shape them. So one lesson I have learned as a teacher in the years since 9/11 is the absolute necessity of distinguishing between the architects of war and the pawns of war. That is to say, my political identity as a Pakistani American Muslim must mesh with the pedagogical imperatives that define me because it is primarily as a professor that I claim space in post-9/11 America.

As a Pakistani American Muslim, I am marked by specific political events since the invasion of Iraq. One came on the heels of the hopeful election of President Barack Obama. Before he had even taken office, his silence as president elect while Israeli attacks killed some 1400 Palestinians in Gaza over the course of three weeks beginning in December 2008 indicated that little was going to change in the increasing polarization of the world as Muslim and non-Muslim. (Not that all Palestinians are Muslim, of course; many are Christian.) Since then, I find myself remarkably free of partisan loyalty. Such freedom necessitates greater vigilance because I have no default position to lean on that acquiesces with a party line. But for that very reason I now have space for a sincerer discursive rapport with my more conservative students. So I do not regret the personal disillusionment. Harder to accept, though unsurprising, is the fact that as a direct consequence of the September 11 attacks, Pakistan itself has become an official war zone. An unidentifiable number of Pakistanis, well in the thousands, have been killed since Pakistan launched its war on terror as a U.S. ally. Of these casualties, the vast majority have been civilians—a fact seldom acknowledged by US officials, who continue to berate the Pakistan government for not doing enough. In July 2007, I was in Karachi during the government's siege and subsequent storming of Lal Masjid (Red Mosque) in Islamabad, which left 108 people dead, mostly young students presumed to be potential militants. Even militants can't be essentialized, as there are diverse groups operating within Pakistan, with very different agendas. As my childhood friend Muna puts it, "We used to wonder how Palestinians and Israelis could carry on their lives in the midst of so much violence; now we are living it ourselves." Apart from the US military "theater" in the northwest, other regions of Pakistan, riddled by inequities, internal strife, and failed leadership, have become sites of unpredictable explosions and shootings, both targeted and random. Among them, my own hometown on the Indian Ocean, the megapolis of Karachi.

Karachi, where I grew up. Site of my mundane joys and trepidations as a child, my predictable teenage rebellions. Though my Indian cousins teased that Karachi couldn't compare with Mumbai across the waters, for us Karachiites its potential endured and endeared. Sprawling city of seventeen million, where, it was said, nobody could die of hunger because one could always find work. Turbulent refuge of the displaced, the ambitious, the hopeless, from all over South Asia. Karachi the resilient, capable of bouncing back from natural disasters and the many more man-made disasters inflicted upon it. Karachi, coastal city of lights and boundless horizons.

It was from Karachi, from my hometown, that ten young men sailed to Mumbai on November 26, 2008.

9/11 and 26/11

They sailed from Karachi—ten young men, almost all of them from villages in Punjab, this side of the border. Ten deadly and dispensable young men who found purpose in Lashkar-e-Tayyaba, the Army of the Pious, which armed them to the hilt and assigned them the one, simple mission of killing as many people as possible in Mumbai. Over the next sixty hours, the ghastly details flashed across the world. What at first seemed like the targeting of Western and well-to-do tourists at the Oberoi and Taj Mahal hotels turned out to be indiscriminate butchery—in boat, taxi, and train station; in a café, a movie theater, a Jewish center, and even a hospital. The savagery knew no religious, racial, or class bounds. Except one: they spared a Turkish Muslim couple at the Oberoi Hotel, using them as scouts. Their rampage left some 170 dead and hundreds injured.

    I did not know any of the victims personally or anyone living in Mumbai; my Indian relatives were safe in other towns. But here in Fresno, the horror paralyzes me. While I listen gratefully to Vijay Prashad's voice on NPR cautioning against rash rhetoric that conflates the Mumbai massacre with the September 11 attacks, the seven years between them collapse and I can not keep the two events separate myself. It is the same bodily reaction—hands, feet, and face ice cold as though drained of blood, and stomach in mutiny. It is the same emotional reaction, that indistinguishable swirl of bewilderment, fear, and outrage; grief and guilt. It is the same intellectual freeze that renders me incapable of processing the event in coherent political terms. But in human terms, I respond to the massacre as we humans often do: powerless in the face of it, I am capable only of despair.

    Among the many things that troubled me was the question of my group affiliation. The ten terrorists were radicalized, as the hijackers of 9/11 were. But they were also Pakistani, every last one of them. And they had sailed from Karachi. Now that I had embraced "Muslim" as a secular political identity, what was I to do with this? How to process the carnage and the Pakistan government's defensiveness about it? How to accept the probable complicity of powerful individuals who had masterminded an attack so sophisticated, technologically savvy, and multipronged? Later, when I hear cell phone recordings of directions articulated in urbane Urdu, in a gentle, guiding voice like my father's—directions to kill—I understand that evil is indeed banal and homey.

I hold on to fragments: the Turkish couple, spared but held hostage by the terrorists, dare to put their hands together in prayer and recite Surah Fateha, the Muslim prayer for the dead, for the non-Muslims shot before their eyes. The killers don't know how to react to this and look away. And when nine out of the ten terrorists are themselves killed, Indian Muslim clerics in Mumbai refuse them a place in their cemeteries. Stories emerge of courage, duty, and sacrifice: the hotel manager and staff who refused to abandon the guests, a chef who sacrificed his life rather than run home to his wife and son, three blocks away, while he had the chance.

In the end, the way out of despair and onto some new plane of consciousness is personal. My mother, calling from Karachi, says that Karachi and Mumbai are twin cities—Mumbai being everything Karachi might have been with greater political stability and less religiosity. She tells me that when Mumbai hurts, as it has before, Karachiites feel the pain. I don't know if many Karachiites feel this way, but I need to clutch at her words. Eventually, I reach out to Rajini, a dear friend of many years, in Massachusetts. Mumbai is her city of birth and remains her spiritual home. They sailed from my hometown to hers. Across the miles, we sorrow together. We fear and hope together for our ancestral South Asia.

In spring 2011, I finally braved the task of teaching a course that struck me terribly close to the bone—a course on South Asian American women writers and filmmakers, Hindu, Muslim, Sikh, and Parsi. It was a course that demanded the confronting of personal and collective histories, from the wrenching divisions of the 1947 British partition of India that birthed Pakistan to our fumblings towards a more holistic South Asian American identity in post-9/11 America. You might say that through my students I have taken a long and circular path back to South Asia, not only as a Pakistani American Muslim woman but also as a South Asian American. Looking back, I see that the September 11 attacks and subsequent—in fact, consequent—events of the past ten years have impelled and necessitated this trajectory.

With astonishing curricular appropriateness, a week before classes end we learn that Osama Bin Laden has been killed by U.S. special security forces in Abbottabad, Pakistan. And I do what I always do as a Pakistani American Muslim professor in post-9/11 America: I perform my consciousness of this Pakistan-centered event in class. By this point in the semester, my students know what many Americans do not: there can be no stable narrative of Pakistan, only a cacophony of mutually exclusive opinions within the country and across the globe. In the classroom, I grapple with my own conflicted feelings about the site and manner of Bin Laden's death—an unsorted mix of relief that Bin Laden is dead; embarrassment that Pakistan had been harboring the author of the 9/11 attacks; a fugitive pride that in the absurdly unequal power relations between Pakistan and the US, a slippery Pakistan had, like David, managed to outwit the mighty Goliath for so many years. As the US government revises its original accounts of the killing, I acknowledge the distaste I feel at the particular brand of justice being celebrated around us. The leader of the most powerful nation in the world sends a death squad not only into another sovereign space but into the home and bedroom of an unarmed Bin Laden, and kills him in the presence of his wife and three children. Then within days, I hear the sobering news of the deaths of eighty Pakistanis killed in a terrorist attack that claims to be the first revenge for Bin Laden's assassination. I must reconcile my feelings with a nascent vision that perhaps this showdown will rend the duplicitous veils that shroud Pakistani politics and betray the most basic needs of its citizens. I feel the first tremblings of a fragile hope: that Pakistan, finding itself at a pivotal juncture, may yet pull back from its General Zia-directed course of Hadood Ordinance and blasphemy laws, and fight back against an overpowerful military, to move towards a more secular society that prioritizes the civil rights of all its people. I share these thoughts, in all their rawness, with my students.

As part of the course on South Asian American women writers and filmmakers, we screened Valarie Kaur's documentary *Divided We Fall: Americans in the Aftermath*. Kaur is a young Sikh American woman from Clovis, California, a town just minutes away from our campus. A sophomore at Stanford when the 9/11 attacks occurred, Kaur was motivated by the backlash against Sikhs, Arabs, and Muslims to travel across America in an attempt to define what it meant to be "American" in that historical moment. An especially poignant segment of the film is Kaur's journey to an Indian village to visit the widow of Balbir Singh Sodhi, the first person to lose his life to the post-9/11 racial hatred of a self-proclaimed American "patriot," in Mesa, Arizona. The film, made by a young person like themselves, moved my students deeply, even as they pointed out to me that they are a generation with no memory of a pre-9/11 America. Neama, a Yemeni American Muslim student, emailed Kaur to thank her. In yet another instance of our curricular and political worlds coinciding, the correspondence between Neama and Valarie Kaur led to our knowledge that Governor Jan Brewer of Arizona was about to decide on a bill to remove Sodhi's name from the state's 9/11 memorial. The bill asserted that Sodhi was not a victim of 9/11. Neama posted a link on Blackboard that would allow us to sign our names to a petition urging the Governor to veto the bill. Several students in the class also posted the link on their Facebook pages, urging their friends to sign. Very soon after, on April 29, 2011, the Governor vetoed the bill. My students, entirely on their own initiative, had added their voices to the protest and exercised their rights in this democracy. They had intervened in the proposal to erase Balbir Singh Sodhi's name from Arizona's 9/11 memorial, grasping the fact that it sought to deny the connection between the terrorist attacks of September 11 and the immediate backlash against Americans of Sikh, Muslim, and Arab descent. That is, my students had intervened in a proposed distortion of U.S. history. I sense that they learn from this their own power as Americans to write an alternative script for America. And I learn from them my own relevance, however small, in this continually shifting landscape.

A dark circularity of events undergirds my narrative, however. At Wheaton College two months after 9/11, I referred to the turban-targeting that had cost Sikh men like Sodhi their lives. Ten years after 9/11, I write in the shadow of the casual killings of two elderly Sikh men, a case that is being investigated as a hate crime. On March 4, 2011, Gurmej Atwal, 78, and Surinder Singh, 65, were shot while out on their daily stroll in the Sacramento suburb of Elk Grove, a few hours' drive from where I live and teach. Singh died instantly, and Atwal succumbed to his injuries on April 15, without ever being able to speak and bear witness.

I am tempted to say that nothing has changed outside of myself and my classroom. But some things have. This time, a Muslim American civil rights group has responded in swift solidarity with the Sikh American community, offering a monetary reward for anyone who will help trace the killers. Perhaps we Muslim Americans have learned from members of the Japanese

American community, who, in speaking out against the racial profiling of Muslims and Arabs immediately after the September 11 attacks when it was not popular to do so, demonstrated their profound understanding of the fact that when we stand up for someone else, we are standing up for ourselves. Perhaps 9/11 taught many of us that as Muslims, Arabs, and South Asians we are all potentially suspect and very vulnerable. I like to think that the ten years since 9/11 have taught all of us that, as Americans living in America, we can choose not only to forge new alliances but, more meaningfully still, to recast our group affiliations in ways that enable us to envision ourselves—and our mutual futures—afresh.

fragment 9

*Oh, but the hauntings in your dreams,
when you stayed at your aunt's,
such fights in your sleep,
the hitting, the kicking,
the hurt.*

*And the hauntings of your pen.
Your A-level essay, on parents who create monsters
and the monsters who lash back at the world.*

*Save my little sister from me, you cried.
Save my brother, my aunt, from me.
Baji, save yourself from me.*

*And I did.
Telling myself that distance would keep our relationship intact,
keep you from destroying it
and despising yourself for it.*

*Yet the panic in my heart that day when you didn't open your bedroom door,
the relief when you finally did.
You'd always open your door to me. All I had to do was knock and say, "Rubina?"*

Why didn't I knock more often?

fragment 10

October's end, and your eighteenth birthday. I arrive with a gift I'm proud of: tan fabric for shalvar-qameez with geometric designs in brown, and—small miracle!—a little round purse that looks just like the fabric. You beam at my Tariq Road finds, and we have cake.

Your mother had a present for you, too, you know—but not the faith that you'd welcome anything from her.
So she set the cake on the table for us but held the present back.

You never knew about her present.

She never knew there'd be no nineteenth birthday.

The Cab-Driver and I

My first fall semester as a tenured professor at Fresno State, and I'm not allowed to drive for six months. This presents challenges on many fronts for our family of four—work, school, and all the ferrying required for soccer, volleyball, and piano. Once the vertigo from my head injury has subsided, I'll be able to take the Route 9 bus straight from my home in northwest Fresno to the university campus where I teach. But until then, I'm getting to know Fresno's cab driving community.

I know the names of both dispatchers of the cab company I call. Desirée, the afternoon dispatcher, will end every sentence with "Hon" and wait patiently for you to recall the name of the campus side street on which your department is located. By contrast, the woman who answers the phone in the mornings will be rude. But she will cry if you sound disapproving. I know the names and cab numbers of the drivers, how many children they have, how long they've been in Fresno. The tall gentleman who has a forehead overcrowded with lines is Nader. He was an airforce pilot in Iran under the Shah and spent two years in prison awaiting execution at the hands of the Islamist Revolutionaries of 1979. A Fresno cabbie for 24 years, he tells me proudly that he's among the few left who can find any street in Fresno without the crutch of a GPS. The youngest of the drivers, Marwan, may enroll in my upper-division writing class next fall. He's the one whose father-in-law was shot dead by robbers in his grocery store a year after he had moved his family to Fresno. It happened twenty years ago, when Marwan's wife was three years old.

So many cab rides, but it's the very first one I think about.

I called for it just a week after my head injury, despite the doctor's injunction to rest. The cab arrived promptly at 12:30 to drive me to my 1 o'clock class.

The driver gets out of his seat, walks over to my side, and opens the back door for me with old-fashioned chivalry. I'm a bit wobbly after the head trauma but manage to mount my bags and myself onto the high perch of the van, albeit with more heroism than grace.

The driver is a slim, small-framed man, and short by American standards. The silver in his hair stands out against his dark skin. I'm not adept at telling people's ages, but I estimate that he's in his sixties. I try to place him ethnically: though he looks like a fellow-South Asian, his accent throws me off.

As the driver negotiates a three-point turn on my street, an exchange begins.

"Fresno State. . . . Are you a student there or a professor?"

"I'm a professor," I reply. "I teach English."

"Ah. . . . Where are you from?"

"Pakistan," I tell him.

The driver freezes in the middle of his three-point turn. Eyes off the road, he gazes up into his rear-view mirror for a better look at me.

"You're from Pakistan and you teach English to *Americans*?" His frown is so concentrated that he looks angry.

"That's right," I say and wonder how long we'll remain suspended in our three-point turn.

The driver's face breaks into a beaming smile, the splendor of fireworks—the way my favorite uncle, my Chotepapa, used to smile. It speaks at once of an unabashed paternal pride and of a child's transparent pleasure in absurdities.

"Where are *you* from?" I ask him.

"I'm from Yemen," he says. By this point his eyes are on the road again, as we navigate the lunch traffic on Shaw Avenue.

He tells me that his son graduated from Fresno State recently and that another one of his children goes there.

"Do you have women students who cover their heads in hijab?" he asks.

I nod.

"Well, one of them is my daughter," he proclaims triumphantly.

The man's candor disarms me, melting our specificities away in an immigrant-to-immigrant moment. It's a moment that compresses the mutual stories of our lives—of what we gave up to be here, in America, in Fresno, California, doing what we do now. In the untold telling, we acknowledge that the road has been a long one, with potholes, dead-ends, and detours we could not have foreseen. That we have sometimes looked back longingly on the terrain we left behind, but stayed. And in the mirror of each other's accomplishments, we are assured that the Dream has not beguiled us.

Then it comes.

"You're Muslim?" he asks.

"I'm from a Muslim family, yes."

"So you're Muslim."

"Well, I'm not religious."

"What do you mean you're not religious? You're from Pakistan."

A voice in my head tells me to take the path of least resistance, to forgo the taboo self-revelation in favor of courtesy and deference to an elder.

But I live in America. I live in America precisely because I can live here authentically.

"I mean that some Pakistanis are believing and practicing Muslims and others aren't. I'm not," I declare.

"What do you mean?" the driver asks again, disbelieving. "Islam is important in every aspect of your life! What good is this"—with a sweep of the hand taking in all of America—"if you don't thank Allah for it?" Then: "Think about your afterlife!" he pleads in the face of my complacency. This time his frown is unmistakable.

The strain of keeping my head from tipping into a vertigo-friendly angle suddenly becomes too much. Eternity is a dizzying concept.

"The reason I have to take a cab," I say, "is that I have a head injury and can't drive. If you don't mind, I need quiet."

He glances at me in the rear-view mirror again but doesn't say anything. I close my eyes and keep them closed the rest of the way.

When we arrive on campus, the driver walks over to my side and opens the door for me again. I say thank-you and overtip him to compensate for my lack of Islam.

He doesn't crack a smile.

I walk towards my classroom as steadily as I can.

So many cabbies of all description in Fresno, and I end up with an avuncular Muslim, reminiscent of the grownups I grew up loving and defying. Next time, I tell myself irrationally, I'm holding out for a non-Muslim cab driver. A turbaned Sikh, maybe—someone who'll have better things to concern himself with than my prospects in the hereafter.

So many cabs since that one, but I've never encountered the

Yemeni driver again.

Just as well, I think. Who needs a cabbie trying to bind me to another space and self? Everything I've tried to get away from!

But every time I get into a cab, I half-hope to see that driver again—the one who binds me to him with wisps of wistfulness.

She Leaves Me, She Leaves Me Not

Yesterday, we drove the three hours from Fresno to San Francisco International Airport together. Twenty-six hours later, you've called to tell me that you made it safely across North America, the Atlantic Ocean, Europe, and the Middle East—back to Karachi, our megacity on Pakistan's southern coast. Sajeda, your housekeeper of fifteen years, has made you a cup of strong, black tea sweetened with honey. Once again your day unfolds thirteen hours ahead of Pacific Standard Time.

I did not permit you any goodbyes in Fresno. As we loaded your bags into the blue minivan, your bottle of water, your string cheese and banana for the journey, and as your face betrayed the weight of the parting, I told you gruffly that this was no time for self-indulgence, we had a plane to catch. I snapped instructions—*use the bathroom*, *put on your jackets*—at my son and daughter, your eldest grandchildren, the ones who have learned from you the right-to-left Urdu alphabet, learned to share your taste for the sweet corn kernels, buttered and peppered, that you'd sauté for them when they came home from school, ravenous. At the steering wheel, I saw without turning my head toward the passenger-seat how you looked at the garage door closing down on our two months of togetherness; how, as we pulled out of the driveway, your gaze lingered on the bountiful oranges peeping out from the backyard, the tips of the tall cypress trees tickling our blue Fresno skies in early February.

Your son, my brother, met us at the International Terminal with a copy of your just-published book, your Urdu translation of *White Bear* by Dan Wegner, your younger daughter Sadia's doctoral advisor, a book on unwanted thoughts and our human attempts to suppress them. My brother and his wife, your daughter-in-law, have brought a chocolate cake and three candles so you can be part of your younger granddaughter's birthday; their San Francisco home with its steep stairs, a world beyond your reach. When we sing happy birthday, two gray-haired women look up from their sandwiches and join in. They are passengers like you, their eyes soft with recognition at your attempts to hold on to the flesh of your flesh even as the plane prepares to carry you eight thousand miles away. The three children who began leaving you thirty years ago, for their undergraduate degrees, their master's, their doctorates; for their careers in the academy, in Silicon Valley, in clinical psychology; for their marriages to Americans, white, Black, and Korean; for their children growing up without thoughts of Karachi. And you have done your best to shrink space and time, to partake of the graduations, weddings, divorces, and births. Except for the five years after 9/11 when the world came between us. In those five years you buried your Apa, my aunt, only a year older than you, and your brother-in-law, my Chotepapa, friend of forty years. In those five years, while shingles torched half your face (and burns you still), rheumatoid arthritis pounced on shoulder and wrist, gnarled your toes, and gnashed at your knees—the searing pain, the contorted limb—a mock rigor mortis, alive and afire. You let go of your school, the one you began in our living room thirty-seven years ago for your four-year-old daughter, my younger sister. You relinquished the love of four hundred schoolchildren. That daughter, my sister, sponsored your Green Card so you would never again be denied entry into our lives. And you sliced your years down the middle, six months here and six months there, the wholeness of hearts bridging the fracture.

But this time Karachi kept you the whole year. This time you arrived at San Francisco airport thinking *Let me see them in their American lives one last time.* This time you arrived in a wheelchair. This time I was glad not to greet you at the airport. I waited for my brother, your son, to bring you to me in Fresno, where you will stay, for the first time unable to visit your other children and your nephew and niece, my cousins. So they will drive to Fresno, a familial Makkah, for hurricane visits from points north and south, including your toddler grandson, my nephew, from San Diego, who will tell you that his knee hurts too. You will look in wonder at the lights on our five-foot Christmas tree, the one we've held on to year after year, though my children, your grandchildren, are catching up to it in height. With your one good hand—the other shriveled up since your crawling days when you dipped it into boiling chai—you will touch the ornaments they made in preschool, kindergarten, fourth grade, and marvel at them with your elementary school teacher's eye. Right before Christmas Eve we will whisk you away from landlocked Fresno for just one night because your son-in-law, my husband, will want you to see the Pacific Ocean again, from the wharf at Avila Beach when the horizon has turned the color of fresh peaches to the west, lavender ribbons flung east.

  At four or five o'clock in the morning, while I press keys on my laptop in the family room, I will hear the hallway door creak open, the sound of your slippered feet scraping their labored way to the kitchen on our hard Mexican tiles. You will not say, and I will not ask, what it took to position your feet on the guestroom floor this morning, how much courage, how much faith that your legs, warped into semi-circles like the necks of guitars left out in the humid Karachi sun, will carry you one more day. When you pass through the family room, I will get up to kiss your cheek, and you will look into my face the way my grandmother, your mother, used to—wistful and wondering, as though I'm a pleasant surprise. I will go back to my laptop and try to measure this morning's pain by the time it takes you to reach for the milk in the refrigerator, unfold the wax paper in the cereal box, eat just enough so you can swallow the painkillers that your stomach will mutiny against all day. When daylight spreads in our backyard, you will raise the shades of the family room, your left hand coaxing the reluctant right arm upward by the elbow, your eyes eager for the sight of our untamed sago palms and our pool shaped by the memory of a lake in Armenia, an exile's imagining of home. You'll make your slow, seesawing way toward the pool's blueness, wrapped in your bunny-pink robe, with cat food for Tub-Tub, the black and white stray who answers your Urdu call as brightly as your grandchildren do. The pain will relent a little in the course of the day, and you will come with me in the blue minivan to see those two grandchildren, my children, on and off the yellow school bus, always vigilant with the remote control so you can relieve me of the task of closing the garage door behind us.

Between the school bus hours, we will savor my sabbatical, have little meals of hard-boiled eggs and steamed edamame together, and you will make me cardamom tea because you know it is a taste of Karachi I'm unable to replicate. We will do our separate readings and writings until late afternoon when the winter sun shines half-heartedly through your window. Then we'll prop ourselves up in your bed, and you will read aloud from the two-volume memoir that your mother, my grandmother, left us so many years ago. The memoir she wrote in her colloquial Urdu over the course of twenty years, which your journalist friend devoured all in one night—*a vivid social history of Bihar!* she raved, of that patch of India my grandmother still yearned for five decades after

Partition. The memoir that was never published in her lifetime. You will read to me for two hours at a time, and we will wonder how she could bear to remember so much, the details as fine as her grape-leaf embroidery on the placemats she made for my table one summer. We will puzzle over the conventions of her time and place, laugh like unruly schoolgirls at her comic sketches. We will read her heartbreaks between the lines. Know ourselves a little better. And when the day draws to an end, when your grandchildren and I have kissed you goodnight, my husband, your son-in-law, will pop his head through your accordian doors and ask if you'd like a new movie to watch. You'll insert the DVD into the player in your bedroom, and Victorian men and women in large hats and flowing garments will flit across the screen all night, a hum barely audible, but companionship enough as you lie on the guest-bed, adrift between waking and sleeping. Then it's five o'clock in the morning again, and on your way to the kitchen you know you'll find me in the family room, pressing keys on my laptop....

Already a memory—our two months together, living as though I never left Karachi, you never grew older, space and time just tricks of our idle imaginations. You leave, as you have left so many times before, but this time you leave me a template for my tomorrows, of grace and tenderness, whatever the pain—*Because if I live long enough, the remaining blessings will disappear, too*—the mind curious, heart eager, eyes singing small beauties. I muffle my goodbyes at San Francisco's International Terminal, as your son, my brother, the one who chose business class to soften what your legs must suffer—*Because when my time comes, how will I spend on my own comfort if I never spent on hers?*—as that son, that brother, waves to the wheelchair attendant, who checks your name off his list with one brusque stroke, and, before I can believe the sight of you in a wheelchair—my dancing mother!—he has whisked you off toward the gate beyond our reach, your grandson, my son the soccer player, running and running on strong, sturdy legs, determined to catch up with you long after I have let you go.

Applause

When Suraiya was not quite two years old, she dipped her left fist into a pot of steaming chai. As a result, her left hand wilted. Suraiya's father would look upon it and worry—at the thumb that barely moved, and the four fingers curled inward, refusing to open up, straighten out, or hold on.

Still, Suraiya found a husband and moved with him from Pakistan to England.

Suraiya used her English words to get a job at the Lyons coffee-packing factory in Greenford. But under the forewoman's stern eyes, her left fist remained closed to the world. The coffee poured onto the factory's cement floor before she could lift the oncoming glass jars from the conveyor belt, smack them into place in the carton, and pass the carton on to the next woman to wrap up in plastic. The torrent of coffee grains rushing through her fingers taught Suraiya to make her right hand work twice as fast, and she kept her job.

When they returned to Pakistan, Suraiya started a preschool for neighborhood children. The preschoolers looked up as they sang and emulated her—row upon row of them clapping with one palm open against a balled fist.

They wondered. All those frumpy women who made it their business to comment publicly on Suraiya's life: how she had discarded, donned, and rediscarded her burqa; walked out on her husband and three children; remarried, redivorced, and married again. How she desired, and acted upon desire, while they made do. Where, they wondered, had Suraiya learned to grab at life like that—or, as the Urdu idioms would have it: to loot with both hands, to make off with sweet, round laddoos in both fists?

Ring In the New

Was I ever young enough to want to go out on New Year's Eve? Or even to just want to stay up until midnight, so the new year wouldn't catch me unawares? I have an occasional memory of venturing out on the T, or subway, as a graduate student, to see the ice sculptures in downtown Boston with my indomitable friend Lucilia, who made a point of resisting the winter inclination to hibernate. And once Alex and I braved an icy First Night on the town, only to discover that others had already beaten us to the free concerts we gravitated to—as much for the indoor warmth as for the music—and that a ten-minute walk between venues on black ice, and with a windchill factor of several degrees below zero, was enough to freeze out our enthusiasm to "do something" on New Year's Eve. Even in temperate California, I prefer to watch the ball descend on Times Square a few feet from the television, as Alex and I huddle with the children by the fireplace. After 9pm Pacific Standard Time, I'm satisfied that I've done my part to ensure the safe arrival of the new year and can retire in good conscience to my room, book in hand.

But I impose a fabricated consistency on my New Year's Eves. The fact is that when I was a teenager in Pakistan, in the Karachi of the late seventies and eighties, Shahina Auntie would beep her horn—two short beeps, followed by three more—after ten o'clock at night and insist we go out on a New Year's Eve drive.

Lively, bold, and resourceful, Shahina Auntie was not related to us. She had been Khalammi's friend since their college days in Dhaka, Bangladesh (then East Pakistan). When the British partitioned India in 1947, carving the new Muslim state of

Pakistan out of it, the lands that formed West and East Pakistan were separated by over a thousand miles of India in between. The two regions shared a majority Muslim identity, which was why they were merged into a single nation, but ethnically, linguistically, and culturally they had little in common. East Pakistan identified mostly as Bengali—though Bengal itself, like Punjab, had been split into two: West Bengal, which went to India, and East Bengal, which became part of Pakistan. Over a million Urdu-speaking Indian Muslims migrated to East Pakistan after the chaotic exit of the British, and many of them were from my parents' ancestral province of Bihar by virtue of its geographical proximity to Bengal. Because Urdu was imposed as the official language in West and East Pakistan alike, the Urdu-speaking of the Eastern wing had an unfair advantage over the native Bengali-speaking population. In effect, Partition for the people of East Bengal meant that they had exchanged the British Raj for colonization in brownface by the government of Pakistan, centered first in Karachi and then in Islamabad. While the country depended on East Pakistan's resources, it remained indifferent to the needs of the Bengali people, and therefore exploitative. Resentment brewed; it came to a head in 1971 when both President Yahya Khan and Zulfiqar Ali Bhutto, leader of the rival Pakistan People's Party, refused to acknowledge the absolute majority of Sheikh Mujibur Rahman's East Pakistani Awami League party. Civil war ensued, and the Pakistan Army's ruthless suppression of Bengali self-assertion, Operation Searchlight, began in March 1971 under General Tikka Khan. India supported the Bengalis, amassing its forces on the eastern border until Pakistan's "preemptive" strike against Indian airbases on December 3 led to all-out war between the two countries. Thirteen days later, Pakistan surrendered to the far superior Indian military. On December 16, 1971, East Pakistan seceded, and the independent state of Bangladesh was born.

Like us, Shahina Auntie is ethnically "Urdu-speaking," though her ancestral province in India is Uttar Pradesh rather than Bihar. While my mother's family had left East Pakistan for Karachi by the time of my grandfather Izhaq Balkhi's death in 1965, Shahina Auntie's family stayed on in the East Pakistani capital of Dhaka. Her father owned two jewelry stores in Dhaka, and she and her younger brother, Parvez, grew up among the Westernized elite of the city in the largely Urdu-speaking neighborhood of Mohammadpur. Statuesque Shahina Auntie, with light skin and light brown hair, was a champion swimmer and table-tennis player, and a heartbreaker. But at Central Women's College, she desired the attention only of my aunt Talat (Khalammi), a poetical young woman, a few years her senior. Talat was married before graduation, however—to my father's younger brother, Ilyas (my Chotepapa)— and, twenty years old and still grieving her father's death from esophageal cancer, moved a world away to London with a man she knew only as her sister's brother-in-law.

When the fateful year of 1971 began, Shahina Auntie was a 22-year-old graduate student of Political Science at Dhaka University. But the family's fortunes, like the country's, would turn dramatically by the end of the year. Between March and December, the Pakistan Army, in its attempt to squelch Bengali "rebellion," raped and massacred anywhere from three hundred thousand to over a million —and by some estimates as many as three million— Bengalis, a horror still to be acknowledged by the Pakistan government. (This despite the fact that, shortly after the war, Pakistan's own Hamoodur Rahman Commission recommended a public trial of the generals involved.) Like most colonial violence in world history, Operation Searchlight was motivated by economic interests but fueled by a potent blend of ethnic, gender, and religious bigotry. The Pakistan Army consisted of taller and relatively light-skinned men, a significant number of whom, like General Tikka Khan himself, identified as Punjabi; these soldiers were conditioned to perceive Bengalis as inferior because of their darker skin, and as effeminate because of their slighter build and scant regard for machismo. Above all, the Pakistan government and its military perceived Bengalis to be unduly influenced by the culture of their Hindu minority. No surprise, then, that a disproportionate number of Hindu Bengalis bore the brunt of Operation Searchlight's terror, and over a million fled to West Bengal, India, never to return.

Grave as that history is, another grim but lesser known history resulted from it, one that finds little space in the textbooks of either Bangladesh or Pakistan. Once Pakistani soldiers had withdrawn in defeat, enraged Bengalis avenged the Pakistani army's excesses by killing Urdu-speaking civilians living in their midst. Most had been Pakistan loyalists; some had actively assisted the brutal paramilitary Razakars. But vengeance has no patience for fine distinctions between guilty and innocent. All Urdu-speaking civilians, including the very old and the very young, became fair game with machetes and bayonets. The Mukti Bahini, lovingly revered by most Bangladeshis as freedom fighters, struck terror in the hearts of this hapless Urdu-speaking population abandoned by Pakistan in December, 1971.

Since my family is ethnically Bihari, everyone in my parents' generation seemed to know of someone who knew someone who had suffered in this second, bloody Partition. In 1972 we lived with Khalammi and Chotepapa's family in the west

London suburb of Greenford, and there we heard of unimaginable horrors: of "Bihari" children fishing among corpses for their parents' missing body parts; of men, old and young, being blindfolded, lined up, and shot at close range; of elderly women brutalized. As a nine-year-old, I didn't dare ask questions, but I'd overhear the adults whispering the rumored redness of Dhaka's rivers, and I'd see their furtive sharing of photographs in the newspapers. Years later in Fresno, California, I'll be looking through British photojournalist Harold Evans's 1978 book, *Pictures on a Page*, and I will shudder, both at the gruesome, full-page image in black and white, bearing the caption "The Bayoneting of Biharis," and at the memory of the grownups' faces as they stared into the *Sunday Times* in Greenford.

Historians emphasize perspective, and they are right, of course. How can these backlash killings, even if in the thousands—and few studies have been curious about their number—compare with the Pakistan Army's state-sponsored atrocities, including the planned and systematic targeting of journalists, artists, intellectuals, and professors (many of them scholars of Bengali and English literature), and the wholesale slaughter of students at Dhaka University, with which Operation Searchlight began?

But the hierarchizing of horrors, though vital for a sense of scale and perspective, is ultimately an empty endeavor for the human heart. In the end, most of us are left only with some personal form of reckoning, some kind of pondering, of the immeasurable effects of a single, individual death. And so, a Bihari friend of my uncle Idris in Islamabad found himself raising a niece who had been orphaned by the violence. And twenty-five years later, my mother would meet and marry an Urdu-speaking man many years her junior who lost both parents and three siblings in this smaller-scale massacre. His is a lifelong reckoning with the haze of memory—of men breaking into their home and shooting the family on sight; an older sister wounded in the hip, her voice urging him to save himself by playing dead.

At the time of this writing, close to 300,000 Biharis remain in the original sixty-six refugee camps in Bangladesh. Initially, when given the choice between staying in Bangladesh and being repatriated to Pakistan, two-thirds had opted for repatriation. According to most estimates, Pakistan admitted some 170,000 by 1974. The majority of these individuals began their lives afresh in Karachi's Orangi Town, the largest slum community in South Asia. But Pakistan, faced with other ethnic strifes, balked at repatriating any more Urdu-speakers, even as it admitted three million refugees from Afghanistan in 1979, and as tens of thousands of impoverished Bangladeshis arrived in Karachi illegally, looking for livelihood. In short, the "Stranded Biharis" had left their ancestral Indian province of Bihar after 1947, either as refugees of religious riots or out of faith in the newly created Muslim state of Pakistan, and had survived the ethnic cleansing that followed Bangladesh's independence, only to find themselves abandoned by Pakistan and unacknowledged by Bangladesh. Occasionally there would be talk of "repatriating" them to Bihar, but what claim could they possibly have on India? Finally, in 2008, Bangladesh granted citizenship to the Bangladesh-born-and-raised inhabitants of the camps, who now formed the majority. But until that point—for no fewer than thirty-seven years after Bangladesh's Liberation War—the Stranded Biharis and their descendants remained a stateless population, not even acknowledged as refugees by the U.N. Refugee Agency (UNHCR), their hopes toyed with by self-serving politicians in Pakistan and Bangladesh.

With neither Bangladesh nor Pakistan interested in the

plight of the Urdu-speaking minority of Bangladesh—either those who escaped to Pakistan or those who remained stranded in the camps—the hush of historical amnesia has, for the most part, enveloped the fact of Bangladesh's early reign of terror. Even if, some day, the government of Pakistan were to do the right thing and make a formal apology to Bangladesh for its terrible cruelties in 1971, who would care to make amends to the survivors of that era's subsequent, and all-but-forgotten, ethnic cleansing?

Yet individual lives, however broken, have a way of defying historical obliterations. The mere fact of their flesh-and-blood existence, charged with memory, challenges the collective amnesia despite abiding national narratives. In March 1971, when the Pakistan Army's Operation Searchlight began in East Pakistan, our family (which, besides Amir and me, now included newborn Sadia) and Khalammi and Chotepapa's (including four-year-old Rubina and toddler Azfar) shared a rented home in the modest Karachi neighborhood of Samanabad, part of Federal B Area, well over a thousand miles away from Dhaka. We had returned from Greenford some months earlier, hoping to resettle in Karachi. One day I answered a knock on our door, and there stood what to my not quite eight-year-old eyes was a paragon of mysterious beauty, one who looked European but sounded Pakistani. A happy commotion ensued as Shahina Auntie and my aunt were reunited for the first time since Talat had left Central Women's College in 1964.

Shahina Auntie had arrived in Lahore (West Pakistan) just a few days earlier with her father and within no time had hopped a plane to Karachi, equipped with a blue aerogramme from Khalammi that bore her Samanabad address on the back. Sensing turmoil in East Pakistan, Shahina Auntie's father had decided to move to Lahore in order to begin the process of re-establishing the family there. His wife remained in Dhaka with their son, 21-year-old Parvez, who was helping his father wrap up the family business. But as luck would have it, the siblings exchanged places by the end of the year. Shahina Auntie, determined to take her two remaining viva voce exams at Dhaka University in order to obtain her Master's degree, flew back to East Pakistan in September of 1971. Meanwhile, Parvez Uncle had flown in the other direction, to Lahore, to get his father's signature on documents pertaining to the sale of their two jewelry stores in Dhaka. On December 16, when Pakistan surrendered, Parvez Uncle's flight to Dhaka was canceled. Father and son would remain in Lahore without news of Shahina Auntie or her mother for ten months.

The day before Pakistan's surrender and the birth of Bangladesh, 22-year-old Shahina and her mother received word from a cousin in the Pakistan Army that they must leave their Mohammadpur neighborhood immediately. He sent an official car with a Bengali driver to pick them up and transport them to the relative safety of the Cantonment area. Shahina and her mother left at once, joined by a caravan of two dozen people, carrying nothing but a single change of clothes each. Their destination turned out to be the house of a Pakistan Army officer—unlocked, empty, and abandoned. The family must have fled suddenly, in the midst of an ordinary day, as nothing showed signs of agitation; even the lipsticks on the dresser seemed to be waiting for the lady of the house without alarm. There was, however, no food in the kitchen. So a couple of men from the group climbed the wall in the backyard and went foraging next door. It was another quietly abandoned house but yielded enough food for the group to live on for two days. Similar stealth excursions to silent homes followed as the need arose, and eight days went by in this way.

Then a young, Urdu-speaking family friend named Mansoor arrives with a trusted Bengali driver to help get Shahina and her mother to safety. Their choices are bleak: they can either throw in their lot with the POWs of the Cantonment or call on old Bengali friends for refuge until the present turmoil is over. Shahina's mother opts for the latter. Rahat Apa, whom she knows through her Tableeghi religious mission, will take them in, she thinks. They get into Mansoor's car and drive towards Rahat Apa's house. But at Ramna Park they are intercepted by two members of the dreaded Mukti Bahini. The two men redirect the car to a nearby house that serves as a Mukti Bahini office, tell them to pull into the driveway, and close the gates behind them. Then they order Mansoor out of the car and into the building for interrogation. Shahina and her mother remain seated inside the vehicle, wondering if Mansoor will emerge from the building alive. Standing a few yards in front of them, a man sharpens machetes. At one point, he looks up towards the striking young woman in the car. Eyes focused on Shahina, and grinning, he holds up the machete and makes a horizontal gesture across his throat, as if to indicate the fate that awaits her.

Some fifteen minutes later, Mansoor returns to the car. Stonefaced, he tells his driver to resume the route to Rahat Apa's. Questions from the women meet with complete silence.

Later, he will tell them of the interrogation, conducted in Bengali. Could all their lives hinge on the answers he gave to such simple questions? Who were they, where did they live, where were they headed. *Give us your wallet. And that watch. You won't be needing them where you're going.* Then Mansoor lets drop the name of a Bengali friend he knows to be a Mukti Bahini freedom fighter.

What he doesn't know is that the youth has assumed a leading role in the movement. His interrogator's face changes. He tells Mansoor to go home to his parents and even hands back his watch and wallet.

But before Mansoor returns to his own beleaguered family, he takes Shahina and her mother to Rahat Apa's house in the neighborhood of Bakshi Bazar. They arrive at her door and ask for refuge—for maybe a week or two, they guess—until the violence has subsided and they can get their exit papers in order. At great risk to herself and her family, Rahat Apa takes them in.

Shahina and her mother spend eight months in Rahat Apa's living room. Shahina is told not to step out of the house, not even to stand in the window. Kidnappings of young Urdu-speaking women abound—vengeance for the mass rapes and abductions of Bengali women by Pakistani soldiers—and Shahina's light skin will betray her instantly.

What compels individuals like Rahat Apa to risk their own security in a violent and chaotic time? To do so without any prospect of personal gain, for no reason but to shelter the shelterless? I marvel that she could resist the national narrative of the day, defy Bengali solidarity, forgo righteous revenge and forgive the brutal, blurry enemy long enough to allow the faces of two women to come into focus, not as Bihari or Bengali, but only as individuals; a mother and her daughter with nowhere to go and everything to lose. Where does it come from, that capacity for human decency that disrupts group affiliations, resists the lulling rhetoric, and intervenes—so quietly yet sure-footedly—in history? Rahat Apa's son was a Mukti Bahini freedom fighter who would come home every couple of weeks, often with loot, and rage against his mother, pointing out that if the Mukti Bahini discovered that his family was harboring Urdu-speaking women, they would kill not only the two women but him as well. Yet Rahat Apa, who must have loved her son, stood her ground. And in doing so, she altered the trajectories of two human lives. Two lives and all their generations to come.

The house next door to Rahat Apa's had tenants on both its levels. The upstairs was occupied by a Bengali professor; the downstairs housed the Punjabi family of Shahina's friend Zeenat. (All non-Bengalis were referred to as "Bihari" at this time, and all were seen as just targets of looting or worse.) Zeenat, who was married, normally lived in another part of town called Motijheel. But a spat with her husband had brought her to her parents' home in Bakshi Bazar, and now she was as confined as Shahina within the four walls of the house. One day, Shahina couldn't resist the temptation to go and see her. She covered herself with a chadar and made her way quickly and inconspicuously to the house next door, and Zeenat let her in.

But it was a dangerous time for tête-á-têtes between girlfriends. The Mukti Bahini chose that day for one of their appearances. The Bengali professor upstairs tried as usual to deflect attention from the Punjabi Khalils while his wife ushered Zeenat and Shahina up the back stairway, into the safety of their own home. She smuggled them into her pantry among onions and potatoes, shut the door, and clamped a hefty lock on it from the outside. There the two young women remained until the professor had persuaded the Mukti Bahini men to leave.

Zeenat's husband, Taufeeq, and his family in Motijheel were less fortunate. Taufeeq and his brother were killed and their younger sister carried off. Their mother eventually found her way to Karachi with her surviving children, but when Shahina Auntie ran into her years later in our Gulshan neighborhood, the mother was still searching for her kidnapped daughter. Every now and then, she would hear a rumor that the young woman had been spotted in this or that part of Dhaka, or seen working as a maid in somebody's house. Once, when relations between Pakistan and Bangladesh had normalized and individual tragedies smoothed over with diplomacy, Zeenat's mother-in-law even scraped the money to follow a lead back to Dhaka. But as recently as 2007, the woman whose two sons were killed before her eyes still cherished the hope that her lost daughter would reappear some day.

Months after the initial killing frenzy had subsided, Shahina and her mother were able to obtain visas for India. By this point, they were staying with the father of Shahina's college friend Yasmin. He had sent his family to safety in Kolkata, India, but himself stayed on in their Kakrail home, near Purana Paltan. Though Urdu-speaking, he looked Bengali, spoke Bengali, and had a Bengali driver. Above all, he had a kind and supportive Bengali employer. In the relative calm, Shahina and her mother even had a source of income: the conscientious West Bengali manager of their jewelry store brought them money from sales for a couple of months until the authorities confiscated the shop and shut it down. The women purchased airline tickets for Karachi, but every time they'd plan to head to the airport, they would be tipped off that Mukti Bahini men were checking for Urdu-speaking passengers trying to escape the country. When the visa was about to expire, they knew they could wait no longer. They had to make their precarious way to Pakistan by road.

A male cousin would travel with them and a Mukti Bahini friend of his would accompany them to Jessore, on the Indian border. Whenever their car was stopped, this friend stepped out and did the talking. In this way, the young Mukti Bahini man did justice both to his nation and to his personal relationships in a time when these loyalties seemed mutually exclusive. He delivered his friend, along with Shahina and her mother, safely to the Indian border.

In Jessore, Shahina's mother and cousin made it through the checkpoint and crossed into India. But the woman inspecting Shahina's papers would not let her pass. The stumbling block was the question of Shahina's ethnicity, which she claimed to be Bengali. Shahina had taken care to dress in a sari, the preferred Bengali attire for women, and another sari was all she carried in her small bag. Having lived her entire life in Dhaka, she responded to all questions in fluent Bengali. Though the border officer was unable to trip her up, she detained Shahina in her kiosk anyway. Shahina could see her mother and cousin on the other side of the checkpoint but couldn't join them, and neither could they cross back into Bangladesh.

As the afternoon wore on and daylight diminished, Shahina's anxieties grew. She was young, female, and vulnerable. The border would be closing soon, and what would become of her then?

Finally, the woman officer relented and told Shahina to go join her mother on the other side of the border.

"But I'll tell you one thing," she said coldly. "I have never in my life seen a Bengali with skin as light as yours."

They got into a taxi on the Indian side of the border and began the four-hour drive to Kolkata. After a week with relatives there, they picked Yasmin up along the way and drove to Kathmandu, Nepal, where they contacted Shahina's father through the Pakistan Embassy. He sent airfare for all four of them, and the

Embassy issued the necessary papers. On an October day in 1972, ten months after Bangladesh's liberation from Pakistan, Shahina, her mother, her cousin, and her friend Yasmin landed in Karachi. By that time, our family and Khalammi's had grown weary of our attempt to settle in Karachi, and, having lived through the bombings of the December '71 war with India, we retreated to Greenford for another couple of years. Shahina Manzoor began the new year in Pakistan, grateful for her life but uncertain what to do with it.

On the eve of 1980, when I was sixteen, we heard the familiar sound of Shahina Auntie's five beeps outside our Gulshan home in Karachi. By this time she was married and had a toddler girl, Usaima, who would come to be a Meadow alum and teacher. (Shahina's husband was an Urdu-speaking man who had been lined up for execution along with his brothers outside their home in Chittagong, Bangladesh, and was saved by the miraculous appearance and intervention of a Bengali friend.) But safe domestic roles couldn't contain Shahina Auntie. She liked to be free, and her fearless driving on the chaotic streets of Karachi was an essential part of that freedom. Luckily, she lived with her husband's large family, and her unmarried sisters-in-law could always be relied upon to attend to the house and toddler. So at the sound of Shahina Auntie's familiar beeps, we said a hasty goodbye to my father and dashed out to meet her. My mother must have pulled out our Volkswagen Beetle to form a caravan because I don't know how else we managed to squeeze in Khalammi and her two children (baby Sheba asleep at home), my mother and her three, plus my older aunt Anjum and her daughter, Naghmi, and Shahina Auntie's friends Yasmin and Arifa. Like these girlfriends, my aunt Anjum was a lonely woman. Long divorced from her abusive husband, she lived with her mother and daughter in a nearby apartment. Eighteen-year-old Naghma-e-Mussarat, whom our poet-aunt Talat had named for the beauty of song, had grown up without a father and was considered fortunate to be getting married in the new year. So it was a particularly poignant New Year's Eve for her and for all of us who loved her. Naghmi had never met her betrothed but, raised by her mother and our grandmother, Amma, on very little, she now stood on the threshold of more possibility than her young life had known.

Our Gulshan neighborhood greeted the Western new year—among Muslims it begins with the lunar month of Muharram—with a nod of acknowledgement but not much more. So New Year's Eve in Gulshan was a far cry from the gaiety that marked the night in richer parts of town like Clifton and Defence. There, young women decked out glamorously in Western attire to attend parties, men and women dancing to Western pop music, the booze flowing freely in a country where alcohol is illegal unless you can prove your non-Muslim status. I was part of that party scene only once in Karachi, in my early twenties, and, uncomfortable around alcohol, felt no inclination to repeat the experience.

Our New Year's Eve caravan stopped outside each house on our Gulshan circuit, Shahina Auntie announcing our arrival with the same distinctive five beeps. If the girlfriend or cousin who emerged from the house voiced any reservations—*so late, possibly unsafe, the elderly to look after at home, and so many chores still to finish*—Shahina Auntie would counter them with her combination of persuasion, charm, and good-natured mockery. If permission was required from a guardian, she would get out of the car and do the sweet-talking herself. Feeling adventurous and daring, the young woman would join the caravan, and away we'd go.

We headed south for Clifton, not to any parties but to the seashore. Along the way, we waved, poked our heads out of the car windows, and shouted, "Happy new year!" at unsuspecting strangers. How must we have appeared to them: carloads of women and children, laughing and hollering into the Karachi night, giddy with a sense of our own recklessness and revelry. We might have stopped at one of the many roadside restaurants that served spicy chickpea chaat on Tariq Road, or the pink semi-liquid dessert of falooda in Bahadurabad, or the carcinogenic after-dinner treat of paan at the PIDC building. Paan, with or without tobacco, has always been favored by Karachiites; for our New Year's Eve caravan, it meant a mix of areca nuts, slaked lime, shredded coconut, and cardamom, wrapped in a betel leaf. Sweet and succulent, it left our mouths and tongues a bright and garish red.

But the real festivities occurred by Clifton beach, across from Sea-View Apartments. In Karachi's temperate winter, moonlight and streetlight illuminate the waves of the Arabian Sea as people from all walks of life converge by its silver-sand shores. In a rigidly stratified society, the long, broad strip of sidewalk and the low wall lacing the shoreline are magical, if momentary, levelers. Big families, their women hidden in white or black burqas, dipped their toes in the same waters as Karachi's Westward-looking yuppies. Turbaned old men, clandestine lovers, and newlyweds—awkward or laughing—nestled together in the city's generous bosom. We emerged from our cars to join them, threading our way through the crowds gathered around the performing monkeys, past the men, women, and children lined up (inasmuch as anyone lines up in Karachi) for roasted chana in paper funnels; beyond the fruitsellers bearing the season's gifts of guavas, or miniature, apple-like bayr, and my favorite cheekoo, which looks like a fleshier kiwi on the outside but is caramel brown on the inside, and, except for its single, black seed, silky sweet. We weren't about to sit contentedly on the low wall and watch. Egged on by Shahina Auntie, we dashed down the sandy slopes, hopped across rocks, and splashed into the sea, fully clothed. In the moonlight, we thronged to the little kiosk-by-the-sea for mango, pistachio, or coconut ice-cream. We shared the waves with chattering multitudes, their saris, chadars, and shalvars flapping in the breeze, and with the occasional camel that clip-clopped by us, squealing children seated between its humps as its trainer held the leash. At the stroke of midnight, fire-crackers resounded, along with celebratory honks from all the cars parked by the low wall, and shouts of "*Happy new year!*" in multiple languages. And shortly thereafter, in an attempt to beat the inevitable gridlock at Sea-View, we made our way past the motorbikes doing wheelies on the roadside, got into our cars, and headed back to Gulshan.

It's the last day of 2012, and I sit in the family room of my home in Fresno, looking at a decade of handmade ornaments on our five-foot Christmas tree. Alex bought this synthetic tree for his company's office in Boston long before the children or I entered his life. Maya and Cyrus have crawled and toddled around it, looking up at its baubles in awe. This year, at twelve and ten years of age, they rival the tree in height but refuse to replace it with a taller one. Instead, for the first time, they take complete charge of decorating this tree that no longer towers above them, and hang ornaments made in daycare and elementary grades on its familiar branches.

I look past their dangling little photo-hearts, glitter-glued stars, and paper angels to that long-ago New Year's Eve in Karachi.

Still morning in California, it is 10 pm on December 31st in Pakistan. Though I rarely call her, tonight I find Shahina Auntie's number among my cell-phone contacts and wait to hear her say hello from eight thousand miles away.

Her cell-phone is busy, so I call my Khalammi instead. After all these years, after the children and grandchildren, and the wayward trajectories of their marriages, it's a safe bet that where you find the one, you'll find the other.

I strain to hear my aunt amidst the din in the background, but we talk for a few minutes, and then I ask for Shahina Auntie. It takes Shahina Auntie a little while to extricate herself from her cell phone—she's still the life of the party for many women—but she sounds happy to hear from me. I remind her of our New Year's Eve thirty-three years ago, and she laughs her hearty laughter. Then her voice grows somber.

"Well, no such drives about town this New Year's Eve," she says. "Sea-View has been closed off. It's amazing we still have cellular connection; they had threatened to cut that off, too."

"Fear of violence?" I ask.

"Always that. When have we ever known a nonviolent Karachi?"

This is true, whatever my defining memory of New Year's Eve in Karachi. Memory is driven by tacit temporal comparisons and, in comparing, oversimplifies. Peace and violence are relative terms, after all.

"But," she continues, "it's become harder and harder for us to bounce back. And now they won't even let us celebrate."

"Who's *they*?" I wonder aloud.

"Hard to say. All part of the Talibanization of Pakistan. We're not allowed to celebrate a decadent Western tradition."

Incredible that the democratically elected but corrupt and godless government of Pakistan has imposed a ban on New Year's Eve. But it's a spineless government, easily cowered by the Taliban on one hand and the all-powerful military on the other.

"No celebration, Samina," Shahina Auntie says again. "They've barred our access to the sea."

They've barred our access to the sea.

The din in the background comes from her three grandchildren. She and Khalammi are looking after them while her daughter Usaima (the toddler of thirty-three years ago) and her husband try to pave a future for their family in Dubai.

"You know that I'll be moving to Dubai with them in March—to look after the children while Usaima and her husband work?"

Yes, I have heard. And I have wondered what will become of my aunt.

"Karachi will be emptier without you," I tell her.

We are both silent for a moment. Then:

"I've lived through the fall of Dhaka," she says quietly.

Shahina Auntie seldom talks about Bangladesh. I let her go on.

"Yes, Karachi has always been a tumultuous city, but it's far more so now. Shia-Sunni killings, ethnic violence, anarchist terror. And there's no protection from the government. I remember Bangladesh, and I'm scared for my daughter and my grandchildren."

Another migration, then. To add on to your parents' and grandparents' migrations—from India to Bangladesh to Pakistan to Dubai. Onward, possibly, to England or the United States, like us. In your sixties, to be uprooted once again and try to re-root yourself in yet another ethnic and linguistic environment. After decades spent defying gender norms, to mold yourself into the domestic role that you know was never your forté.

But you mustn't look back. Forget independence. Forget your life with my aunt. Forget even mobility and driving for a while. Live through the children and grandchildren who will grow up with fewer and fewer memories of any land you ever called home.

I hear sounds of rambunctious play in the background.

"It will be hard at first. But I'm sure you'll find your way, Shahina Auntie."

Shahina Auntie agrees.

Happy new year, we say.

World Cup Mama

I am a professor of American literature, and as such I do all the predictable things such people do: during the academic year I read, teach, and grade papers, and during the summer I read, write, research (and sometimes teach). When I'm not actually reading, writing, or teaching, I like to talk about reading, writing, and teaching. My 14-year-old daughter, Maya, and 12-year-old son, Cyrus, know this about me. Cyrus, who loves soccer, long ago resigned himself to the fact that though his mother will show up dutifully at his games, she understands little and cares less about sports. He has even had to grow up without cable, without ESPN. I have never played a team sport, never understood how people squander hours in front of a screen, watching grown men chase after a ball as though their lives depended on it. Long ago and far away, there was cricket. Pakistan, like many former British colonies, has always been cricket-crazy. While my brother played cricket with other boys in the street—evening matches often punctuated by the loud smashing of this or that neighbor's window—and while my staid and dignified father's face transformed into a barometer of how well or ill Pakistan was doing in some International Test Series (especially if it was against India), my own contribution to the national fervor did not get beyond fleeting teenage crushes on individual hottie players.

But this Californian summer I have lost count of the number of World Cup soccer matches I have watched on television. While countries played in the group stage, I sat through three matches a day for five days straight, and the only thing that tore me away from the TV was a long-planned drive down to my sister's in San Diego to pick up my mother and aunt, who are visiting from Pakistan. Even in San Diego I managed to catch the Argentina-Iran game, and during Ammi's and Khalammi's week with me in Fresno, I watched a few other games while my guests sat politely beside me. Since they left, I have missed only one match—the quarter-final between the Netherlands and Costa Rica—in order to ferry Maya to her writing workshop, reminding myself to keep sight of parental priorities. I have not been altogether irresponsible: I did inform the editors of the anthology for which I'm writing a scholarly piece on war and literature that they will have my revised essay when the World Cup is over.

In the two days between Round of 16 and quarter-finals, when no matches were scheduled, I became a model of efficiency. Got up early and presented myself at Quest Diagnostics for my annual blood test precisely at 6:30 a.m. when their doors opened. Drafted the Table of Contents for the prospective publisher of a collaborative project, paid bills, got the mammogram done that I had skipped last year, and took Cyrus for a haircut before the crown of his head had grown a mid-sized mountain. I made other appointments, with dentist and therapist, thinking deeply and carefully so as to avoid collision with the upcoming quarter-finals and semi-finals. When Maya's summer AP-prep course began at Edison High the week of July 7, I made carpool arrangements that ensured I'd be doing the 7:45 a.m. drop-offs, since afternoon pickups would conflict with the World Cup semi-finals.

How did this happen?
One could point to the addictive nature of sports, of course. Or chalk it up to a middle-age identity crisis. My need to fill the void my father's death has left behind with something new and different. Or to a philosophy I have often shared with my students: that life

is only as interesting as the degree of interest you take in it (so why not take an interest in the World Cup?). Certainly, we invested in cable this summer for the express purpose of being able to watch the matches. It made sense because Cyrus had just qualified for a competitive soccer team, and if we were going to become a traveling soccer family, I was going to throw myself into it wholeheartedly.

And yet. None of these explanations accounts for the intensity, the passion, the intellectual preoccupation that the World Cup has become for me. Even before the tournament began, I fell in love with the Brazuca ball, handmade by gifted, underpaid rural women in Pakistan. There's something about that arc, about the ball's trajectory from the painstaking hands of these anonymous women to the cleats and clout of Messi, Robben, and Ronaldo. I've seen images of these women—heads covered, eyes focused, and slender brown hands holding a ball that will be kicked around by millionaires in stadiums throughout Brazil, the world watching the ball but not thinking of them. There's a lesson there in gender, race, and economics; it's a lesson in global inequities, yes, but also in global interdependencies.

Mostly my thoughts center on smaller things. I'm awed by the World Cup's power to evoke strong, conflicting emotions in me and challenge what I thought I knew about myself. I, who bristle at nationalist rhetoric, have been enjoying the often amusing manifestations of nationalist sentiment in the stadiums. Moreover, I find myself deeply stirred by the anthems preceding the game. My sympathies bewilder me. I may start out supporting Belgium in honor of my husband and children's ancestry, but the moment the Algerian players press their foreheads to the turf in a grateful post-goal sajdah, my father's face flashes before me and I root for Algeria despite my secular self. Indeed, I discover that all my loyalties are relative. I cheer for Portugal against Germany, the US against Portugal, and am thankful not to have to choose between Pakistan and the US. I support the Americas over Europe because the weight of colonial history is palpable during the World Cup—unless, irony of ironies, the European country in question is England, where I spent my childhood.

And then there's the existential dimension to the World Cup. I know nothing about the Iranian team but am crushed at its elimination from the tournament—and Australia's, Ghana's, Chile's, and Costa Rica's— because in the end no amount of energy, brilliance, and dedication could save them from whimsical luck. I learn that soccer is about as fair as life, that shooting stars take all. And sometimes the shooting stars fall to earth with a thud: Neymar with a fractured vertebra, Jozy Altidore pulling a hamstring. There are also shocking examples of the moral frailty of human beings on the field: deliberate head butts, punches, and bites by grown men for the glory of winning. Sneakier strategies—a dive here, a foul there—to see what one can get away with, because the referee is only human and even indisputable replays have no power to rewrite the wrongs. What is done cannot be undone.

Nothing prepared me, however, for the tournament's spectacles of defeat. One team's victory is not only tempered by, but dependent upon, another's loss. This is an obvious fact; don't all our privileges come at somebody else's cost? Yet, I didn't expect to see that social dynamic played out so nakedly on the field. I didn't expect to be rooting for Brazil against Colombia in the quarter-finals but stop short of celebrating at the sight of James Rodriguez in tears. Then to be moved by Brazil's David Luiz comforting him, urging the crowd to acknowledge the Colombian star, exchanging shirts.

World Cup champion Spain's early defeat by the Netherlands seemed harsh until we witnessed Brazil's unraveling at the hands of Germany in the semi-final. I'm still processing this one—not tactically or technically (because I lack that sort of know-how) but emotionally. The shock of five goals against them within eighteen minutes was reflected in the horrified faces of fans throughout the stadium. You could see that they experienced the relentless pummeling viscerally. Children covering their eyes, sobbing, as their idols crumbled around them. By the apocalyptic 7-1 end, it was David Luiz's turn to cry, to beg his nation's forgiveness for having humbled them in so appalling a spectacle. For me, much of the heart went out of the World Cup after that. Three days later, Brazil's loss to the Netherlands in the third-place match sealed the sadness, silencing any possible narrative of redemption.

Today, we will watch the final between Germany and Argentina. Friends will come over and we'll settle with our pizzas in front of the TV for a game that may well extend into extra time and penalty kicks. I will wait to see where my loyalties emerge. By 3 p.m. it will all be over. I will go back to reading, writing, and teaching. To being the person I know myself to be. And when the World Cup happens again in 2018, Cyrus will be a junior in high school and Maya about to take flight for college. Family life as we know it will come to an end as the tournament ends. As all things must.

But this year, for once Santa will not have to hear my rants about the commercialization of Christmas. If he's any good at his job, he'll know to come down my chimney bearing a bonafide, made-in-Pakistan Brazuca ball.

The Sky That Didn't Fall

The most shocking thing about grief is that the sky doesn't fall. The unspeakable happens, the news reaches you across two oceans, the world is about to fold in on itself and collapse as it must, as you must. You shiver, you shake. But in the end you don't end. And the sky is still there—serene, expansive, indifferent.

So a life ended, as all lives do. What's so special about *your* loss? Nothing. Absolutely nothing. So many people don't have a father at all. Others have fathers who leave them with little to miss. Some fathers die young, a tragic disruption of the natural order of things. Yours was none of these.

In 2013, Abbu had just turned eighty-one. That was longer than anyone in his family had lived. His mother died in her thirties, his father in his forties, one brother at fifty-two, another at sixty-eight, two half-sisters in their fifties and sixties, and a much-loved nephew at forty-five. So Abbu had been expecting to die for forty years. And the end, when it came, was at the hands of a familiar opponent, heart disease. There was nothing extraordinary about Abbu's death.

As reliable in death as he was in life, Abbu left us clues with which to reconstruct his final hour. His alarm was set for 3:57 am that morning, for the extra-credit Tahajjud prayer before dawn. Predictable, reliable, in death as in life.

And yet, there has been nothing predictable about grieving him these four years. The sorrow balls up in my throat without warning, sometimes without context—while I'm teaching, or while engaged in an assigned, three-minute conversation with a fellow Summer Arts student at Fresno State. Abbu was about to visit his children and grandchildren in California in two and a half weeks. Instead he died alone in his bed, leaving us a list, in his precise and pleasing hand, of items still to pack. Four years later, I have accepted that nothing will bring him back, but the heart mutinies because he deserved better than to die eight thousand miles away from his flesh and blood. This is what remains indigestible, what won't go down but wells up through the eyes and in the cracked edges of my voice. This, finally, has taught me jealousy. This is what makes the third Sunday in June, Fathers' Day, a day of avoidance, of self-imposed social media blackout, because those images of fathers with still-beating hearts smart the eye and sting the still-grieving heart, and suddenly it's possible again—and again—for the sky to heave, cleave, come crashing down.

Part 3

Benign Baggage

He is moving brusquely about the house, opening this closet and that, gathering his personal belongings. Clothes mostly, but also a few magazines and cookbooks, cutesie figurines and trinkets I have known him to collect over the twenty-four years that we have been together. It's a predictably warm Fourth of July in Fresno, the air conditioning blowing its labored breath through the vents of the house by ten o'clock in the morning. Our fifteen-year-old daughter, Maya, focuses on the SAT prep that is her mission this summer and will be again this time next year. Cyrus, two years her junior, remains in his room, peering into his cell phone, most likely reading articles about global transfers of soccer players from one club to another. I feel the absence of my brother, who took a week off from his work at Google in order to be here for my surgery a month ago—a hysterectomy to remove uterine fibroids. My mother will remain until I am fully recovered. Her own fibroids shrank with menopause many years ago. Now she occupies the white vinyl armchair in the family room as she writes, clench-jawed, about the possibility of leaving Pakistan permanently and beginning life afresh in California in her seventies.

This summer I have made it my business to read in the formal living room where Maya studies at least four hours every day. I look forward to this peace, this enforced rest. In a little while Cyrus will tire of his cell phone scrolling and move to the piano bench in his room. Then his renderings of a Beethoven rondo will waft down the hallway, and I will hold the moment, cup it in the hollow of memory, against the day when both he and Maya will be gone. Holding it, I will drift off to sleep on the red couch—I, who, in able-bodied arrogance, had scorned naps. But today I am distracted, not by my convalescing body but by the sounds of things being dropped into cardboard boxes and the periodic slap of the packaging tape sealing them shut. They are the sounds of the finally purposeful presence of my husband preparing to move out.

How do you drop twenty-four years into a box and seal it?

It's possible that twenty-four years ago I already had the uterine fibroids.

Uterine fibroids are noncancerous growths of the uterus that often appear during childbearing years. . . . Fibroids range in size from seedlings, undetectable by the human eye, to bulky masses that can distort and enlarge the uterus. . . . As many as 3 out of 4 women have uterine fibroids sometime during their lives, but most are unaware of them because they often cause no symptoms. – Mayo Clinic

So, not only are most women oblivious of the fibroids they carry, but nobody knows why they happen or what a woman might do to prevent them. Genetics matter; a mother or sister with fibroids puts you at greater risk. And Black women are more likely to get them—larger growths, more numerous, and at a younger age. My own fibroids first became a concern in 1999 when we lived in Taunton, Massachusetts, and I conceived Maya. One fibroid in particular, towards the bottom left of my pelvic cavity, had acquired the size of the proverbial tennis ball. Miraculously, the fibroids didn't cause a miscarriage in either of my pregnancies, but they did obstruct my babies' movements enough to keep them from turning head down, in the cephalic position. Breech babies who did not have space enough to respond to the manual guidance of "external cephalic versions," Maya's and Cyrus's only way out into life was via cesareans. Maya, in the last weeks before birth, had been sitting on her feet like an amateur Buddha, to emerge from the womb with her right foot perpendicular to her leg. Luckily, her foot straightened itself out in a few weeks, as the doctor had said it would. In Cyrus's time I opted for the cesarean without subjecting myself to the pointless discomfort of an attempted manual "version."

Then in 2005, when my children were five and three years old, I got so tired that moving a few feet took enormous effort, and conversation required more breath than I had to spare. It was not something I expected my husband or anyone else to really notice. That summer, on the eve of my birthday, I dreamed that I longed to lie down and be allowed to die—gradually, as in a bloodletting—but I couldn't because Cyrus needed my attention. It turned out that I had a severe iron deficiency. Whereas the normal hemoglobin range for women is 12-15 grams per deciliter, mine had fallen to 7. I didn't know then that such low hemoglobin levels can lead to heart attacks. That fact came to light eight years later when my father died. His last email to his children, sent from Pakistan a day before his death, mentioned that his hemoglobin level had dropped to 7. I was younger and luckier than my father. But though fibroids are technically "benign tumors," in my case they were agents of malicious blood loss until my doctor in Taunton finally thought to put me on the birth-control pill. While the pill curbed my symptoms and arrested the bleeding, the fibroids themselves, with wry medical irony, thrived on the estrogen and progesterone in it. Yet I deferred the surgery year after year for all the wrong reasons: because I was too busy, unfocused, and afraid.

I've learned that a single uterus can sport a variety of these benign tumors: from the most common intramural fibroid that grows within the muscular uterus wall to the subserosal that flourishes on the outer wall, to the least common submucosal that develops just under the mucous membrane or lining and, in some internet images, resembles the outline of a toddler's head hiding under a rug. Then there's the pedunculated fibroid that sprouts bizarrely on a stalk, within the uterus wall or outside it. Its descriptions are often macabre: *A fibroid that hangs by a stalk inside or outside the uterus . . . can trigger pain by twisting on its stalk and cutting off its blood supply* (Mayo Clinic). So it blossoms on a stalk like a flower but is neither benign nor beautiful in its sadomasochistic twists. My fibroids, twelve to fifteen in number, were mostly intramural. By the time of the hysterectomy, the largest of these was ten centimeters in diameter, heavily calcified, and, according to the pathology report I later saw, showed "ischemic-type necrosis," meaning that its blood supply had been cut off, causing it to degenerate. The multiple fibroids would chafe against my uterus lining and resulted in such bloodletting that I became acutely anemic.

Anemia: noun

1. *Pathology.* A quantitative deficiency of the hemoglobin, often accompanied by a reduced number of red blood cells and causing pallor, weakness, and breathlessness.

2. a lack of power, vigor, vitality, or colorfulness.

— Dictionary.com

What I hadn't realized a decade ago was that my marriage, too, had begun its long, anemic decline. The symptoms were so subtle as to go undetected. We were different to begin with—in age, race, religious background, politics, priorities, and temperament—but thought we could overwhelm the odds. In the mid-1990s we were also at different stages of our very different careers: while I wrote my dissertation in American literature and braved the whims of academia as an adjunct professor, his leasing company still employed several people. But he captained a ship that had once sailed with the rising economic tides and now drifted, only half-aware of the shoals that would sink it before we even married. Then with two children born twenty-one months apart, it was easy to see ourselves as just getting through the daily tasks to do our best as parents. How eagerly we—I?—blamed these pressures and held on to the hazy thought that we would get beyond them, to a day when we could bring each other into focus again. In the meantime, if we weren't going to the movies or to dinner together, we explained it to ourselves as owing to a lack of money or babysitter rather than a lack of inclination. That the marriage might have paled before the children were even born—that is a possibility I am allowing myself to register only now, in this act of writing. The mind conspires to not see. It's only now as my fingertip retraces the thread of time and fumbles its way back to the spool that I detect the silent, stealthy unraveling. But who can account for the death of a love, or the disappearance of a former self? Who can see an invisible hemorrhaging?

    I wish I could identify the benign tumors that drained the lifeblood from my marriage. The enemy within the walls, or hiding against it, or stalking on the outside, biding its time until one suicidal twist cuts off its own blood supply and, in bitter anguish, it strangles itself and the marriage. The marriage a uterus, full of the possibility of life—indeed delivering on its promise until one day a sudden clap of clarity reveals that it has outlived its purpose, that the thought of its surgical removal is more welcome to both parties than the prospect of bearing the burden it has become.

Or had the marriage itself become a benign tumor? A fibroid pressing against vital organs, distorting the shape of the uterus on which it preys, and gradually robbing the entire body of red-blooded vitality. Our growing habit of inattention has taken distinct forms: mine an easy immersion in children and students; his the constant busy work in the house, the exacting perfectionism in small things, even as he ignores the financial precipice toward which we are edging; the brooding at the dinner table with eyes closed as the children chatter. When did my shoulders learn to relax with his absence, like a tide receding, every third weekend when he visits his mother in Carmel?

Carmel, that fairytale setting for weddings, including ours almost nineteen years ago.

I think now of his relationship with other things and seek clues to the mystery of our story there. The Pace Arrow motorhome he drove alone, devoted and determined, across the continent when we moved to Fresno in 2006, the 38-foot vehicle already eighteen years old and clambering breathlessly as he coaxed it over the Rockies and the Sierras. Once in Fresno, it was parked in storage and never seen again. Dues paid faithfully every month for nearly nine years, the joy of it forgotten.

And then his equivocal relationship with the yard: at once a passion, an escape, and a life sentence with hard labor. *No thanks* he says to the gardeners who maintain our neighbors' homes. Hours poured into work that is never complete, yet all the trees left untended. The palm that sold me on the house in Fresno so overburdened that it hangs threateningly over the children's heads in the pool. Voluntary oaks shoot up in the front yard; oleanders rise jarringly amidst the junipers. The olive tree near the entrance, into whose outstretched and welcoming arms my four- and six-year-olds had run at first sight of their new home, still standing, its limbs now gnawed away by termites. But its roots grow powerful beneath the ground we tread, and treacherous—undulating the surface in concrete waves that reach for Maya's bedroom. A few feet away, a young Japanese maple threads its trunk through the wrought iron gate, one of its thicker branches resting against the house and a crack spreading like a sardonic smile on the inside of the arched wall overhead. It is a landscape both cared for and neglected, loved and resented.

Was that a separation in 2003 when I took three-year-old Maya and one-year-old Cyrus with me to Pakistan for an open-ended stay? To give him time to find employment and me a chance to escape the Iraq War fervor in America—in my own home, in fact—and make memories with my parents, so we said. We talked on the phone twice a week over what turned into five months, his note cards supplementing our scattered conversations at regular intervals. He even visited us in Karachi for a week. But if either of us said *I miss you*, I have forgotten it.

A mystery, too, *when* precisely cards and flowers languished into bloodless rituals. Each year before our anniversary there I am, staring blankly at the offerings in the Target aisle. He goes for the cute and funny, but I strain for the right tone. Valentine's Day matters less—a manufactured holiday that marginalizes most people. But he will have a card and flowers for me, as he will for the children and for his mother, all the cards bearing similar cheery messages in his unique, oversized handwriting that quickly covers the space.

On Valentine's Day weekend, 2015, there happen to be no cards. For the first time in fifteen years, there are no children at home either because my family has flown them out to San Diego for Cyrus's thirteenth birthday. That Friday evening after I return from dropping our young teens off at the airport, he tells me it has been three weeks—time for his drive to Carmel. He doesn't ask what my plans are. I don't ask to accompany him. We kiss each other on the cheek, and I spend the weekend alone. And happy—a morning walk, an idle peek at a house for sale in the bohemian Tower District, a little dancing by myself as my mother used to when I was Maya's age.

Marriage as a benign tumor, then. It's what one calls "baggage" in a more familiar metaphor. Over the past two decades I have learned that there is no such thing as benign baggage because, one way or another, you pay to lug it.

The fibroids I had been lugging all those years were removed in an abdominal hysterectomy. My surgeon was also my gynecologist of four years. An earth-toned African American woman of faith and grace, she has moist eyes, a deep, gentle voice, and a powerful handshake. Her small, silver-and-pearl cross gleams beneath her collar bones. Though she appears spacey at times, I am convinced that I can trust her with a knife. Perhaps I do so because she is the only doctor ever to tell me, "I like words. I like their precision." Or perhaps I trust her because she isn't afraid to show emotion. At my pre-op appointment I sit in her office as she peers into a computer and asks me a series of routine pre-surgery questions. Then she poses one that I'm not unexpecting:

"Are you married?" she asks.

"Yes."

"How long?"

"Eighteen and a half years," I say. Then add: "But it's about to end."

Still facing the computer, she closes her eyes and takes a

deep breath. In that moment she is taking in the whole likely story. When she opens her eyes again, something between sorrow and exasperation crosses her face.

"I like to know," she says.

She also tells me that my uterus has grown dramatically due to the fibroids; it is the size of a thirteen to fourteen-week pregnancy.

During the abdominal hysterectomy she cut into the very incision that was made years ago for my two cesareans. In order to rid my body of the fibroids, the uterus that had been harboring them, as it had harbored my babies, had to go, too. My cervix, ovaries, and fallopian tubes were also removed in what is called a total abdominal hysterectomy with bilateral salpingo-oophorectomy. There was no point in holding on to them. At my age these reproductive organs, simply by virtue of time, had lost their life-giver status and become potentially treacherous sources of cancer. And when the ovaries go, they take with them the woman's primary source of estrogen, so menopause arrives immediately and unceremoniously, ready or not. Second to cesareans, hysterectomy is the most common form of surgery performed on women, and one in three American women have the procedure by the time they are sixty. Major surgery, demanding six to eight weeks for recovery, but routinely performed nonetheless. As in my case, the most common reason for hysterectomies is unruly fibroids—those benign tumors that three out of four women carry, though they may not realize it; their cause unknown, and their prevention virtually impossible.

For a time after the hysterectomy, I am uncomfortable even when the pain has diminished. Distended stomach, lower-back ache, easier to sleep sitting up. When I lie on my back, a weight settles on me; as I try to turn on my side, I feel a movement, something shifting, and I support my drum belly with my hand.

"It's weird to feel pregnant when you don't have a uterus," I say. Maya is so amused by this statement, she tweets it.

I imagine how my pelvic cavity looks without uterus, cervix, fallopian tubes, and ovaries. An empty cave? More space than the remaining organs know what to do with, but in time they will adjust to the absence of that presence that had seemed an inevitability. I wonder what has taken the place of my reproductive organs in the immediate aftermath of the hysterectomy. Gases? Fluids? Emptiness is not nothingness. Sometimes at the bottom left of my abdomen, where once I could touch the well-defined tennis ball, I feel a twinge of pain. A phantom fibroid. Will it always haunt?

Loss and hope converge in my hysterectomy. That word "womb"—a lone syllable, wistful; its long vowel shaping the mouth in a wind-blown kiss, its consonant cluster mellifluous and lingering. The womb that had held my babies, grown them in cramped quarters and brought them safely to term, is gone. All that remains of it is captured in a photograph that I had asked my doctor to take for me (not an usual request, she said). Cyrus is fascinated by the pulpy, pear-shaped mass, its tennis ball glistening.

"Your first home," I say, and he smiles.

With ovaries gone, the hormonal shock to my system has rendered me instantly menopausal. And no woman was ever as excited about this phenomenon as I. Lying in the hospital bed a night or two after the hysterectomy, I realize that I'm breaking into a sweat. Through my morphine-muddled consciousness, an exhilarating thought breaks through: *Hot flashes! These must be hot flashes!* I bid the moment stay. After years of blur, I am giddy with gratitude for menopause's sudden and unequivocal arrival, for its contours sharp and bold. The womb is gone, the ovaries, too, but in one summer I have freed myself of all benign tumors. Welcome then, menopause. Welcome the clarity of this transition, the crisp outline of the end of an era. And the beginning of a new one—just my babies and me.

fragment 11

The final fragments flicker only in memory, no photographs to make them real.

On a sweltering May afternoon, before the cooling monsoons, you come up the stairs looking for me. You took the yellow minibus all the way to Tariq Road and back, saw a handbag you like for me. Does it sound like something I'd want for my 22nd birthday? It does: coffee-colored faux leather with diagonal lines; multiple compartments for my college notebooks, yet small enough for style. The minute you have my approval, you turn right around to catch another minibus back to Tariq Road. Another long ride, back into the heat, the dust, the crowds. You won't even stay for a glass of cold water.

Tomorrow? It might be gone tomorrow, you say, and disappear.

The body notwithstanding.

One hundred and six degrees, and ninety percent humidity;
thirst and fatigue, but
the body notwithstanding.
What you could put yourself through for something you wanted.
Wanted for me, because I wanted it.

Early June, and my home is festive; friends to celebrate my birthday. You are among them, but in the shadows. Your face has thinned and darkened since I saw you last, your stylish "boy cut" hair left untrimmed. I see this, but I don't. I'm twenty-two today, I'm happy and in love. We gather around Irum, who reads palms and tells us our futures. You've been waiting for your turn, too. But at the last second, you pull your palm away.

Did you see the lifeline snapping eleven days later?

First Thanksgiving Without Them

I'm riding Amtrak from Fresno to San Francisco, towards Amir and Linda's home, grateful that my brother and his family eagerly await me. But I am thinking of my two teens and wondering: when did it begin to feel like a love relationship? If it's true that we know our experiences by analogy, that's the closest parallel to this state of desperate missing, this yearning for the sight and touch of them, their absence a great heaviness that settles within me like a dense, Central Valley fog.

As they pulled out of the driveway with their father in yesterday's afternoon light, I thought I saw my own longing reflected in their faces—their smiles in place but a momentary dimming of the eyes as they waved from their windows. I picture what their eyes beheld: the solitary figure of a middle-aged woman still in her teaching attire, the eyes behind her glasses tired from having been up since 4:00 am to finish grading the papers she wanted to hand back before Thanksgiving break. Smiling as she waves, as she recedes with the cypresses that line the entrance to their home.

All three of us smiling because there's nothing to be done about the car driving away, the mother staying behind, the children waving goodbye.

They will be back on Friday; I will be back on Friday. They go with a father who cares about them, though for now he has absolved himself of responsibility for the day-to-day and moved three hours away. They go to continue the one tradition we used to have with their father's family, who will be glad to see them. There is no dark and terrible story here.

Why then does it hurt like this? Not a dull, constant ache but darts of pain—abrupt, focused, incisive. Three nights without them, that's all. Yet the yearning, the hankering to be around them, bewilders me. True that many a mom has felt this way about her newborn baby. But about her teenagers? Who *does* that?

I am after all a single parent, the primary parent, the parent who, by mutual agreement, has full physical custody with all that that means—from the eggs, oatmeal, and vitamins on the table by 6:30 every morning to the last pickup from soccer or choir at 8:00 at night. My own work, the students in whom I am so invested, in between. I'm supposed to look forward to this "me" time. After all, I did seek it out at distant conferences in the past.

Back when they were little, I needed to get away every so often—needed to be able to hold a thought and test it out on an academic audience, to assure myself that I was still me. Motherhood, for all its highs, felt like a constant state of siege of the self. Perhaps I wanted so much to do parenting "right" that I forgot to savor its intense flavors, its elusive joys. I breastfed my babies on demand, pumped on my teaching days, slept for years on the crack between two little beds to keep childhood fears at bay. So when people would tell me, "It goes by so fast," I'd be creaking from my exacting nights and days and marvel at their delusions. If only I had grasped then that painstaking parenting isn't the same thing as mindful parenting. No wonder I never knew how to strike a genuine note about motherhood, my tone always sounding either falsely celebratory or falsely flat to my ears. No wonder I needed a break now and then. And not just for conferences: once I even took off to Oaxaca, Mexico, with my sister, leaving my four- and two-year-olds behind with my husband. And I did so at a time when my daughter was sorrowing over the babysitter next door, the warm and cheery woman who had cared for her since she was a year old and then dumped her suddenly because of something my husband had said, though she kept the other children in her care. Even as I observed how the brightness had vanished from those four-year-old eyes, even as I hurt to see my daughter look longingly out the window at the children gathered around the tire swing next door, I left her for five nights to go on a vacation.

The past, as someone said, *is a foreign country. They do things differently there.*

Since my husband moved out five months ago, our lives have been transformed. But it's not about him. It's about the three of us: Maya, Cyrus, and I. A cohesive whole, as complete and defined as an isosceles triangle. Yet the lines that hold us and give us shape seem porous, pulsing with possibility and a sense of our own expansiveness.

That is how we are when we're together.

My first Thanksgiving without them. The first of many. I experience time as compressed: three years while both still live at home, three years in which to make up for all our lost days and all the years of empty-nesting ahead. Let there be candlelight and laughter at the table, let me teach during the summer so I can whisk them off to Paris in springtime. Future Thanksgivings will be a ritual of waiting—waiting for them to come home from college, to eat well and catch up on sleep and studies before the frenzy of finals. Goodbyes until winter break, until spring break, until finally the delicious stretch of summer once more.

If, as my sister says, I am living mindfully, then to live mindfully is to live as though you're in love with the present. Maybe that's why four days without Maya and Cyrus hurt as they do. Maybe that's why it feels like first love: intensely lived in this moment, for a lifetime of looking back. I'm looking through the two ends of the telescope at once—at the faraway tomorrow from this end and the faraway past from the other. Both remote. Meanwhile I seize on the present through a microscope, see it larger, fuller, its every detail clearly delineated, its wondrous immensity so close and so intimate as to sweep out of view all befores and afters. This is what it means to be in love. This must be the ever after.

Here—And There—Lies Home

Once as a young teen, I found a poster of a brown, Western-looking house, with slanted roof and abundant springtime flowers canopied by a blue sky. It didn't matter that those orange and yellow springtime flowers—tulips and daffodils—didn't grow in my hometown in southern Pakistan, or that our homes were made of concrete rather than wood. Nor did it matter that slanted rooftops never appeared on our city's skyline; we had flat, balconied roofs we could stroll on because, except for torrential downpours during monsoon season when water stood a foot high in the streets, it hardly ever rained in Karachi. What mattered was the ideal that the image projected, however removed from the reality.

But I loved, above all, the English words that accompanied the image in slanted white print, as if sprouting among the flowers: *Home is Where the Heart Lies*. It was the first time I had come across that expression. I purchased the glossy poster with my pocket money and had it framed in nearby Kamran Market. I intended it for my mother, on her birthday perhaps. On the back I wrote in my best cursive: "For Ammi, the heart of our home," and encased the words carefully in the curves of an oversized heart. The framed image hung in our living room for some time before it succumbed to gravity, fell to the floor and smashed.

I was twenty-one and living at home like most young women my age when my mother moved out. She didn't move far physically, but she had outpaced her marriage and followed her heart where it led her. It was a brave, even scandalous, move for 1980s Pakistan, and because Ammi didn't seem like "that sort" of woman, people didn't know how to account for her actions except to say she might have taken to drugs. After all, opium abounded since the influx of Afghan refugees fleeing the Soviet occupation of their homeland, they said.

My younger brother's departure had preceded Ammi's. Not quite seventeen, Amir left home in pursuit of the outsized dream of Stanford and called California home thereafter. My father and younger sister, Sadia, continued to live at 379-A/1, as did I for the most part—until we sisters, too, answered the seductive call of America, cast in the ideal of a Western education. Ten years later, Ammi and her husband rented the house across the street from Abbu, and all of them lived as amiable neighbors for eight years until Ammi moved across town, the ocean beckoning. Abbu remained in our Karachi home—his home—until he died. He never married again. When asked why not, he'd say he wanted us to always have a home to come back to. Eight months after his death, Amir, Sadia and I returned to Karachi for a week and sold 379-A/1, the house that he and Ammi had purchased together, its first owners, forty-three years earlier.

I have spent most of my American life in Massachusetts. But in 2006, the promise of a tenure-track position at California State University, Fresno, lured me westward. I was married then, with two young children, including four-year-old Cyrus who sorrowed over the loss of the only home he had known. There was no way to tell him then that his was but the latest of multigenerational migrations in our family: from his great-grandmother's yearnings for Patna, in her native India, after Partition, to his grandparents' attempts to belong in the London suburb of Greenford in the sixties and seventies, to his grand-aunts' and uncles' years spent in Denmark, Malawi, and Nigeria. His own mother's growing up in London and Karachi, like her adult years in Boston, were marked by that twoness of home—the twoness that is sometimes the expansive feeling of belonging equally on two different patches of the earth; more often, the feeling that wherever you are, you hold on to one half of a whole.

This past summer I worried how Cyrus, fourteen now, would react to losing the second home he had known—the beautiful one on San Jose Avenue in Fresno, with the adobe walls and red tile roof, the tall cypresses in front and a pool in the backyard. Clementines and kumquats to the east of the house, and lemons, grapefruit, and—most exciting to my parents—figs, to the west. It was a beauty we could no longer afford—never could, really, but now as a single woman I could make the decision to give it up without having to accommodate anyone else's dreams or delusions. Still, it was a hard thing to let it go, knowing I was not likely to live in a space that beautiful ever again.

But every time you move—be it 1100 miles between Patna and Karachi, 4000 miles between London and Karachi, 7000 from Karachi to Boston, 3000 from Boston to Fresno, or 1.7 miles from one home to another within Fresno—every time you move, you let go of some beauty. You let go of some ugliness. You hope that in the end beauty carries you over the threshold without your casting too many a glance backward.

Backward, forward. The weight we give to those words: "backward" implying a retreat, submission, failure; "forward" always somehow better because the future is home to possibility. Lucilia, my best friend from grad school, who was born and raised in the Azores, once said she thought no one should ever leave home because there is no going back even if you go back, and there is no moving forward without the weight of memory impeding your progress. There is no leaving behind your home. Or homes.

Sometimes at Fresno State I teach Sandra Cisneros's story "Eleven," in which the child narrator says that when you're eleven, you're also ten, nine, eight, seven, six, five, four, three, two, and one years old, like the layers of an onion or a doll inside a doll. I think when we live inside one home, we are also living in all the other homes we have ever inhabited. We live among those smells, those surfaces, those different dawns; we breathe the air of those homes populated by faces we will never see again.

When Amir and Linda drove down from San Francisco with their daughter, Naïla, to visit our old home in Fresno for the last time, I streamed a song for them by the Bangladeshi singer Runa Laila. The song, "Dil Dharkay," had been a hit in the summer of 1970 when our parents had moved us back from London to Karachi—a move that proved temporary because we returned to London in '72, after the war with India and Bangladesh's hard-won independence from Pakistan. Amir was not quite five years old at the time, but that day in Fresno his face brightened at the sound of the lively tune. He named the singer immediately and commented that she was a favorite of Chotepapa's, our beloved uncle who had blazed the trail to England, and who died the year my son was born. And then Amir startled me with the observation that, quite literally, the face of the map had changed since we first sang that song because East Pakistan no longer existed on the globe. As East Pakistan, Bangladesh had been Ammi's home, the patch of newly created Pakistan (which was itself envisioned as a homeland for India's Muslims, though most stayed in India) to which her parents had migrated after Partition. It was the site of her growth into womanhood, she and her sister Talat together, in Bengali and Urdu and a smattering of English. And it no longer exists. It was wiped out in blood. The memory of that home is, for these two sisters, enmeshed with a memory of collective trauma on both sides of the violence.

As I write, I'm looking forward to my brother's first visit to my new home in Fresno, where we have been living for almost a month now. Just west of Fig Garden Village, it's a pretty, spacious, and well-located condo on Calimyrna Avenue that I have been able to buy with his help a year after the divorce. My teenagers still have a pool but without the worry of upkeep because it's communal, and a tennis court to boot. Most glamorous for them is the proximity of Dutch Bros with their boutique drinks, which has made our home a popular congregating point for their friends.

I search the meaning of "Calimyrna" and discover that the word refers to the Smyrna fig as it is cultivated in California—in Fresno and the San Joaquin Valley where we live, in fact. Trace the ancient history of the fig and you find that it, too, has come a long way, a native of west Asia. It figures among the first plants ever cultivated by human beings—by some accounts, it may be the first domesticated plant of the Neolithic Revolution, some twelve thousand years ago—and it thrives even in inhospitable environments. Which is to say, transcends time and space.

In California, it was Junipero Serra and his fleet of Spanish missionaries who introduced figs—the dark, so-called Mission figs—in the eighteenth century. The Smyrna fig, however, didn't find its way to California until the late nineteenth century, and it took another generation to figure out how to get it to bear fruit. In fact, figs are not really a fruit but inverted flowers that store their pollen inside. It turned out that the Smyrna fig had to be pollinated by a special fig wasp from west Asia that lives inside wild "capri figs." The tiny, two-millimeter female wasp has a symbiotic relationship with the capri fig: it provides her a home while she provides the pollen for the fruit. By a fascinating process, she is driven to leave this home in order to lay her eggs elsewhere. When she comes to a Smyrna fig, however, she doesn't realize that she won't be able to lay her eggs there because Smyrna figs have only female flowers. Spurred by instinct, the fig wasp is lured by the false promise of a home for her eggs.

But here's the thing: in the process of making her way through the opening in the fruit's crown, crazed by some desperate dream, her wings are torn. Once inside the Smyrna fig, there is no going back. So the fig wasp tries to go forward, from flower to flower, in vain. But no, not entirely in vain. According to author and natural historian Wayne P. Armstrong, longtime professor at Palomar College: "In her desperate attempt to lay eggs, she inadvertently pollinates the flowers." Inadvertently. Seeking one outcome and failing to secure it, she creates another. But "eventually she dies from sheer exhaustion, or old age." She's swallowed up by a protein-digesting enzyme and serves to provide the nuttiness and crunch of the Smyrna fig. Acre upon acre of fig orchards on Highway 99 just north of Fresno testify to her enormous contribution to California's economy, and to the economy of the San Joaquin Valley in particular. That's her future. The fig wasp is programmed to self-destruct for the sake of her tomorrows.

The Smyrna fig gets its name from its homeland in Smyrna—now known as Izmir—in present-day Turkey, where it has been cultivated for centuries. And the fig cultivated at about the same latitude in Fresno, California becomes the Calimyrna fig in celebration of its dual origins: its present home in California and its ancient roots in Turkey, a country that itself straddles two continents on which I once lived. And yet the species is not a hybrid; rather, the Calimyrna fig traces a direct line of descent from those original cuttings brought to California from Asia well over a hundred years ago.

    My daughter, Maya, loved the condo the instant we saw it and has loved it consistently since. My son was won over by the time we moved in. I like it well enough and love it in moments when I see it through their eyes. It's ours; a home for just the three of us. True, my daughter will leave for college in less than two years, my son in four. But for a space in time we will be rooted here together, and this Calimyrna condo will be home.

Yellow Coat

This is an essay I don't want my son to read.

When Cyrus first arrived at the daycare center, a handsome two-year-old with dimpled cheek, he refused to take his coat off. For weeks the battle raged. Even when he could be persuaded to walk into his classroom and sit at the communal table, he would not permit anyone to unzip his puffy yellow coat or slide the hood from his head. His teacher, a no-nonsense young woman concerned about the hazards of overheating, insisted. Cyrus would back away, clutching at his chest as she approached, but stronger hands than his pried his fingers away and retrieved the shrinking arms from the yellow sleeves that cocooned them. He'd crumple in the corner, then, his body hiccuping with sobs.

By the time Cyrus was four years old, he was already a staunch creature of habit. Every morning he climbed down from the top of the bunk-bed, one careful step at a time, with a plush animal or two ensconced under his arm, and at the end of each day he gathered his critters and climbed back up the ladder to bed. No matter how late the night or how tired his legs, Cyrus never left his critters behind.

But then his mother accepted a tenure-track position in the English Department at Fresno State. During the five months in which our family of four had to pack up our lives in Massachusetts and move to California, Cyrus sorrowed for what he was about to lose: the bedroom lined with bookshelves that he shared with his older sister, Maya; the swing-set in the sprawling backyard with grass that his father mowed on a mini tractor, sometimes with Cyrus sitting ensconced between his knees; the above-ground pool he would venture into only with a yellow float that resembled a lifejacket; his preschool friends and teachers who had been part of his world for fully half his life—in a word, everything he knew.

I helped as I knew how: by buying children's books on the subject. Together we followed the Berenstain Bears' move from mountain cave to tree-house and Tigger's move to a new home; we read about a human family's sudden accumulation of cardboard boxes from the perspective of their dog, Boomer. In fact, I discovered scores of stories about animals whose families were about to relocate. The one Cyrus asked me to read most often featured a little boy mouse and bore the title: *I'm Not Moving, Mama!*

Ten years later Cyrus would have to move again, this time within Fresno, following his parents' divorce. I'll worry about its effect on him, but though he'll be more tentative about the condo than his sister, he will be surer of it than I. At fourteen, the relief of not having to water backyard trees or skim a pool, and the coolness factor of having the boutique drinks of Dutch Bros nearby will outweigh any sense of loss. This time it will be our four-year-old cat, Winnie, who'll spend the first months after the move huddled in a cardbox box in our new garage.

But back then as we packed for the transcontinental move, Cyrus refused to part with any of his belongings, so we paid to have them all—not just the stuffed animals but every building block, every monster truck, every long-lost board-book, old socks, and worn shoes—we paid by the pound to have all of them driven three thousand miles in a big moving truck that sported the word *Atlas* on a blue wave across its breadth.

On the six-hour flight from Boston to San Francisco, Cyrus sat somber and resigned, like a kitten in a carry-cage that had stopped meowing but couldn't be made to purr. An enthusiast about every mode of transportation, he allowed himself to be distracted only briefly by the airplane's wing or the terrain below it. Often I'd look up to find his eyes holding the tears that would neither quell nor drop.

A single photograph captures the moment of Cyrus's arrival at Fresno airport. He stands with his older sister at the top of the downward escalator in the terminal, a giant "Welcome to Fresno" sign visible above their small frames. Maya looks around her with bright, inquisitive eyes and a smile forming on her lips. Cyrus, on the other hand, wears a wary expression and a navy blue t-shirt with B-O-S-T-O-N in big red letters across his chest.

That first year, in addition to my new tenure-track job, the family had to adjust to the fact that dad was no longer working from home. This was especially hard for Cyrus. "I wish Daddy didn't have a job," he said more than once. (Until, within the year, his wish came true.) I arose at 5:00 am to prepare or overprepare for my classes and get myself and my children ready for the day. I'd drop Maya off at Malloch Elementary and Cyrus at Kiddie Kare—the preschool he had picked over the more prestigious Fairmont on account of the quality of its playground (and yes, I gave him the choice because he had so few choices). Then I made my way twenty minutes east to Fresno State. I was teaching new courses and adapting to the rhythms of a large public university where the culture differed significantly from the small New England colleges I had taught at until then. I was being tested and I didn't want to fail.

Cyrus added to the challenges of my first year on the job by dragging his feet every morning. The day would begin pleasantly enough. He'd be the first person to awake after me, and as soon as he did so, he'd climb down from the bunk-bed with the stuffed toys du jour and come looking for Mama in the family room. He'd find her predictably reading on the couch, pen in hand. Our unspoken ritual dictated that I set my tome aside for a few minutes while he rested his head on my lap, and together we listened for the birdies. I didn't know then how abruptly such rituals end, or how often I would return to that morning communion between us when the teen years came. There are days now when my son will emerge from his bedroom and walk at brisk, preoccupied pace right past the living room, unseeing. But back then I would have to say, "Time for us to get up now, love." And somehow as soon as the moment of idyllic stasis was behind us, as it came time to get dressed and head out of the house, the morning demanded some combination of coaxing, humoring, arguing, and reprimanding to get Cyrus out the door on time. Somehow, we managed.

Until one day, six months into the new school year, it got to me. And it was the morning of Cyrus's fifth birthday.

He had come looking for me in the living room that cold February morning, his footsteps soft against the Mexican tiles of the hallway. But instead of bounding toward the couch, he paused at the threshold with smiling eyes, clutching Pinkie, the plush poodle, in one hand, his slender body wrapped in the fleece robe his Granny had made him for Christmas. I went up to hug him before we returned to the couch together. That morning at the breakfast table he laughed at everything. He was the Birthday Boy, dimples deep with the giddiness of turning five.

I don't know when it began or how it escalated, but an hour later, the scene had shifted. Maya was dressed and ready, as was I. Also ready to go was a half-sheet marble cake for Cyrus's classmates with strawberry filling and a miniature Lightning McQueen parked atop the icing. Then Cyrus was protesting—was it about wearing a sweater? putting his shoes on?—and I was trying to reason with him. Next thing I knew, I was shrieking at him in a voice I couldn't recognize as my own. It wasn't even the worst of his procrastinations, but I couldn't scale back. My words, whatever they were, bounced off the dark floor tiles and resounded throughout the high-ceilinged house. Maya stared. Six months of practiced patience at home and nervous diligence at work had erupted in unaccustomed volume that terrorized the five-year-old boy before me. His shoulders shook from the force of his sobs.

I like to think I didn't let him cry for long. That I recovered my sense of proportion, abandoning whatever had seemed important to insist upon a few minutes ago. I held him until the sobs subsided, led him to the bathroom to wash his face and pat it dry, my fingers smoothing his dark hair.

I loaded the Lightning McQueen cake into the minivan. We dropped Maya off at Malloch and within five minutes we had arrived at Kiddie Kare. As I reached for the sheet cake on the backseat, I wondered if Cyrus was a tad too quiet. The teacher took the cake from my hands and assured me that the children would enjoy it. "Cyrus makes everyone laugh," she said.

Alex and I had gone all out for our son's fifth birthday, his first one in Fresno. We even colluded in buying him the big, red motorized All Terrain Vehicle he could only imagine owning. After Kiddie Kare, there was Pump It Up, an extravagant space where brother and sister bounced their hearts out together. The following day we hosted Cyrus's four close friends from preschool, all of them boys who displayed good-natured envy of his new ATV and took turns driving it around our backyard. Photographs show Cyrus and his playmates with exuberant expressions, intent on their fun. All evidence suggests a happy birthday.

So why has that morning been on my mind these past few weeks of summer? Cyrus and Maya appear to have no memory of it. Does that mean it didn't happen? That I didn't ruin the day—didn't make my son cry on the morning of his fifth birthday?

Moments after that moment, six-year-old Maya had said quietly, "He wasn't really arguing with you, Mama. I don't know why you got so upset with him."

Maya has always been communicative—to a fault, her teachers might say. "Why not try to sit with silence?" I'd ask her at the kitchen table sometimes. "It's not the same thing as nothingness, you know." Now, in her last summer at home before leaving for college, she does yoga and we hang out at cafés together, as comfortable with quiet as with chatter. Our conversations move across varied terrains. She's my window into contemporary pop culture as shaped by artists of color—Solange Knowles, Childish Gambino (whom I once recalled as "Childish Bambino," much to my children's mirth). I can't get into the macabre crime shows she loves, but *Jane the Virgin* reels me in with such vehemence that within weeks I've caught up on all eighty-one episodes available on Netflix.

Maya was a junior at Edison High when Cyrus entered his first year there. Many in his class looked up to his sister as part of the cool set, one of those tweeting juniors and seniors who have their fingers firmly on the pulse of their times. She made a formidable opponent in debates at Model United Nations conferences and performed in Edison Tiger Theater Company's productions of *The Wiz* and *The Lion King*. She's also a freelance journalist for The kNOw Youth Media, and Fresnans have seen her pictured in *The Fresno Bee* among a small group of young people speaking up for their right to meaningful sex education in Fresno Unified schools. Maya has an opinion on most things, including high school robotics, which her brother loves.

Robotics. Cyrus's first year of high school, robotics became the wall between us that I couldn't scale. He's been loyal to soccer and piano since he was little, but neither of those shut me out like robotics, perhaps because sports and music make room for an audience. By contrast, the robotics club at Edison High gathers in an extension of the lab that is a warehouse—a metallic room cramped with tools that I can barely name, let alone use. This unbeautiful space fires my son's imagination. During the six weeks of Build Season, he and a few other hardcore robotics students like him spend at least as many hours in the warehouse after school as they do in class. There they feel the rush of the hands-on, head-on thrill of designing and building a robot that can compete at the prestigious First Robotics regional, national, and maybe even global competitions. A tireless teacher stays with them as well as parent-mentors who have both the time and know-how to make themselves useful.

I am not one of them. But during Cyrus's sophomore year I spend more money than I should to tag along to Houston when Edison's team, Mindcraft 3495, is invited to the World Competition, sponsored by major tech companies, including Google. Their robot's unique four-bar arm design, which Cyrus had worked on with a senior, had won the Engineering Award at the Central Valley Regional and caught the attention of the First Robotics judges. They didn't win the global tournament, but they were there. And cheering them on, I felt for the first time that I understood something of First Robotics culture, if not of mechanical engineering.

Still, the mother seeks traces of the little boy who loved his stuffed animals and never failed to scoop them up at the end of the day.

Is the boy who held on to his yellow coat there in the sixteen-year-old whose teammates trust him not only to design and build their robot but to drive it in the tense, adrenalin-charged arenas of a tournament?

Maya has her own take on her younger brother. With the vantage point of a just-graduated high school senior, she casts a suspicious eye on "STEM kids" as likely robotic themselves. And as an enthusiast of psychology, she has been known, half-seriously, to call her brother a sociopath—*as distinct from psychopath*, she tells him; *more like the profiles of CEOs*. I recoil from the noun and admonish her for typecasting. What does she know of Cyrus's capacity for tenderness, his vulnerabilities, and his loyalties? Mine is the memory.

Perhaps the memories of Cyrus's early years press on me this summer because Maya is about to leave home. I have spent the past few years anticipating what her absence will mean for me, for Cyrus, for our home life. We've moved twice before, but as a family; now Maya will be moving out. She will be moving on. For the first time in our world, it will be just my son and me. We'll have only each other to greet first thing in the morning and last thing at night. Until, in two years' time, Cyrus moves out, too.

As the stern hand of time reaches for me, I shrink into my yellow coat.

I want to be the critter who won't be left behind.

Mourning Dove

The Mourning Dove flutters between its nest in the neighbor's tree and the small, rectangular patch of my backyard brimming with grass seeds. In the early light, I detect another bird stationed in the nest, but its perch is too high up for me to see much of anything else in it. That must be the male, incubating the eggs for a few hours before he hands the job over to his female partner for the rest of the day. From among all the possible locations he showed her when he wooed her, she chose my neighbor's tree as the site of their new home. They built the nest together—he, the gatherer of the raw material, and she, the one charged with making meaning out of it.

I hear Mourning Doves are monogamous. I marvel but don't envy them.

Maybe the eggs have hatched already, and he is babysitting the fledgelings up there while she gathers the rye seed below, to chew in her own mouth before feeding it to her young. They can't handle the business of living full throttle just yet. Every seed she picks is a dot of green that will be missing in the lawn I have allowed myself this spring.

I watch her through the glass panes of the slider between my bedroom and backyard. I see her in profile, dark semicircle under her eye. What will she do when the fledgelings, plumped with grass seed, outgrow her space and falter into their own? Dizzy with dreams, and longings fueled by flight.

Is that when the mourning begins?

Café Convo

Maya and I resolved to create more café time for the two of us this, her last year of high school. Busy as we both are, we're averaging only once a month so far.

But what a special day it is when your almost-eighteen-year-old, sipping her latte, remarks that the conscious choices you made for her earliest books and toys were a good idea. Astonishingly, she remembers that when you read stories to her, you would ask her what she'd like the gender of the protagonist to be, and that invariably she'd superimpose a "she" where the animals were almost always "he." ("Non-binary" hadn't yet expanded our options back then.) She remembers that you'd invite her to retell the fairytales, so that in her version Cinderella became a nurse after marrying her prince. And that any dolls she had were made of different shades of plastic.

She says you always commented on the "beautiful brown skin" of the darkest girl at Mulberry, her preschool in Taunton, Massachusetts, and on her own "beautiful brown hands."

You listen, stunned.

Because you had forgotten,

because she remembers.

Because today she's sitting in a café with you,

telling you that

it mattered.

Trinità

After years of envying parents who could afford it, I made it happen. I took my two teenagers, born in Boston and raised in Fresno, California, to the cities in Bella Italia I most wanted them to experience with me: Firenze and Venezia. It was a feat to have found a time in 2019 that worked for all three of us. Maya, it turned out, would not be coming home from college her first summer but staying in La Jolla to work, and Cyrus, a rising senior in high school, had his hands and head full with other ambitions. That's when I realized that our summers of assumed togetherness had ended, as abruptly as all eras end, that I could, with patience, replenish the savings in my bank account, but I'd never find an ATM to retrieve the hours that have accrued to the past. It was two months before Venice's worst flooding in fifty years, five months before the coronavirus pandemic struck Italy.

That one precious week in early September, stolen from all our other obligations, I watched my children's interactions with the landscape, and with each other in that landscape—Cyrus expecting at any moment to step outside this "old town" Florence into some modern downtown and marveling that that never happens. Because in Firenze the present inhabits the past and fills it with flesh, like young children growing into the clothes their parents have picked out for them. The light of recognition in Maya's eyes as she stands before Botticelli's *Birth of Venus* at the Uffizi, which, until now, she knew only as an illustration in her Art History textbook. At once enchanted and disconcerted by the canals of Venice—a visual wonder at every turn, but utterly unreal. (And *how sustainable?* my Gen Z children wondered.)

There is recognition for me, too, from my visit to these two cities some seven years prior. I had come seeking asylum from grief after my father's passing. He died suddenly in Karachi that March, his much-anticipated visit to us in California suspended in the never-to-be future, though his packing list sat in readiness on the night-stand. I had had no plans for such extravagance in grief, for choosing that moment to realize a banal, if dearly-held, dream of seeing Italy someday. But my own fiftieth birthday followed a few weeks after Abbu's death, and it was also the date stamped on his passport, June 4, marking the expiration of his visit visa to the US. The knotting of desire, death, birth, travel, and expiration date struck some barely registered chord, but with sufficient power to delineate the finiteness of things, including the shape of our own longings. And so, casting aside concerns about future college expenses, and leaving Maya and Cyrus with my sister, Sadia, and her family in San Diego, I had come to Italy with my husband of sixteen years, unaware that it was a last-ditch attempt to resuscitate a dying marriage. As I looked out on the Grand Canal from the crowded vaporetto that warm July, the mists of mortality enveloped me more closely than I knew.

In that sense, this long-coveted, September visit to Italy is a conscious reprise. Happier times of togetherness for my children and me—long, exploratory walks, which they navigate with Google Maps on their phones, technology for wanderlust that Marco Polo and Cristoforo Colombo could not have dreamed of. Firenze makes a particular impression on them. Our hotel stands a whisper away from the Renaissance sculptures in the Piazza della Signoria, the public square where Neptune poses for selfies with the tourists, where the story of the abduction of the Sabine women by Romulus and his men is carved out of a single marble slab for viewers to gaze on from every angle, and where Medusa's head dangles in perpetuity from Perseus's grasp. I imagine the Signore looking down on them all from their seat of government in the Palazzo Vecchio, the sculptures pulsing with particular meaning for the Florentines of the day and still speaking to us of power and passion, and our own appetite for violence. We have our afternoon cappuccinos across from this ever-accessible outdoor gallery, and one tender night my children and I sit on some steps nearby, licking our gelati.

At nineteen and seventeen, Maya and Cyrus move through the Basilica di Santa Croce unencumbered by time. There they stand, reading plaques, as close as they will ever get to the bodily remains of Michelangelo, Galileo, Rossini, and—excitingly for kids who have been involved with Model U.N. in high school—Machiavelli. But the goosebumps are all mine. It's the same when I see them sitting among other students at the Biblioteca delle Oblate, Cyrus peering into his laptop, Maya scrolling on her phone, and the cathedral's rust-red dome observing their preoccupations from the open balcony. What the Duomo must know about aspirations of becoming, itself a hundred and forty years in the making, until Brunelleschi's eye gave its beauty a long-awaited, half-hoped-for completion, with the strength to endure.

My children appear racially ambiguous. Matrilineally Pakistani, they have a Belgian grandmother and are Italian on their paternal grandfather's side. Livio "Lee" Vagnini's mother, Margarita Avondo (or Rita, as she was called) left Turino for New Jersey in the early years of the twentieth century, married an Italian American named Frank whose parents had migrated from Sorrento, and whose name echoes in my ex's. But grandson Frank Alex altered the spelling of his last name to make it phonetic in English, and so my children becameВанninis.

Not that names are reliable routes back to our ancestors anyway. My own last name came not from a clan but from my paternal grandfather in pre-Partition India, the poet who chose *Najam*, the Arabic for "star," as his pen name. *Najmi*, literally "my star" but implying "of Najam," was the name he gave to his children and, in the South Asian custom of the day, to his poet apprentices. After years of considering ourselves unique, I was startled to discover in my thirties how many Najmis exist online with whom I have no familial ties.

No familial ties, but yet a connection. Because when you huddle in close proximity under a single umbrella, it hardly matters in the long run how you got there. So Maya googled "Vannini in Firenze" and found a pasticceria with the name. We made the pilgrimage by cab to have our lattes in that hallowed space beyond tourist attractions. The women who worked there spoke only Italian but gleaned enough from Maya's driver's license to be tickled by the thought that they were welcoming "back" one of their prodigal own. We walked home because we were out of euros and the taxi we called didn't accept credit cards. And wouldn't you know it? Barely a mile down the road, on the same Via del Ponte alle Mosse, Maya's eagle eye spots yet another Vannini business—easy to miss as we tread the narrow sidewalk past all the other small businesses in the big, concrete building. The small, unpretentious store is closed for the day now, but its watches and clocks of disparate shapes and sizes are prominently displayed on glass shelves in the narrow, arched window. *Vetta Vannini*, the sign says, inviting passersby to linger by the window. The simple display defies us to go digital; it appeals to our yearning for something tangible to touch, something beautiful to behold. Something to distract us from the intended purpose of the window's wares: to mark the minutes as they go by. Because to wrap time around our wrists is to forget that it eludes even Perseus's grasp.

But nothing absorbs time as the river Arno does, gathering our todays into its yesterdays, to flow swiftly and silently into someone else's tomorrows. Long before I ever visited Florence, I imagined the Arno as Keats and Shelley evoked it in their poetry almost two hundred years ago. The name itself appealed, its open vowels calling me across some great distance. *Arno* . . . To say its name is to open wide and deep before you breathe it out again, tongue touching the palate like a furtive piano key—deft, soft— without the lips ever sealing your mouth against the air.

No matter where we roamed, the Arno framed Firenze for me. Even while I stood inside the Uffizi, amidst the art collection of the Medicis, it beckoned from the upper-story windows of the South Corridor, and I turned my back on the treasures within to photograph it. The river sparkled like jade in the sun, arched by bridges and edged by an unbroken line of buildings in amber, gold, and dust. But my favorite site from which to view the Arno was the Ponte Santa Trinita, a Renaissance-era bridge that once had a life as a medieval wooden structure. Its name—without the accent on the "a" in Trinita—echoes an older time when Florentines referred to the Holy Trinity with an emphasis on the first vowel rather than the last. In 1259, when the Arno's flooding frenzy washed the wooden bridge away, it came back reincarnated in stone. But stone had its vulnerabilities, too, it turned out, and the bridge was swept away again in 1333. Rebuilt by the Florentines and destroyed again by the river, the bridge had to wait until 1569 for the architect Bartolomeo Ammannati (who also sculpted the Neptune of our selfies) to design its three-arch structure. Like Brunelleschi,

Ammannati imparted strength to beauty, his design directing water away from the structural support for the bridge. So this time the bridge survived almost four centuries, only to be blown up by the retreating Nazis one night in August, 1944—all of it, including the four marble statues representing the seasons, two on each side of the bridge, which had been added in 1608 as part of the wedding celebrations for Cosimo II de' Medici. The people of Florence rebuilt it yet again in the 1950s. They retrieved the original stone, piece by piece, from the Arno, and what the river wouldn't return, they replaced with stone from the same quarry as the original. Only Primavera's marble head remained missing—until the Arno relinquished that 350-year-old treasure, too, in 1961.

Like so many other people whose lives intersected with ours on the Ponte Santa Trinita, Maya, Cyrus, and I gazed at the peach and purple hues of the sun setting on the river, the skies reflected in it. At night the lights shimmered golden in the waters while we indulged in our daily gelato ritual. My marriage was four years in the past, all bitterness behind us, but that particular gelateria immediately south of the bridge that Alex and I had favored was still there, and I could still order a black sesame gelato inside and eat it on the Ponte Santa Trinita amid the teenage banter of my two children. Who can say we weren't a flesh-and-blood trinity then, indistinct among the other tourists, but with a sanctity all our own?

On our last night in Firenze we watched the sun set on the city from the height of the Piazzale Michelangelo. It was an aerial view of the red rooftops, the Duomo distinct among them, and the Arno flowing by. As night fell, we strangers danced together, celebrating . . . what? That life was ours in that moment—small, insignificant, and as vulnerable to time as the wooden bridge was to the river, but part of something larger, a historical human stream, to whose existence the panoramic landscape bore witness. We had formed a flash community on the Piazzale Michelangelo that night—our lives converging, precious, on a hill above the Arno; our laughter and dance a timeless toast to our own effervescence.

One song that the street musicians didn't play on the Piazzale that night, but which we heard many times in the course of our week in Bella Italia was Andrea Bocelli's "Con Te Partirò." I remember when the tenor, child of a small town close to Firenze, made himself known to us in Boston, before Maya and Cyrus were born. Bocelli has his fans and detractors—the latter find him too popular for opera, too operatic for pop—but Alex and I loved the song the moment we first heard it, over twenty years ago. Bocelli seemed to pour into his voice some hard-won knowledge. It was perhaps what he knew from having once been able to see, and then not. Wherever it comes from, the yearning reaches us in song and evokes in the sighted a wrenching recognition, the certain knowledge of loss.

The song unsettles me. In 1998, Alex and I didn't have children but we did have our gentle tabby, MoeMoe. Two weeks before Alex discovered MoeMoe dead outside our doorstep, his radio kept playing Bocelli's song over and over again. It's hard for either of us to hear it now without the weight of memory pressing on us as superstition. As beautiful as Bocelli's voice is, sadness overcame me when a gifted woman cellist on the street corner played the tune—not once, but twice—as we ate our last dinner, outdoors on a patio, in Florence. And later, the same sadness intruded again on that Venetian night when the orchestras on opposite sides of the grand Piazza San Marcos switched from Beethoven to Bocelli's song. Suddenly, like an orchestral tag team, they took turns playing "Con Te Partirò" to the throngs that had gathered to listen—some, like us, seated at their circular tables, others standing, and a few couples slow-dancing to the music as midnight approached.

I couldn't shake that sadness off for a couple of weeks after our return to Fresno. For the first time, my curiosity about the lyrics compelled me to do a little research. And I discovered that the song doesn't translate. My limited knowledge of Italian told me that "Con te partirò" means "with you I will leave," and yet the English title, which generated instant fame for Andrea Bocelli, is "Time To Say Goodbye." But now I learned that the disjunction goes beyond the title. Some critics have pointed to the incoherence of the lyrics themselves when translated to English. I'm riveted by one section of Bocelli's duet with Sarah Brightman in particular, which has been translated as:

Horizons are never far
Would I have to find them alone
Without true light of my own with you
I will go on ships over seas
That I now know
No, they don't exist anymore
It's time to say goodbye

People point to the absurdity of the last four lines, of going on ships over newly discovered seas that don't exist anymore. (In fact, "they" could mean both the ships and the seas here.) How can they both be true: "seas/that I now know," which, in the next moment, "don't exist anymore"?

But the very incoherence of the lines makes my sadness

intelligible to me. Every time I chanced upon the melody during our week in Italy, I need not have succumbed to a superstitious foreboding, or even to the heft of a twenty-year-old memory. The English translation articulates a paradox, two mutually exclusive, yet inclusive, truths: in the very moment that we're discovering the preciousness of something, we are also losing it. We may well visit Bella Italia again someday, the three of us together. But as my friend Kathee put it, we won't be the same people.

I hear Bocelli's song in Fresno. It has become a chorus to that week in Italy, a time of increasingly rare togetherness with my young adult children. The melody plays somewhere in my consciousness, soft and subtle, between Maya's phone calls from La Jolla—those calls that allow me to share in her excitement about her Clinical Psychology and Ethnic Studies courses at UC San Diego, her work at the VA, the events she has planned for the Pakistani Students Association on campus. *Mama*, she says, her voice in my ear brimming with the cadences of the four-year-old she used to be.

I hear Bocelli's song as Cyrus works on his college applications. He's seated at the same circular, cherry-wood dining table where he constructed his very first sentences on the page, shortly after our move from Boston. Today, his reach is eager for worlds beyond Fresno, beyond California and the western bounds of this vast country. This time next year, neither of them will be sitting across from me at the dinner table. This time next year, who knows how else the earth will have shifted?

Con te partirò, I think. It has always been time to say goodbye.

fragment 12

A week to go, and Sadia has a dream:
Our whole family gathered around the table, playing cards.
The ceiling fan.
A face beneath the ceiling fan,
shadowed,
looking down on all our cards.
And we,
oblivious.

The last time I saw you, we were at a wedding reception. Our Shahid Phuppa proudly telling his guests about your scholarship to Smith. Your face thinner yet. I followed my new husband around; you followed me. A small sense of belonging I did not reciprocate. We might have had a conversation. I might have asked about your plans for Smith. Instead, I spent our last evening together pandering to the ego of my angry young man.

The sound of your voice, with two days to go. I call for Hasina, some mundane question about meat or cilantro. And you answer the phone. How are you, Roob, I ask off-hand. "Teek," you reply. But you're not okay; your voice is desolate.

I hear it, its bleakness.
Last call.
But I ask nothing further.

Was it a week earlier that we had rented a VCR and an American movie at my mother's place—Azfar, Sadia, and I—and left you out? We had not wanted to, but my mother, newly single, did not think you'd be able to keep her secret. What you didn't know wouldn't hurt you, we thought.
What were the odds?

You found out. But asked us no questions.
Never asked why you had been excluded from the special sibling treat.
For once, you chose not to fight it.
Just held six-year-old Sheba close on your last night alive.

You knew you were never really one of us.

Odd one out

Black sheep of the Najmis

Odd one out.

Who would miss you?

Out! Out! OUT!

Brew

Noun:

A mixture of several things - *Cambridge Dictionary*

Verb:

To cook, steep, or simmer

To concoct

To conspire

(of tea or coffee): To become stronger in taste in the container in which it is made - *Cambridge Dictionary*

All those years that I was chasing after them, wiping their noses, reading and singing them to sleep, I was brewing. I was trying to concoct the perfect brew. You're handed the raw material you have to work with, but brewing is by definition an interaction among those ingredients, the brewer, the cup, and what the brewer pours into the cup.

Take tea, for instance, the South Asian chai. You have limited control over the quality of the tea leaves; geographic, economic, historical, and sociopolitical forces greater than you have grown, picked, packaged, and transported them. But they await the labor and attentiveness of your one little self. You must make sure the cup has been warmed in anticipation before you drop the leaves into it because the cup is the crucible. And the water you pour over the leaves—has it boiled sufficiently, to the point where its vapors find expression through the kettle's spout for a solid thirty seconds? Then, too: have water, tea, and cup been allowed their full four minutes of togetherness?

And who are you, Brewer? Do you make this cup of tea for yourself, to keep you company on the patio on a lonely afternoon? Do you make it for the friend who will scatter the loneliness with conversation? Or are you the artist whose focus in this moment is not on yourself at all, but on creating the one perfect cup as though nothing else in the world matters? And in so doing, you've poured your dreams and demons into the brew. The Carnation, the cardamom—who are they, but you?

Brewer Mother, what have I learned? That besides the leaves, the cup, the brewer's hand, there's the reckoning with Time. All measurement is temporal. The brew evolves, unfurls, blossoms or blights, in time. No ambition may rush it, no yearning slow it down. In brewing, all proportion is temporal. Too little, and there's no strength, flavor, or aroma. Too much, and the strength alights as bitterness on the tongue. Patience and vigilance, yes. Know your leaves, know your water, know your cup. Know the steadfast gentleness of your own hand. But Time seeps and steeps, infuses everything. Vital and exacting, it concocts the brew. Not you.

Let me know that. And let me savor the cup.

One Summer in Gaza

Sometimes you fall for the narrative. You fall so hard that the narrator, the conduit through whom the story reaches you, escapes your scrutiny. That's how I ended up married to a curly-lashed Palestinian student in the Journalism Department while still an undergraduate English major at the University of Karachi, in Pakistan.

His was a gripping narrative of home and the sudden violence of its loss, a communal loss of freedom and autonomy for an indigenous people. The narrator had a six-year-old's memory of the 1967 annexation of Gaza—of people fleeing helter-skelter, of his not being able to carry the baby brother, of laying him down in the stampede. Is every detail true? Probably not. After all, this storyteller often favored the genre of fiction in his day-to-day conversations. But teaching and writing memoir now, I'm more adept at identifying something between fiction and nonfiction—a fictionalized memory that is, in the main, true. Later I would meet the narrator's mother and learn for myself that the loss of this baby boy in the Six-Day War with Israel was among her many heartbreaks.

At twenty-one, I defied the expectations of my elders and married this bearer of the story, a testimonio from a faraway place that made the headlines of the *Dawn* newspaper real to me. The one good thing I owe directly to that too-long marriage of six years—from which I had to literally sneak out—is that it enabled me to visit the foreign and forbidden land of Gaza. What seemed like a feat in 1986 is almost an impossibility for any non-Gazan today.

Ghaza in Arabic, as in Urdu. *Ghazawi,* the one who belongs to *Ghaza,* and to whom *Ghaza* belongs. You make that initial consonant sound as you would the French "r"—from the throat, the back of the tongue almost closing off the windpipe, cutting off breath. Almost.

Ghaza as in "ghazal," the genre of Arabic poetry that dates back to the sixth century and, in another six centuries, had found its way to my ancestral land, the Indian subcontinent. In India, the ghazal thrived in the courts of the Mughal emperors; it witnessed the arrival of the Europeans in the seventeenth century, their fierce competition for the resources of a bountiful land and its gradual colonization by the British. It became the favored form of urbane Urdu poets in the nineteenth century. The ghazal is a genre that has traveled beyond its place of birth to find a home in other languages, including English. From the sixth century to the twenty-first. And little surprise, as its lyrical tradition speaks a universal language of love and loss. Subtract the final "l" and *Ghaza* is that language.

I visited Gaza in the summer of 1986, having just graduated from Karachi University—a couple of years later than I should have because the school shutdowns of the past decade had interfered with what was once a precocious trajectory. It was two years after my Nikah to the storybearer, and a year after we lost my cousin Rubina to suicide. Four years after the massacre in the refugee camps of Sabra and Shatila. It was two years before I arrived in Boston as a graduate student at Tufts. And just a year before the first Intifada, when children raised under twenty years of occupation rose up in protest.

We were a young married couple in Karachi, living first with my father and then with my mother, but sharing lofty dreams of a wider world. The storybearer had no passport, only the Travel Document issued to refugees. He had a home without a homeland, the refugee camp of Khan Younis in the Gaza Strip, a twenty-five mile long strip of land that borders the eastern Mediterranean, measuring seven-and-a-half miles at its widest point and separated from the West Bank by the state of Israel. Before Israel, Egypt occupied the Gaza Strip, and before that the British, and before that the Ottomans, or Al Othman in Arabic.

Today almost two million people live in what has been described as the world's largest open-air prison. It has no army. Although technically Israel withdrew from the Gaza Strip in 2005, it maintains control of air and sea access, and six out of seven points of entry by land. Egypt keeps its seven and a half miles of border with the Gaza Strip sealed for the most part. The tunnels into Egyptian territory, which, like any conduit, may be used for good and bad, have been destroyed. Hamas remains in power since 2007, at loggerheads with Al Fatah. Since then, Israel has launched three air wars to punish Hamas for rocket attacks, causing mostly civilian deaths. Its fierce fourth attack is happening at the time of this writing (May 2021), in response to protests against the forced evictions of Palestinians from their homes in East Jerusalem, and rocket fire from Hamas. While power relations remain acutely asymmetrical, all sides seem locked in their sliver of the story. Meanwhile, generation after generation of ordinary people wanting ordinary things like water, electricity, medicine, building materials, education, jobs, and mere mobility—to work, visit loved ones—must do without them. And extraordinary people with extraordinary talents, like the gifted soccer player Mahmoud Wadi, remain unknown. Wadi waits year after year for permission to leave this twenty-five mile strip, so he can avail of the opportunity to play the sport he loves on international fields.

Gaza is a throttled windpipe. Almost.

In the summer of 1986, Israeli officials sent me back from the border with Jordan twice before they allowed me in. We had flown from Karachi to Amman, Jordan, and stayed with friends before making the road trip to Khan Younis. A mere hundred or so miles, but worlds away for most. The first time we crossed the Allenby Bridge over the River Jordan, which separates Jordan from the Israeli-occupied West Bank, I wore my best Western clothes: a rayon burgundy dress with a paisley design that gathers by the waist, its hemline just below the knee. It had been picked out for me by my brother's girlfriend Debbie in Palo Alto, a young Jewish American woman who would visit us in Karachi later that year. Less to accessorize than to transport safely, I wore my incongruous South Asian wedding jewelry: 22-karat gold jhumkis dangling from my earlobes, a close-fitting filigree necklace, and an assortment of rings with little rubies, emeralds, and other gems studded in them. They were gifts from my parents, and I was going to wear them for the reception that my parents-in-law were surely planning in our honor. (The latter had no phone and couldn't read or write, so we seldom had news of them, or they of us, except via Palestinian students traveling between Gaza and Karachi.) Amma, my grandmother, had sewn me a silk purse pieced with triangles of vivid colors and golden edging, and in it I carried my eye pencil, blush, and lipstick, and a few U.S. dollar bills. I don't remember much about the bus ride from Amman, beyond the fact that I was sitting next to a blond, ponytailed woman in blue jeans who looked out the window as we crossed the River Jordan and said, "It looks more like a creek."

Bridges fascinate me. They seem so vulnerable, suspended in the air, a narrow spine over a body of water or a roaring highway. And yet they perform the Herculean task of linking two divided spaces, a conduit for connection that wouldn't be possible without them. They pay the price for this role: because of it, they become targets in times of war.

The Allenby Bridge goes by other names, depending on your orientation; it's also the Gesher Allenby, the King Hussein Bridge, and Al-Karameh. I don't know what it was called under the Ottomans, but it became the Allenby when the British rebuilt it in 1918. Since then it's been destroyed by an earthquake in 1927 and by two targeted destructions: the first in 1946 by the Palmach (who were freedom-fighters or terrorists, depending on whether you sympathized with the Jewish activists or British imperial power), and the second by Israel in the Six-Day War of 1967. It was then rebuilt as a truss bridge, and that's all it was in 1986 when my bus drove over it from Jordan into the occupied West Bank.

Once we arrived at the Israel border, the storybearer and I were separated. I was directed to Passport Control with other tourists and visitors, and he joined all the Palestinians holding the Travel Document for refugees.

When it came my turn to approach the window, I handed the Israeli official my emerald-green passport with gold lettering that read ISLAMIC REPUBLIC OF PAKISTAN in Urdu, English, and Arabic. The man, who appeared to be in his late thirties and had a phenotype and coloring not unlike those of the many Palestinian students I had come to know in Karachi, looked at it closely.

I wonder now what he was thinking. Did he know how often the Pakistani passport had changed in appearance since the first, beige-colored one issued in 1947? Within seven years, green had become the favored color, based on its traditional association with Islam, the color of Paradise as described in the Quran. Over the decades, the passport became a lighter or darker shade of green depending on where we stood between secularism and theocracy as a nation. Initially there were two flags, one each for West and East Pakistan, until Pakistan recognized Bangladesh in 1974, at which point the flags were dispensed with altogether in favor of Pakistan's coat-of-arms, and the Bengali script disappeared. In various eras, English and Urdu have vied for the top line of the cover, reflecting a familiar struggle of postcolonial linguistic identity, as neither language is native to all Pakistanis. In an illuminating 2016 *Dawn* article on this history, Nadeem Paracha surmises: "The Pakistani passport has been a mirror of the persistent existentialist tussle in the country itself."

The passport I handed to the Israeli official in 1986 was the latest iteration, under the religious orthodoxy of General Zia-ul-Haq, of the face we presented to the world. Although Pakistan's first constitution had declared the country an Islamic Republic, the religious qualifier had not appeared on our passports until 1984. Also under the General's regime, the Arabic script was added on the passport cover and, within its pages, a declaration of the holder's religion. While the former was abandoned in the 1990s, the latter remains. And there also remains an explicit notification that the passport is not valid for travel to Israel.

Pakistan and Israel: Abrahamic siblings and two post-World War II countries envisioned as a religious ideal that materialized on the map within months of each other. True, the creation of Pakistan did not become an open invitation for Muslims from all over the world to immigrate to the land at the cost of the indigenous population. Nor does it possess anywhere near the kind of power Israel has in its region, armed and funded as it is by the United States. Over the course of seven decades, Pakistan's territory has contracted rather than expanded. Still, families like mine—Muhajirs from India—though they brought much with them in the early years after Partition, can not be said to have integrated with an eye toward the equitable distribution of resources. And whatever vision of inclusiveness the founders may have had, Pakistan's religious minorities, including some non-Sunni Muslim sects, have been marginalized by a combination of policy, public sentiment, and vigilante violence. Those who can have fled. Pakistan and Israel, penned into existence by the British imperial hand in its dying days. A greedy, grasping hand, grown lazy and impatient with age, but consummately self-serving to the last.

Now the Israeli official furrows his thick, dark brows as he peers into my passport. His voice is calm and curious as he looks up at me.

"You know that your country does not have diplomatic relations with Israel?"

I did know. But I had assumed that the marriage papers, testifying that my spouse was from the Occupied Territories, would be enough to grant me a visit visa upon arrival. They were not. And here I was now, a frightened 23-year-old woman, by myself, with no idea what would happen next.

I was told to return to Jordan. But I had no idea how to find my husband. I knew little Arabic at that point, and it was clear that most people around me, Israeli or Arab, did not speak English. I was told to wait in a specific area, and wait I did. An Arab man in Western attire offered to drive me to Amman in his cab. As I weighed my options, an elder shuffled up to me in his long jalabiya and checkered kufiyah, and, in a low voice, advised against trusting the younger man. He said I would be safer with him and his family. Until I finally saw a soldier approach with my husband in tow, I stood there, terrified.

Back in Amman, everyone told us my mistake had been to attempt to enter with the tourists; as the wife of a Palestinian, I should have lined up with the Palestinians. A few days later, we tried again.

This time I was among Palestinian women, as we were segregated by gender. This time I received very different treatment. No pleasantries exchanged, no courtesy or curiosity. I have an Arabic name and could pass for Arab, so when I didn't heed a command—was it to come here or go there?—a soldier yelled at me, and I cowered. This time I was searched bodily. This time they took away my eye-pencil as a potential threat to security. This time they confiscated my wedding video. I pleaded. The officer screening my belongings explained that entering as I was "on the Arab side," video cassettes were not permitted. He averted his eyes as he said this. He was American, and we had language in common.

But after all that, I was denied entry for the same reason: my passport wasn't valid for travel to Israel and the proof of my marriage to a Travel Document-bearing Palestinian was worth nothing.

By this point enough officials understood that I wasn't Arab and that I spoke English. I was told, not unkindly, that it was illegal for me to be standing there at all. A soldier who had been witnessing my interactions was assigned to stand with me while they located my husband again.

This young man was about my age but at least a foot taller. He was clean-shaven, light-skinned, with reddish brown hair. He didn't say much as we stood side by side in the heat of the day, both of us looking straight ahead as though hope would arrive from that direction. But he must have asked for my story because I told him why I was there. It was a small wish, really, to meet the family of the curly-lashed man you had married.

The soldier was silent at first. Then he said softly, in clear and slightly accented English: "This is against humanity. This is not what Israel was meant to be."

I glanced up at him then and saw his clenched jaws and moist eyes.

His name was Endal. Thirty-five years later, this brief encounter remains a defining memory. It cautions against collapsing a people, even soldiers, with their governments. It's a reason to read the *Ha'aretz*, to support the human rights work of B'Tselem, to follow Jewish Voice for Peace.

We very nearly gave up on my ever meeting the family in Khan Younis after that. We decided to make the best of it and played tourist in Amman, an inviting modern city where you might walk casually by Roman ruins. In another two weeks I had acquired enough Arabic to follow the gist of a conversation in the Ghazawi vernacular of our hosts. And I loved the food, including shawarma bought from street vendors—these were my carnivore days—carved hot off the vertical spit and bundled up in pita with a well-seasoned salad and yogurt dressing.

Then one day someone suggested that I present my case to Jordan's Ministry of the Interior, which issued permits to West Bank Palestinians. Nobody had ever heard of the Jordanian government issuing a Travel Document to the spouse of a Ghazawi (as opposed to a West Banker) because Gaza documents were Egypt's responsibility. But what had we to lose?

I walked into the big stone building at the appointed hour and awaited my audience with the Minister (at least that's who I remember him to be). The meeting was brief. He sat in a large, imposing room full of portraits, behind a daunting desk, while I stood twenty feet away from him. I said my piece in English. The man eyed me without a smile. But his tone, when he spoke, was incredulous.

"You really want to go that badly to *Khan Younis*?" he asked. And I nodded.

As we approached the densely populated refugee camp, the taxi driver had to honk to disperse the crowds and thread his way toward the unpaved road where my in-laws lived. Big, seemingly unfinished cement houses sat next to much smaller ones. None was painted. Our taxi stopped just beyond the alley where my husband's family lived; it was too narrow for a car. Immediately, children ran up to us, asking excited questions. As we walked, they surrounded us, leading me as though in a reverse enactment of the Pied Piper story. A couple of men who had been sitting outside rushed towards us. There was much laughter and embracing as they grabbed our bags. We walked up to a humble home, constructed with sandstone blocks and plaster and topped with a tin roof. Several children ran inside to tell the parents that their son and his bride were home.

We stayed in Khan Younis for almost three months, until September.

I came to love his family—the parents, the six brothers

and sisters who spoiled me and wouldn't let me lift a finger to help with anything. I grew fleshier for lack of exercise but devoured the food anyway. My favorite meal was our breakfast of fava beans (fool) and homemade hummus and feta, with a dash of zartar in olive oil or red chilis on the side, all scooped up with pita bread. While the storybearer was out telling other stories to cousins in the neighborhood, I got to know his youngest sibling, Issa (Arabic for Jesus), whose physical and mental age you'd guess to be five or six years old, though he was twelve. His mother had been sick while she was pregnant with him. Issa's head was disproportionately large for his body. He had big eyes that often looked amused, with thick lashes like the rest of his siblings. When we first met, he held back, taking a few days to size me up before flashing his wide, dimpled smile at me. After that, he and I would sit beside each other on the floor mattress. Issa had what we call emotional intelligence. Although my Arabic quickly outpaced his, he understood more than he could convey in words. He understood the language of hugs and valued the moment, the physical presence. When I'd emerge from the bathroom, I'd often find him waiting for me quietly outside the door. Together we made our way back to the floor mattress, to family chatter, while Issa's older sister made strong, sweetened black tea with mint leaves on the two-burner stove, poured it into miniature glasses, and brought them out to us on a circular aluminum tray.

    Life was hard in the refugee camp, and prospects for anything more than a basic education, daily wage labor for the young men and marriage for the young women, were almost nonexistent even before the Intifada. Every home knew loss, and some knew horror. But it was life nonetheless, and people found ways to tailor their dreams and joys to their circumstances. To hope, to anger, but to not ask for more.

Looking back, I realize that I grasped only the surface of things. Just beneath it lay the despair that would erupt the following year in a shower of rocks from the fists of children. At the time, movement was still possible, though it seemed terribly circumscribed to me. Some of us could drive not just to Gaza City but to Ashkelon and beyond, as long as we carried our papers on us at all times. I visited Tel Aviv, Nazareth-Al Naasira, Bethlehem, and Jerusalem-Al Quds. Also many towns in the West Bank: Jericho-Ariha, Hebron-Al Khalil, Nablus, Ramallah. I learned to address my husband loudly in English when we stopped at military checkpoints because it meant less harassment for the driver and others in the car with me. Invariably, the sound of English aroused curiosity and shifted the tone. When it was my turn to produce documents, I'd look the checkpoint soldier in the eye and make small talk. I was treated with courtesy, and by extension, everyone in the car was let off without the customary humiliations. On one occasion a soldier smiled as he handed back my papers and said, "Speak well of us when you go back to your country."

I never saw Issa or the rest of the Khan Younis family again. Four and a half years later, I stole out of my Somerville, Massachusetts, apartment while the storybearer was at work because he would have barred my exit, had he known. I took no photographs with me. Only the bit of earth I had scooped up from outside Issa's home the day we left and poured into a small glass jar. A bit of Gaza I had carried with me from Khan Younis to Karachi to Boston. And which, fifteen years later, I would bring with me to Fresno, California.

Yet every time Gaza appears in the headlines, and

sometimes during the long spells when it remains forgotten, I think of Issa. Watching the World Cup with my children in July 2014, I froze when I read of the bomb dropped on Khan Younis that killed eight members of a single family. It was during Ramadan, the month of fasting, at 1 o'clock in the morning. They were watching the World Cup, as we were in Fresno. I could tell from the victims' last names that they were not Issa's family, but I grieved as though I had known them.

This morning there's news of fifty-two air attacks on and around Khan Younis. Given five minutes of warning, a house that was home to forty members of the Al-Astal family was destroyed. The Associated Press article quotes Ahmed Al-Astal, a professor like me. Splayed across my laptop screen is the image of men in jeans and t-shirts gazing down at the rubble. What did it take to build that home? And given the scarcity and staggering cost of construction materials owing to the blockade, what will it take to rebuild? Why even try when this will likely happen again in a few years, probably during another Ramadan and Eid season? In the background, unnoticed by the men, a boy about ten years of age balances himself on the rubble. He wears a black t-shirt and black athletic pants with RAVE printed in white letters on the side. His facial expression is absorbed and focused. Right foot on the ground and left leg bent, he raises his arms at different angles—cautiously, as if treading a tightrope; gracefully, as though poised to take flight.

In *The Truth About Stories*, Cherokee writer Thomas King says that stories are all we have. They shape who we are and how we see others as well as ourselves. It's a truth that many Indigenous Americans besides King, like Laguna Pueblo writer Leslie Marmon Silko, have long known and tried to share with us. We must be careful which stories we tell, they say, because once we put them out into the world, there's no taking them back.

It matters, too, how we hear a story and how we give it meaning. When we let a story in, it takes root in us. It grows with us, its stems and branches extending upward from our core, through heart and lungs, to frame our vision, and reaching into whatever new stories we will tell. It's possible to feel seduced by a narrative, to regret the years of your life you invested in the narrator, and yet to cherish what the story itself gave you: the humanity of a people dismissed as roadkill, not worth stopping for. It's possible, during a global pandemic, for the heart to drop when you learn that an occupying power that boasts the highest vaccination rate in the world denies the life-saving vaccine to the occupied. It's possible, long after the storyteller himself has become an almost-forgotten history, to think of Ghaza with tenderness, to read the headlines in Fresno and weep.

Author's note: I wrote this essay in May, 2021, during one of Israel's periodic attacks on Gaza that barely made the news in U.S. media. The essay has seen republication in 2024, as we register both the continuity of a long history of occupation and the unprecedented scale of its violence.

Seduced by the Story

Sometimes you fall for the narrative. You may be intelligent and highly educated, you may be the daughter of educators, you may be an educator yourself. You may even talk with your students about critical reading and thinking, about close analysis of characters, situations, and language; about power relations and point of view. About gender, race, and colonization. You can provide your students with theoretical and historical frameworks for the personal. You know all about reading the world as text. And yet, you fall so hard for the romance of the story, for the possibility of a protagonist's role in it, that you *will* yourself into illiteracy. Into a state of unknowing and unseeing. Unreading. And you do so for years, and sometimes for decades.

In his 1817 nonfiction work *Biographia Literaria*, the British Romantic poet Samuel Taylor Coleridge refers to the reader's "willing suspension of disbelief" when engaging with the fantastical elements of a poem. In real-life interactions, it's more apt to call it the willing suspension of close and critical reading. And it has staggering consequences for our lives.

Pueblo Laguna writer Leslie Marmon Silko's *Storyteller*—a groundbreaking work of creative nonfiction before most people in the literary establishment even recognized creative nonfiction as a genre—emphasized the power of both story and storyteller almost a half-century ago. The stories Silko tells remind us that we *are* our stories, that they shape us, and that once they are released into the world, they can't be taken back. Then again, *Storyteller* implies, we have it in our power to intervene with an alternative story. Along those lines, Cherríe Moraga's essay "Looking for the Insatiable

Woman," which begins with an epigraph from Silko, retells the story of La Llorona from the perspective of a queer Chicana feminist, intervening in what she sees as the story's oppressive implications for Chicanas. Like Silko, Moraga emphasizes the role of both story and storyteller in our lives. I'm struck by her opening line: "Most of us can name the story that came into the town of our hearts which changed our lives forever."

Yet it took me thirty years to become aware of the most beguiling story in my life, perhaps because the story reached me through no specific storyteller. Rather, it was a communal story, a national narrative, so widely projected, exported, and consumed that it had become something like religion—specious if inspected up close, but firmly held together by faith. It was the story of America.

When I came to the United States, when I chose to make it my home, I wasn't thinking that I'd like to be part of a nation state built with the labor of stolen bodies on stolen land. That's not the story of America that's disseminated and internalized across the globe. No, I was drawn by that other narrative, of a land of opportunity, of personal freedom, where I could become the best that I could possibly be—by dreaming big enough, working hard enough. In a word, a meritocracy where one isn't held back by gender, ethnicity, or class. In my personal experience, this narrative has proved mostly true; I have felt closer to all my possibilities here in the U.S. than in any other country where I have lived. It's important for me to acknowledge this, and also to acknowledge the privilege inherent in my ability to say so. But the fact is that that's only one story of America out of many. Yet this version dominates all the others like an invasive plant, choking out other realities. The narrative doesn't qualify, critique, contextualize, or nuance. And so, not only does it become self-serving, but it renders injustices, past and present, invisible. American Indians become characters in a remote history or caricatures in Hollywood, their vanishment a fait accompli in which we played no role. We keep arriving at these shores, some more recently than others, none of us indigenous to this land; not thinking of how we inherit all the histories of this country the moment we or our forbearers choose to live here. Instead, we adopt its collective amnesia.

Thirty years an academic in the United States, I have read and taught many American Indian authors and become well acquainted with the history of genocide, removal, and forced assimilation in North America, along with what Ojibwe writer Gerald Vizenor has called the survivance of Native peoples. So not only have I been aware, but as a professor I've been spreading that awareness with a sense of urgency all these years. But somehow none of that sincere, mindful, even passionate, work in the classroom translated into a sense of my *personal* accountability as an immigrant to the U.S.

It had begun to happen dimly, haltingly, when Maya started taking Ethnic Studies courses as a first year student at UC San Diego. It was 2018, before the national reckoning with race that's been part of the collective consciousness since George Floyd's murder at the hands of a white police officer and the resurgence of the Black Lives Matter movement in May 2020. Maya would talk about her readings and writings in long conversations with me over the phone. I never had the chance to take Ethnic Studies in college, but I knew many of the literary and theoretical works Maya was reading by virtue of my training in "multiethnic" U.S. literature. My American-born daughter had been clear-eyed about her country's oppressive political structures early on—she would often ask me why, of all the countries in the world, I had chosen the United States—

but she now also had the language to support her feelings about it. And that language had an inescapable directness that literary studies couldn't claim. During one phone conversation, in the very moment that I was ready to cut through the fog of unreading and unseeing to formulate the words, Maya gave them formidable shape over the air waves: "Mama—do we live in a settler-colonial state?"

People talk about epiphanies as imbued in light, but sometimes the truth that dawns on you illuminates a shattering darkness. The wonder is that you had managed not to see it in the present tense before. Of course, given your academic training, in the next instant you recognize that unseeing as manufactured by your privilege. The settler-colonial state never stopped being present tense for the people whose trajectories it so violently altered. You knew that, didn't you? But the refusal to connect the dots all the way up to your own present moment allowed you not to implicate yourself in the story. To evade responsibility.

The shockingly belated realization had a paralyzing effect. *What had I done?* In choosing to make a home for myself in the United States, I had opted out of a postcolonial country to become part of an ongoing colonial project. But now, three decades after I first arrived in Boston as a graduate student, and having thrown down roots here, where was I to go? It's not as though I'd rather live anywhere else. And what good does it do for a lone individual to jump ship in atonement, even if that were possible or desirable?

In her essay "Disloyal to Civilization," the poet and cultural critic Adrienne Rich makes a distinction between guilt and accountability. For Rich, a Jewish lesbian, the primary audience for that 1978 essay was straight white women, to whom she suggests, along with queer Black feminists June Jordan, Audre Lorde, and

Barbara Smith, that misogyny springs from the same source as racism and homophobia. (Jordan went further in her vocal critique of imperialism and, specifically, of the settler-colonial ideology of Zionism as related forms of oppression.) Rich anticipates the guilt that her white feminist readers might feel in being made to see this confluence of power relations and shows them a responsible way out of it by arguing that guilt is not the same thing as accountability. Whereas guilt is self-indulgent, accountability is *usable*. I had often invoked this distinction for my students before; I needed to focus all my emotional energy on it now.

The paralysis of the epiphany eventually led to my *seeing* that there was work to be done in the here and the now, beyond the classroom, and in the community. I had already been trying to leverage my position as a full professor to engage Fresno State in greater outreach to Edison High School in southwest Fresno, the historically Black neighborhood where Maya and Cyrus went to school. It was high time I educated myself on how to amplify the voices of my Yokuts and Mono neighbors in the Central Valley. I taught some of the origin stories Chief Ron Goode (North Fork Mono) had been known to teach at Fresno City College and assigned the PBS show *Tending the Wild*, in which Chief Goode teaches us how to manage wildfires with controlled or "cultural" burning. I looked for opportunities to crosslist courses with the American Indian Studies program at Fresno State. Finding social media connections to the Fresno American Indian Health Project, and to individuals leading the fight against demeaning school mascots, was a small beginning out of the paralysis. But I didn't know what to do with the multigenerational implications of the story that had brought me to this country in the first place.

A First Nations storyteller came to my rescue: memoirist

Terese Mailhot of the Seabird Island Band, who led a week-long CSU Summer Arts workshop in 2019. I had heard American Indian writers give talks before and had helped to bring Gerald Vizenor and Hopi-Miwok poet Wendy Rose to Fresno State as keynote speakers for our undergraduate conference, UCMLA. The conversations had enriched us all. But there was something about Mailhot's way of hosting this workshop for our huge group of thirty writers that held significance beyond that specific context. During our week with her, she showed us how to share on micro and macro levels—everything from communal snacks to time and space. For the first time, I felt that someone with ancient roots on this continent was welcoming me, a seeker from afar, into her hearth and home. Mailhot demonstrated how it was possible, if we were mindful of one another, to share the resources available to us, including what she herself had to give us as writers. She called us out on occasion, but mostly what stood out to me was her generosity, her faith that even after all this time, after all the violence of history and the everyday erasures, a different way of inhabiting our own historical moment was possible.

Terese Mailhot offered us another narrative of America. I have a long way to go, but I move a little differently on this continent because of it.

I'm helped along by the occasional immigrant writer who asks the hard questions and takes responsibility. The 2021 memoir *Northern Light*, by queer South Asian American poet Kazim Ali, throws me a rope. It's an account of Ali's return to Cross Lake in the Canadian province of Manitoba to see for himself how the construction of a hydroelectric dam on the Nelson River, which his father helped build forty years prior, has impacted the lives of the Pimicikamac Cree people. At one point, Ali quotes his friend,

Lakota Pueblo poet Layli Long Soldier, as telling him: "To be cut off from [the land] is not a small thing; but honestly, Kazim, when you think about how few years it has really been since the Europeans came to this continent and changed things so much, we are only at the chronological beginning of this trauma. There is still time to work against the disconnect, to reconcile with both land and people" (25).

We are only at the chronological beginning. There is still time.

I read Layli Long Soldier's words again and again. It's as though she's speaking directly to me.

Sometimes the willed illiteracy is not a matter of ignorance but of a lack of accountability—which is itself a refusal to implicate yourself in the story. It's a refusal to position yourself as an active agent rather than as a passive listener. To see that the life you yearned for and have in great part realized, the future you envision for your children, and the very home you claim, are built on the backs of specific communities, individuals whose lives were not in your range of vision when you embarked on your future. And *seeing*—not as an ableist trait, but in the figurative sense of open-eyed reading—is, as I learned from the author Doug Rice, who coordinated the very first CSU Summer Arts course I took in 2011, not just an aesthetic imperative but a moral one.

Potawatomi writer and botany professor Robin Wall Kimmerer indicates a way forward for all of us as inhabitants of a common earth, and addresses especially those of us who arrived in the New World as immigrants, recently or generations ago. Her widely read collection of essays, *Braiding Sweetgrass* (2013), opens with the origin story of Skywoman, who falls to the earth, pregnant and clutching only a handful of seeds. She survives with the help of the animals who were there before her, and in turn she does her part so that they can all thrive together as a community.

"It is good to remember that the original woman was herself an immigrant," says Kimmerer. "She fell a long way from her home in the Skyworld, leaving behind all who knew her and who held her dear. She could never go back."

And the lines that fling open all the windows of my eyes and heart to let in the light:

"It was through her actions of reciprocity, the give and take with the land, that the original immigrant became Indigenous." Kimmerer asks her students, and in turn asks us: "Can a nation of immigrants once again follow [Skywoman's] example to become native, to make a home?"

Sometimes the fog lifts suddenly. The storytellers you didn't even know you were waiting for arrive in the town of your heart. And there appears before you a path that was always there, a path home, perhaps—and with it, the possibility of stepping into a new story.

The Crow and the Keys

The day we say goodbye to 379-A/1, our childhood home in Karachi, a single crow bears witness. It sits in the gulmohar tree that Abbu had planted for me out front during my sabbatical visit, a year and eight months earlier. The crow remains perched on one branch or another for hours without a caw—black beak and feathers in the vibrant green of the leaves and the orange splashes of the gulmohar flowers. Whenever I happen by, the crow is there, patient and still, and facing the house. Inside, Abbu's Californian children go through his books and papers and paraphernalia—all three of them together under his roof again, as he had yearned to see them.

I didn't make it home to Karachi in time for Abbu's funeral. But I see it all: the living room at 379-A/1 Gulshan-e-Iqbal so packed with menfolk—neighbors, friends, relatives, and former students, colleagues, and employees—that the overflow fills the front patio where Abbu's car is normally parked, the Honda City he was so proud of, not only because it was the only brand new car he ever owned, but because it was a gift from his youngest, most beloved child, Sadia. People spill all the way to the back where the deafening water-pump is situated. Extra chairs have to be brought out from Abdul's room in the backyard, which has served as a storage room in the years since his death from tuberculosis. Women crowd the bedrooms on the ground floor—Sadia, Sheba, and Khalammi among them. Khalammi, who was only eighteen when Abbu married her sister Suraiya, and twenty when he mediated her own marriage to his brother Ilyas, has lost more a brother than a brother-in-law. But she privileges the children's grief over her own—the five of us who remain, formed in the shadow of her first-born, Rubina's, death at the age of eighteen. Khalammi and all the other women say their goodbyes before Abbu's male kin, his son and nephews, heave the takht on which his body lies to their shoulders. Amir, Azfar, Khurram, and other sorrowing men carry Abbu's weight reverently, walking him to Masjid-e-Noor one last time. They carry him through the dusty lane toward Kamran Market, as Abbu had carried Abdul fourteen years before. After the Imam's address, which reveals how deep and abiding was our father's connection to this neighborhood, and after the communal namaz-e-janaza, Abbu is taken to the same cemetery where his sister Shakira, Khurram's mother, is buried. There Amir, Azfar, and Khurram step down into the freshly dug grave to receive him. They lay Abbu in the earth, his body facing east toward Makkah, nothing but a white, cotton kafan between him and the earth's embrace.

In his lifetime Abbu had seen to the legalities that would leave 379-A/1 to us. He had taken this trouble despite his assertion that the assets would be worth "a peanut" when converted to U.S. dollars. His own father had not been able to leave his children anything. We didn't know it then, but my share of the money from the sale of 379-A/1 would pay the bulk of college expenses for Maya and Cyrus. There's poetry in that, and I like to think that Abbu would have savored it.

So in November of 2013, eight months after Abbu's death, Amir, Sadia, and I returned to Karachi from California to sell our childhood home. While Abbu lived, we had not been at 379-A/1 together for fourteen years. It was our father's favorite fantasy, one that made his eyes shine: to have all three of his children visit together, the whole family in his house again. Now we were making his dream come true for a second time within the year, but only because he was no longer alive. We had found a buyer for the house prior to our arrival; on this trip we had five days in which to sift through the accumulations of forty-two years.

We knew the house would be empty. Khurram and Paras had moved out of the second floor with their infant son, as planned. Azlaan, born a month before Abbu's death, arrived in time for his great-uncle to hold him. Over four decades, through all the comings and goings of lives lived on different continents and converging on this house, Azlaan is the only one in the family who can claim 379-A/1 as his very first home in the world.
As the taxi carrying the three of us and Khalammi turned the corner at Kamran Market, we braced ourselves for what lay ahead. And then two small miracles greeted us at 379-A/1: the vermillion of a bougainvillea vine I had wished aloud for on my sabbatical the year before cascading down the short front wall, and a glorious young gulmohar tree outside the gate, of the kind I hadn't seen there since I was a teenager.

We had only that day to clear everything out—to decide what to give away and to whom, what to carry back to California, and what to discard. My father was not the worst of hoarders, but in a life that had taken much from him, he liked to hold on to things. Thanks to this preference, we found fragments of our forgotten trajectories that day: a notebook full of poems I had written as a fourteen-year-old, Amir's first Urdu primer, Sadia's doodles chalked on the inside of the closet doors in the upstairs bedroom we three had shared growing up. We held the physics textbooks Abbu had authored, copies of his father's poetry collection that he and Chotepapa had compiled and published.

There was also his own memoir in Urdu, *My Family and I*, written over the years, mostly on the extended trips he made to the United States to be with us, which did not see print until a few weeks after his death. It's an account of his ancestors in Bihar, the Partition that snatched him away from his father, his own journeys that took him from India to Pakistan and Bangladesh, then to England and America. It's an account marked by enormous endeavors and accomplishments, but also by staggering losses: bereft of mother, father, and older sister by the time he was eighteen, as an adult he lived to see the deaths not only of the grandmother who had raised him, but of many others he had loved: his older brother Idris, his niece Rubina, his nephew Ashar, his younger brother Ilyas, who was my Chotepapa, his sister Masooma in India. And six months before his own death, one final heartbreak: his nephew Khurram coming downstairs to tell him that his mother, Shakira—Abbu's younger sister, the one who had married a Karachi man and left Bihar so she could live closer to her brother—was dead.

Haroon Najmi lost his wife to divorce, his children to America. But ultimately it is the love rather than the loss that overwhelms Abbu's memoir—for his elders, his siblings, his many nieces and nephews. For his children, of course, but also for their spouses, all of different races, whose entry into the family had stretched his heart's capacity beyond its known limits. Above all, for the five grandchildren he had lived to see, ranging in age from three to thirteen.

We go through the books, the photographs, the luggage, the linen, and the odds and ends from the nightstand drawers. We find Abbu's packing list, prepared in anticipation of his upcoming visit to California to see us once again, perhaps even to think about making California home because it is home to Sadia and the rest of us, and to his children's children. I ask to have the metal plaque bearing Abbu's name and address taken off the entrance. I want to carry it with me to California. It's been drilled into the decorative stone wall adjacent to the gate, beneath one of the two rectangular lamps. Like the stone wall, the lamp is an original; it has been shining a light on the entrance to 379-A/1 for forty-two years. The rusted nails securing the plaque have to be coaxed out with a mechanical screwdriver. I can't recall now who does that; perhaps Dolly's husband—Dolly, who kept house for Abbu for seventeen years. But there's one nail that holds on with ferocious tenacity. When it finally yields, the violence of that wrenching leaves an undulation in the metal. But it doesn't break, and I put the plaque among my keeps. Later Khan Sahib, across the street in 388-A/1, tells me how much it pained him to see Professor Haroon Najmi's name torn from his home.

      With most of the furniture gone, there is hardly any place to sit. By the end of the day we are weary. But Khalammi sustains us; without her parental presence we would have felt orphaned. At last we have packed things into plastic bags and are ready to call a taxi to transport us all back to Khalammi's home in Clifton. But when we go across the street to say goodbye to Khan Sahib, he won't hear of our taking a taxi. He asks his son to drive us all the way across town on his one day off. His son does so readily, his wife and daughter hopping into the car with him to make an excursion of it. We understand that Khan Sahib's gesture is more than kindness towards us; he is seeing to it that Najmi Sahib's long tenure in the lane ends decorously, with the grace and generosity that had marked all his interactions in it. I doubt Khan Sahib knows the extent to which his send-off has gentled the forlornness of the day.

Leaving our Gulshan home for the last time, I brought with me Abbu's cotton shalvar-qameez, plain and white, that had been hanging up in his room. He had worn it the day before he died, hoping to go to Masjid-e-Noor for Juma prayers. Dolly tells me she offered to iron a fancier shalvar-qameez, but Abbu said that this one was more comfortable. He showered and dressed for the communal highlight of his week, the sabbath prayer. But ultimately he was unable to walk to the masjid on that last Friday of his life. He prayed at home in simple but clean, pressed clothes, appropriate for Juma. On that last day, as throughout his life, Abbu was attentive to his priorities, mindful of custom, accepting of his limitations, and devout.

Back in the U.S., I hang Abbu's shalvar-qameez among my own clothes in the walk-in closet of my bedroom. From time to time, I touch and feel the fabric. Some days I rest my head where Abbu's shoulder would have filled it, plant a kiss on the sleeve where his shapely brown hand would have emerged from the cuff. One morning, almost a year after Abbu's death, I walk into the closet for the mundane task of selecting something to wear. But then, resisting the imperatives of the present for just a moment, I reach instead for my father's white shalvar-qameez on the hanger. I hold the qameez to my cheek, smell it, and stroke its cool, soft surface with my fingertips. Then my hand feels some unevenness on a part of the tunic to the left where his heart might have been. I discover that the breast pocket holds his angina medication and a piece of tissue. Curious, I now slip my hand into the deep side-pocket on the right and immediately feel a weightiness. When I pull my hand out again, I see what I have grasped: a set of keys that we had been looking for after the funeral in Karachi but couldn't find anywhere. They are Abbu's house keys, the ones he carried with him every day to Masjid-e-Noor and Kamran Market. Eight thousand miles away from home, the keys to 379-A/1 have found their way to Fresno, California.

Memoir in Dust

Nostalgia is Karachi dust
gleaming on the shelves of Mister Book.
Watching from the balcony as lives converge in Kamran Market,
the muezzin's call to prayer a periodic refrain to other imperatives:
live chickens to sell from wire cages and mangoes
ambering on a wheeled cart.
Cumin cookies crumble in our mouths as we walk
staidly to the Kodak studio for a family portrait.
Nostalgia is filmee songs blaring from the barber's radio,
guts on the ground,
the stench of slaughter,
feathers scattered at our feet.

Dust Bowl has echoes of ruin and nothingness,
of land laid bare by fate and folly.
Lives rendered unlivable where they had been rooted.
Migration, the reset button!
The toil, the journey, a new patch of earth—
alien and inviting—from which to sprout a future.

"You just take care of the dusting," he says. "I'll mow the lawn."
Just? Dusting is delicate, diligent work.
Approach each piece with reverence:
pick it up, caress its contours, and place it back
exactly where it asks to be,
a little shinier for your touch.
How is that *not* heavy lifting?

Dust bin—an anomaly in my present life, on this continent.
It makes my children laugh to hear me use the term;
it annoys me to hear them laugh in the face of my urgency
to take the trash out before we miss the weekly pickup.
Dust bin stays, reverberates through the decades—
memento of a tongue acquired in a land
that wasn't mine and couldn't keep me.
It holds the things I never asked for, never wanted,
and the dust of everything dear.

Let me get up, then, dust myself off, and move on.
From love? From motherhood?
From home as I have known it for twenty years?
It was dust I cultivated,
dust I planted,
dust that blossomed and bore fruit.
Let it linger a while longer on me.
I don't know how to breathe without it.

Learning Distance

My mother's email, with the subject heading "Cycle of Life," sits in my inbox. The first line is visible without my clicking it open; it's the curvy, right-to-left Urdu script—beautiful to look at in the Rumicode software my brother created, but a little slow-going for my now unaccustomed eyes. She often shares her meditative and eloquent micro-essays with me this way. I make a mental note to come back to the email at the end of my grading day.

Suraiya Jabeen writes every day. She has done so for as long as I can remember. Growing up, I'd see her fill big, lined notebooks that resembled the attendance registers in Meadow Secondary School. Those handwritten records of her "sorting out" her life and loves fell casualty to the moves, fears, and distances of the past half-century. But still she writes.

Ammi has been sheltering with her younger sister, my Khalammi Talat, since the coronavirus pandemic struck in mid-March. For the past five years Ammi's home has been with her youngest child, Sadia, and her family, in San Diego's University Heights. But immunocompromised as Ammi is, we all think it safer for her, and less lonely for Khalammi, if the two sisters stay together in my aunt's Hillcrest condo, a short drive away. Days later, when I drive the five-plus hours to La Jolla to move my daughter out of UC San Diego housing—her academic term cut short by the pandemic—I do it as a day trip, without seeing Ammi and Khalammi, or any family, in San Diego. Already, love means staying away.

Grading in May is always frenzied and exhausting, coming as it does not only at the end of the semester, but at the end of a long academic year. This year, with teaching as we knew it suspended in mid-March by the threat of COVID-19, the depletion I feel seems self-indulgent. My students have lost jobs and livelihoods. One lost his father. In some cases, these young people have no choice but to brave the coronavirus threat and pick up hours as essential workers. At least one, whose family members have lost their incomes, is supporting his entire family on what he earns as a tutor at the Writing Center. Many find themselves physically displaced, in living situations that inhibit their ability to learn. For all of Fresno State's offers of electronic devices and hotspots, they have problems with access to online instruction. Some students are also parenting and schooling at home. With these hardships in mind, I opt to teach asynchronous classes, without Zoom meetings, so they can participate in online discussions and submit assignments in their own time. The effort to translate the dialectical mode of learning to the written word results in an exponential increase in class time for me. There is no absolute start or end time to classes, seldom a moment when I feel caught up. But two weeks into this online "transition"—a misnomer because there could be no transit time, only an abrupt launch into another dimension—my students respond to the survey I give them with overwhelming preference for the asynchronous model as the least stressful in their new lives. And so, I stay the course until the end of classes in early May.

In the afternoon, I take a break from grading and call Ammi. I ask her to read me her emailed essay. I'm startled to hear her Urdu title for the piece, which translates to the paradoxical

"Welcome, Departing Springs." In brave and beautiful voice she articulates the reality that, though she's still only in her seventies, mortality stares her down daily. The chronic pain of the past six months, and her gradually diminishing physical abilities, sound a friendly warning to savor what's left of her time in an imperfect but still serviceable body.

The first epidural shot of steroids did nothing to ease the pain. The second becomes a challenge to schedule during the lockdown. Besides logistical impediments to an in-person appointment at the clinic, Ammi has to choose between the risk of exposure to a potentially lethal virus and the certainty of immobilizing pain. As hope subdues fear, she goes for the second epidural, in mask and gloves and wheelchair. Sadia can accompany her only so far; social distancing measures mean she has to wait in the car during the procedure.

Three weeks later, the pain still rages.

As a friend with greater experience of remote instruction puts it, there's so much wandering and herding in online teaching. The metaphor lingers with me, though it obliterates the individuality and mindfulness of my students. I do indeed expend a lot of energy taking count—who appears, who disappears on the Canvas discussion board; how often, and for how long. It isn't to be punitive but to know who is still there, still hanging on. If they have *wandered*, from what? Toward what? Or does the verb by definition imply a lack of purpose in either direction? And what, then, is the role—the point, even— of the shepherd?

Meadow Secondary School flourished in Pakistan's megacity of Karachi for thirty-three years. It began as a preschool in our two-bedroom home and grew with Sadia, one grade at a time. Ammi tells me I came up with the name as a twelve-year-old. *You mean like a pasture?* someone asked in disbelief. But Ammi loved its implications. When I enrolled at Karachi University, Meadow gave me my first, part-time employment as an English teacher.

In 1975, Suraiya Jabeen had a vision to bring psychologically savvy teaching methods to the austere and outdated classrooms of our struggling-to-be-middle-class neighborhood, and to make that education affordable. Without much capital, success was slow but steady and, eventually, staggering, though Ammi never grew rich. Throughout those years, Madam Suraiya knew the name of every child who walked through Meadow's gates, a vital bit of every child's history. For the younger ones, she emphasized learning through play. She reasoned with the older ones, teaching them to question and persuade rather than simply obey. Fathers leaving for employment in Jeddah or Dubai trusted her to watch out for their sons and daughters. Madam Suraiya was known to waive tuition for the needy, to press with promise the hand of a dying mother and make it easier for her to go.

But Meadow Secondary School finally closed its doors in 2008. Ammi's rheumatoid arthritis had gotten the better of her. The new owners, educators who had promised to continue the legacy, instead shut it down. Devoted alumni have posted Facebook images of the sad, empty building and grounds. It's one thing to grow up with fond memories of the school you left behind. It's another to have that physical space erased. But for students, staff, and principal alike, it's a different kind of loss altogether when the physical site of memory still stands, weathered, worn, and crumbling. Like the aging body of a loved one—still beloved, still greeting each spring as though it might be the last.

I wasn't able to see all my students through to the end of the semester. There were six I couldn't get back after we moved online, though I tried and they tried. I had feared the darkness that would swallow them. But the shepherd's vigilance proved futile, the proddings failed.

The morning I submitted course grades for the semester, my son walked in on my grief for the distances I couldn't bridge. When I told him, through sobs, that I had lost six students, he thought I had lost them to COVID-19. And, in a way, I had.

Emergency remote instruction, we called it. *Distance learning*, we say.

It's a hard thing to recognize, let alone accept, when remoteness becomes a receding—a wandering into meadows that lie beyond the sight and call and reach of love.

Teaching as a Pakistani American Muslim Feminist: Ten, Twenty Years On

My first thought when invited to revisit the essay I wrote for the *Asian American Literary Review*'s 9/11 commemorative issue ten years ago was that I couldn't. It had been the kind of essay you write with your whole body, which leaves you limp, your energy sapped for a long while.

My second thought was that I must.

Lately, I keep returning to the idea that all linearity is circularity in disguise—a shape that becomes visible only when we zoom out through the lens of time. To read the essay I wrote on the eve of the tenth anniversary of 9/11 is to realize that not only are our apparently linear trajectories circular, but those circles are superimposed upon other circles. Whatever progression we may see in history, its material reality is layered and textured.

Just as it was impossible for me to speak of the decade since 9/11 without circling back to Afghanistan and Iraq on the one hand, and to Pakistan and India on the other, today my thoughts are those of both an American and a South Asian. Twenty years of the United States in Afghanistan—South Asian neighbor of Pakistan, with 1,640 miles of shared border and less than 300 miles of road between Kabul and Islamabad. Twenty years of an effete and apathetic presence at best, distracted by the more lucrative aggression on Iraq, and no accounting for all the Afghan lives lost over the course of the occupation. Twenty years, to end as abruptly as empires do when they must accept defeat. No vision, no exit strategy that takes full responsibility for those left behind. No acknowledgement that most would have preferred to stay, had America's sudden departure not made them unsafe. So reminiscent of the British, who, when forced out of their 200-year plundering spree of the Indian subcontinent in 1947, made their escape in five swift weeks. Then they sat back and watched, as if on a screen, the tumult of the largest mass migration in human history, the sectarian violence, the trauma of brown peoples that subsequent generations have inherited. Our communal memory of Partition demands that we work through its political and psychic legacies wherever we find ourselves on the globe today.

And what of South Asia now, as Afghanistan reels from President Biden's arbitrary withdrawal date of August 31, 2021? Already thousands have become refugees, walking across the border into northwest Pakistan, as they did after the Soviet occupation of 1979. And then throughout the eighties, the Reagan administration supported the theocratic Mujahideen with the help of Pakistan's General Zia-ul-Haq, under whose orthodox vision of Sunni Islam I came of age. General Zia and I left Pakistan in August 1988, within days of each other: I, for graduate school in the US, and he, violently, in the plane crash that killed him. He may have nurtured the Taliban originally, but in ironic circularity, current Prime Minister Imran Khan's elected government also aligns itself with the Taliban, prompting his critics to nickname him "Taliban Khan," regardless of his Oxford-educated, cricketing history. The Pakistani Prime Minister not only seeks a workable relationship with the Taliban, which may be understandable given Pakistan's own vulnerability to Taliban violence, but his government also aims for so-called strategic depth in Afghanistan in the name of national security, a mini-imperialist venture in its own right. Meanwhile, Prime Minister Modi has intervened in India's democratic and pluralistic trajectory with a potent mix of legislation and demagoguery. His assiduous efforts to disenfranchise Muslims and other vulnerable communities in India have resulted in jeopardizing their very safety in India.

And what of South Asian *Americans* ten years on? Hate crimes against Muslims and Sikhs never ceased. Besides the horrific 2012 massacre at the gurdwara in Oak Creek, Wisconsin, fatal attacks on Sikh elders, in particular, have been widespread. In fact, they have happened right here in Fresno, home to some 35,000 Sikh Americans. As in the rest of the country, the violence has escalated in my hometown since the 2016 election. That year in Fresno began with the New Year's Day murder of 68-year-old Gurcharan Singh Gill, who was not even wearing a turban at the time. Other attacks, non-fatal but terrorizing nonetheless, have continued to occur, prompting some Sikh Americans to urge their elders not to go out on walks.

Today we South Asian Americans hold our breaths against renewed backlash as the twentieth anniversary of 9/11 approaches. Valarie Kaur's *Divided We Fall* appears on my syllabus again, in a graduate seminar on the literature of the San Joaquin Valley. This time it's assigned along with her book, *See No Stranger: A Memoir and Manifesto of Revolutionary Love.* The Punjabi-Sikh lawyer and civil rights activist, with deep roots in this patch of earth where I have made my life as a Pakistani American Muslim feminist professor, is also deeply invested in doing what she can to mitigate the desperation of Afghan people in the present moment. I share the links she posts on Facebook of reliable places to donate, petitions to sign. I have assigned Kaur's work on our September calendar because I know that both my students and I will need it in this heavy anniversary month.

My ambivalence about group affiliations, so painfully

personal during the Mumbai terror attacks of November 2008, remains. If anything, I find group identities more entrenched the world over. But I claim my place in the American landscape, apocalyptic as it sometimes appears, literally ablaze with wildfires in the West. I'm often the outsider-insider and sometimes a bridge. But always I am shaped and reshaped by my students, with whom my two children have now caught up in age. These young people are diverse in background—many of them Latinx, others Armenian, Hmong, and Punjabi—with a tacit grasp of the portability of collective trauma. They don't need to be taught the porousness of the line between the local and the global, a lesson brought so brutally home by the coronavirus pandemic. Others come from rural places outside Fresno, from families of farmworkers as well as farm-owners. Many are churchgoing Christians and right-leaning. Inasmuch as I believe in my three feet of influence, I am invested in them all. With my students, those in the classroom and those who have ventured far beyond it but stayed in touch, I will think and feel my way through the 20th anniversary of 9/11, as I have every major national and global event in the past twenty years. Fresno State affords me the space to address such moments in course offerings like "Literature of the US-Iraq Wars," but any US literature course opens up the conversation. The night of November 8, 2016, when Donald Trump won the US presidential election, is a case in point. While my colleague Kathee and I sat in front of her television, hands clapped over our mouths in dismay, an email from Jacob, an undergraduate student in my Multiethnic US Literature class, threw me the lifeline I so desperately needed that night. Sometimes when hope ebbs, I read that email again:

"I wear work boots and jeans. I want to show the world around me that a man can wear boots and love literature. A man can love

Johnny Cash's music while supporting progressive agendas. I know there are social assumptions made about me, about people who look like me. In certain ways, I am cut from the same cloth as many of the people who've potentially elected Trump to the White House, with regard to financial, social, and racial station. I'm embarrassed.

. . . .

I believe that you teach a very important class, especially here in the Central Valley. This is my home. I've grown up here, and I want the best for the area. . . .

Thank you for making our country a better place in which to make a life."

In happy circularity, this young man is now a much-loved teacher at a high school just outside Fresno from which he himself graduated, doing the daily work of making this Valley and this country "a better place in which to make a life."

As I write this, a suicide-bomber affiliated with ISIS-K has blown up part of Kabul airport in the midst of the chaotic evacuations. Thirteen US military personnel are dead, and over a hundred Afghans have lost their lives in these closing days of America's bipartisan imperialist venture in their country, fueled as it was by vengeance for the 9/11 attacks. President Biden has promised the terrorists: "We will not forgive. We will not forget. We will hunt you down and make you pay," the string of monosyllables stressed for chilling emphasis. His words reverberate back in time, echoing those of President George W. Bush in 2001, and I wonder what fresh cycle of violence we may see ten, twenty years from now.

The intertwining of our mutual histories has never been more sharply delineated than in this historical moment. Of all the wrenching scenes from Afghanistan flashing across our screens, the most indelible are those of a US Air Force plane, a C-17, determined to take off almost as soon as it lands, on August 16. The aircraft doesn't even linger to unload its cargo, much less evacuate anyone. Scores of people cling to it in desperation. I pause the video before I can see what happens next. But later my heart breaks to hear of a youth named Zaki Anwari among the dead. A handsome 19-year-old, the same age as my son, Cyrus, both of them born within months of the 9/11 attacks and America's subsequent bombing of Afghanistan. In the images I see of him, Zaki has a slender frame like Cyrus's. The two appear similar enough in phenotype to look like cousins—even sharing a love of soccer. In fact, Zaki was a soccer star, having played for Afghanistan's national youth soccer team as a sixteen-year-old. That same Monday, August 16, my son boarded a plane from Fresno airport, on his way to Houston to begin his sophomore year of college. Boarding a plane—an ambition so mundane, yet so cruelly out of reach for another mother's son in Kabul.

The details of Zaki Anwari's death are still unclear—whether he was among those who fell as the C-17 took off, or if his were the bodily remains found in the wheel well when the plane landed in Doha. But a youth resembling my son is dead, and those details seem irrelevant.

What terrifying vision of the future compels a gifted young adult, beloved of his family, to seek such impossible escape? *What hope in America?*

Striking images layer our interconnected histories, bend the linear into the shape of a circle. Few are as salient, as staggering, or as tragic as human beings falling out of the sky.

fragment 13

*Your last gift to Sadia, on her fourteenth birthday
a novel that opens with the mythical thorn bird
who sings one exquisite song
before she impales herself
upon a thorn*

*One exquisite song
for the rest of us to live on
ever after*

Between Cave and Canyon

  Year fifteen at Fresno State: empty classrooms and empty nest. I begin the online semester in August of 2020 fearing that my efforts of the past two years to gain institutional support for outreach to southwest Fresno, our historically Black neighborhood, are stalled and sputtering in a new era of budget cuts, even though the Black Lives Matter movement has garnered attention in the national consciousness. The virtual Democratic National Convention is on, its tone as somber as the threat to democracy feels real. Someone I knew in graduate school has died suddenly of a heart attack in Boston. America's death toll from COVID-19 stands at 175,000, and the Central Valley is a hotspot. In California, an existential crisis, an apocalypse. Triple-digit heat, rolling blackouts, and over 11,000 bolts of lightning in 72 hours. As I begin the first week of virtual classes, more than five hundred wildfires rage in Northern California, covering an expanse greater than the state of Rhode Island, and leaving the skies above me opaque with smoke and thick with ash. Ancient redwoods, witness to fifteen hundred years of history, have died a terrible death. With 120,000 people evacuated, Governor Newsom has ordered all Californians to be ready to up and go. (But go where, Governor? How do we empty out the entire state of California?)

  Disasters on a scale too vast to take in. Fires I don't know how to put out.

  Yet somehow, come Friday afternoon, I must tend to the one little flame that is my life. I have never lived alone before now—now that both my children have left for college. My writings have been anticipating the empty nest for the past five years, but

I never imagined that it would coincide with a pandemic. No students or colleagues in the flesh, no café, no library. No family nearby, and friends isolating indoors because a masked, socially distanced visit outdoors is unthinkable in the record heat. This Friday—even as I have virtual meetings with Fresno State's tech staff for Zoom and Canvas help, conclude that my Kaiser Permanente health insurance won't suffice for Cyrus at Rice University, mail the vehicle registration sticker to Maya in La Jolla, and make the virtual physical therapy appointment I should have made weeks ago for my impinged shoulder—I know that I draw closer and closer to the cavernous mouth of the weekend. I must walk into it alone, unseeing. I'm determined not to run away from my life, but I am afraid.

    I place one foot and then another into the daunting darkness of the cave. There's no telling which rock might trip me up, what creature tear into me. I don't know where I am, where I go from here. The ground feels unfamiliar underfoot and my hand has no muscle memory of the craggy surface of the cave's walls. The silence threatens. Faces I have loved, that tell me who I am, are out there somewhere, but this absolute, untethered aloneness is the only thing that's real.

    I recall the terror of driving east on Route 152 from Los Baños one winter's night in a tule fog so dense I can't see five feet ahead. There's no safe way to stop or turn back or determine where I am. I can't tell if I've veered off the route because nothing is visible—not the highway signs, or billboards or any other marker that locates me in space. Not the dimmest of tail lights to assure me that even if I don't know where I am, I follow a road that others are traveling with me.

Eyes on the ground, Samina. Don't try to see beyond five feet. Because if you look up now, the immensity will swallow you whole, and you will indeed be lost. Trust the tires on the road, your hands on the steering wheel, the momentum that carries you forward. And know that the fog will lift as suddenly as it has descended on you.

Eyes on the ground. Surely, I come prepared for this moment? Think, what resources have I brought with me, neatly packed or randomly thrown into the backpack of the years?

The therapist I saw for a few years after my father died emphasized the vital necessity of keeping the body moving. But I knew that already as a young teen watching my mother dance solo at home to Fleetwood Mac's "Say You Love Me" or Boney M's "Rasputin." I knew of no other mother in the Pakistan of forty years ago who did that. Ammi would insert my cassette into the player, turn up the volume, and go. Too shy to join her, I marveled at the unselfconsciousness with which she would twirl and flail her limbs, alive to the music and nothing else. Today I know that what might have looked like unconventional, goofy abandon to her children must have been an often desperate attempt to find meaning in the mundane. What demons of isolation was my mother confronting even before any of her children had left to study in America?

Now, the moment I feel the heart hollowing, I reach for the headphones my son has left me, stream "Say You Love Me" on my cell phone, and dance.

In an episode of Krista Tippett's podcast *On Being*, the sculptor Dario Robleto speaks in soft tones about memory as a creative response to loss. Don't I know the truth of this from years of reading and teaching literature? Let me call it up now: memory activated with intention. Let memory show me that loss demands invention to survive it. And once we emerge on the other side of it, that loss itself becomes a memory to be activated creatively in response to something else we will inevitably lose some day.

 I have memories honed from loss. Surely, I am strong.

 Like most students at Karachi University, I commuted from home. The rest of my adult years—American years—I was either married or had housemates, including my children, Maya and Cyrus. Having grown up sharing a room with my siblings, I didn't know the preciousness of having my own bedroom until, at twenty-seven years of age, I left my first husband and rented an apartment at Medford Hillside, the lone graduate student among Tufts undergraduates. The exhilaration of furnishing it in mauve—a small rug, a printed comforter, solid mauve bedsheets from Sears, a lamp to read by, and a boom-box from which to play Enya and float away on my exquisite aloneness. The gift of certainty that no man who said he loved me was going to smash the small things I held dear, in a rage exceeding all reason. Profound peace wafted on that aloneness because it was hard-won.

 Alone. It had been a mere two years since I had left Karachi for Tufts' graduate program in English literature and suffered terribly from homesickness. And yet, I had not arrived alone but had brought with me, on a spouse visa, the angry young man I had insisted on marrying while still a junior at Karachi University. For the first six weeks we lived with his brother and sister-in-law in the Boston suburb of Reading. That meant a commute of two and a half hours each way to Tufts: on commuter rail and subway, green line to red line, and then the walk through Powder House Square and up College Avenue, to my classes on the hill. Fall in New

England, beautiful as it was, sounded the warning of shorter, grayer, colder days to come. But it was the cumulative effect of multiple alienesses that got to me—alien faces in an alien landscape, and I, a stranger to myself in Western clothes and no break from the English language. My home, my family, all my frames of reference gone. And this was before email or text, when the cost of a phone call home was too high to entertain. Some days I would dial my father's number in Karachi just to hear his phone ring and hang up quickly before he picked it up and AT&T charged me $1.22 per minute, plus tax, for the call. Just knowing that I was hearing Abbu's phone ring in real time connected me to home for vital seconds. That first year on this continent I understood the line between sanity and insanity to be membrane-thin. If there's nothing around me to tell me who I used to be, how do I know that I'm real?

And how did my parents do it—let their children go so far beyond sight, and quiet their protesting hearts because this was what the children wanted and therefore what they wanted for them? Those childhood Saturdays when it was just Ammi and her three children at home, we would have free and open conversations that felt significant. I remember them as cheery and light, but an image stays with me: my young and beautiful mother in her cotton maxi dress, having just finished dancing perhaps, rests her hand on the door frame, her voice shaking as she anticipates a future in which her children will be gone and she is left all alone.

We didn't know then that absolute aloneness would be my father's, who never remarried after the divorce. He was my age when my sister, Sadia, and I left Karachi, as our brother had six years prior. For most of the twenty-five years that he lived after that, Abbu sought meaning in the Creator he looked up to, in the neighborhood community that looked up to him, and in the accomplishments of his children and grandchildren overseas. Following retirement as principal of Urdu Science College, the big revolution in his life, as Sadia reminds me, was the arrival of the satellite dish. Now he was no longer bound by the offerings of Pakistan Television. Entire evenings could be anchored in a sequence of local and Indian dramas. It amused me that his viewing schedule wouldn't budge for our visits from the US, but he would be greatly pleased if we watched with him. Fragments return to me now—conflicting, but belonging together—of Abbu lying on the couch in the cold and dark night, the television blaring; Abbu belly-laughing in his bedroom, where he later moved the television, at some farcical scene; Abbu speaking matter-of-factly of loneliness chasing after him, to bite him to bits.

Loss resists hierarchizing. While you're in the cave, it hardly matters how you got there.

Only three years prior to my arrival in the U.S., my family suffered the staggering loss of my cousin Rubina. She was three years my junior, and we had grown up together, living many years under one roof in Greenford and Karachi. At eighteen, she opted out of life—snuffed it out with a knot tied in her dupatta by her own hands, in a room that she shared with no-one. With all of us around her, how lonely was she? In the Karachi of 1985 we had no real concept of mental health—its complexity flattened into two categories, "sane" or "insane"—much less any thought of tending to it with professional care. We saw behavior problems and attitude problems, and there was enough blame to go around, but we could not imagine Rubina's suicide. Her violent absence has lingered with her mother, who keeps her long grief to herself, the anguish flaring into visibility only on the page, in her sporadic but prolific poetry. Rubina's self-erasure has also shaped the rest of us in our own ways, including the generation we raise after us, the nieces and nephews Rubina never knew. That includes my firstborn, Maya Bina, whose name echoes her Rubina Khala's, and whose choice of Clinical Psychology as a major in college is prompted in part by this particular legacy of loss.

How did we survive it?

Did we survive it?

The family that has endured without Rubina is, for better and worse, not the same family. Recast in the kiln of memory, our glass lives, molten, have flowed into the void to assume unintended forms. But if we can withstand so agonizing a transformation, what matters the crucible of an inevitable empty nest? Rubina, who had been admitted to Smith College in Massachusetts, with financial aid that's so hard to come by for an international student, would have been the first girl in our family to study in the US. On that pitiless June afternoon as her body was being carried out of her home—465-A/1 in Gulshan, where, as little girls we had survived bombs—and amid a throng of family and friends, the mail carrier handed me a big white envelope from Smith College, addressed to Rubina Najmi. I stared at the letters, struck by the absurd irony that they no longer referred to a living person. Rubina never left for college, as Maya and Cyrus have. In our family we don't take for granted that our children will turn nineteen.

A month after I began writing my way through the cavernous unknown, I had to flee from the smoke of the Creek Fire burning in Shaver Lake, just an hour northeast of Fresno. I didn't lose my home to the wildfire as colleagues of mine did who lived in the Sierra Nevada foothills, and I didn't have to be evacuated as a student of mine had to, who kept going back to help extended family, neighbors, and livestock out of there while he was housed in a temporary shelter in Fresno. But the smoke was making me sick despite my sealed, air-conditioned condo in the city. Taking advantage of the portability of online teaching for a couple of weeks, I am nestled amid close family in San Diego, in the home of my aunt Talat—my Khalammi, the poet, Rubina's mother. After thirty years of scattered lives, my family is concentrated here, including Maya, who goes to UC San Diego. On Friday evening, Khalammi's younger daughter, Sheba, wants us all to go out, masked and socially distant, to see the sun setting over the canyon in the neighborhood where my mother lives with the daughter who was only thirteen when Ammi moved out of 379-A/1. Ammi's quest for love rests here—in Sadia's gentle care; sharing laughs with her son-in-law, Kip, that make sense only to the two of them, and fueled by the proximity of her two grandchildren, Armaan and Amara.

There's 19 and then there's 79. Ammi is a buoyant, youthful, forward-looking elder, though her body often refuses to carry her. Denied her youthful passion for song, she takes singing lessons at home now with an Ustaad who accompanies her on the harmonium. Songbird Suraiya. In Pakistan, she broke molds and blazed trails for ensuing generations—not just in the family, but for all the students in her care in the school she founded in her early thirties.

And she danced.

At a moderate pace, the canyon is a five-minute walk away, some of it steep and uneven, but Ammi wants to test the strength of her legs and walk the distance herself instead of letting Sheba drive her. Caned and sneakered, she places one tentative foot before the other as we—niece, sister, and daughter—slow our pace to match hers. We take photos to document the rare moment of Ammi's excursion on foot and our togetherness on the sidewalk. At one point my mother, in her teal top and black pants, and hair pulled back in a no-nonsense ponytail, passes under an arch of bougainvillaea across from a little bench. She is framed by its fuschia splendor. Even in slow motion it's a fleeting moment, seized only by my cell-phone camera for a digital eternity.

By the time we arrive at the canyon, able-bodied people, forced by the pandemic to take life at a slower pace, have gathered on their feet and on bikes to see the sun go down. They are oblivious, as Ammi cannot be, to the absence of benches around them. She watches the peaching sky for a minute or two before she says, in a voice as shaky as her legs have become, that she can't stay for the sunset; we must see it for her.

"Where's that bench?" she asks in Urdu. "It had seemed so much closer."

I see Ammi turn her back on the setting sun and make her way toward that elusive bench. Trees line the sidewalk, some sporting hibiscus flowers as orange as the skies above the canyon she has left behind. My mother rests her weight on her clawed cane. She places one foot and then another into the daunting distance.

Say you love me.

Cacti, six feet tall, obstruct our eastward view, but I know how far she must go.

Eyes on the ground. Don't try to see beyond five feet. If you look up now, the immensity will swallow you whole.

Across from the bench we cannot see, a burst of fuschia beckons.

Acknowledgments

"Here—and There—Lies Home." *In Writing the Golden State: The New Literary Terrain of California*. Ed. Carribean Fragoza et al. Angel City Press, 2024.

"Sweet-and-Twenty." *Under the Gum Tree* Issue 49, Fall 2023.

"Memoir In Dust." In *New Moons: Contemporary Muslim American Literature*. Ed. Kazim Ali. Red Hen Press, 2021.

"Mourning Dove." In *New Moons: Contemporary Muslim American Literature*. Ed. Kazim Ali. Red Hen Press, 2021.

"Teaching as a Pakistani American Muslim Feminist—Ten, Twenty Years On." *The Margins*, Asian American Writers Workshop, 30 Sept. 2021.

"Trinità." *Under the Sun*. 29 May 2021. Pushcart nominee.

"One Summer in Gaza." *Entropy Magazine*. 20 May 2021. Reprint: Doubleback 6:1, April 2024.

"The Straight Lines of a Circle." *Split Lip Magazine*. 15 April 2021.

"Yellow Coat." *Manifest-Station*. 4 April 2021.

"Between Cave and Canyon." *Entropy Magazine*. 19 Feb. 2021.

"The Cat Connection." In *The Ordinary Chaos of Being Human: Tales from Many Muslim Worlds*. Ed. Marguerite Richards. Penguin Southeast Asia, 2019. US edition: 2024.

"Brew." *Thin Air* 11 Oct. 2019.

"The Sky That Didn't Fall." *Thin Air* 11 Oct. 2019.

"Café Convo." *Thin Air* 11 Oct. 2019.

"Amma." *The Massachusetts Review*. Special issue on Asian American Literature. Dec. 2018.

"Benign Baggage." *Entropy Magazine*. 12 Sep. 2017.

"Triptych." *World Literature Today*. Mar. 2017.

"First Thanksgiving Without Them." *Mothers Always Write* 29 Feb. 2016. Reprint: *SugarSugarSalt* 20 Oct. 2024.

"Ring In the New." *Warscapes* 12 Nov. 2014.

"The Little Room on the Roof." *Gargoyle* 61 (2014). Print.

"How I Became the *Other* Type of Soccer Mom." *Paste* 21 July 2014.

"Blind Date." *Mom Egg Review* 12 (2014): 35.
Reprint: in *M.A.M.A.* no. 15. 1 March 2016. n. pag. Web.

"The Cab Driver and I." *Jaggery: A DesiLit Arts and Literature Journal* 8 Nov. 2013: n. pag. Web.

"Applause." *damselfly press* 25. 15 Oct. 2013. Reprint: *SugarSugarSalt* 20 Oct. 2024.

"Greenford's Gift." *The Rumpus* 5 Aug. 2013.

"Skydying." Chautauqua Journal (2013): 167-9. Print.

"Hiding Osama bin Laden." The Progressive Oct. 2012: 32-3. Print. Reprint: Our Stories: An Introduction to South Asian America. South Asian American Digital Archive (SAADA), 2022.

"She Leaves Me, She Leaves Me Not." *bioStories* 7 Aug. 2012. Reissued in *Mothers and Other Creatures*. Ed. Mark Leichliter. Create Space, Feb. 2015. Print.

"Burglar in Braids." *Pilgrimage*. 36: 2/3 (May 2012): 10-13. Print.

"Abdul." *Map Literary: A Journal of Contemporary Literature* 1, Spring 2012.

Winner, 2012 *Map Literary* Nonfiction Prize. Reprint: *Glint*, Dec. 2024.

"Membership Dues." *SALA* (South Asian Literary Association, an allied organization of the MLA). Winter 2011: Newsletter, Personal Essay, 26. Print.

"Teaching as a Pakistani American Muslim Feminist." *Commemorating the Tenth Anniversary of September 11*. Ed. Parag Khandar and Rajini Srikanth. Spec. issue of *Asian American Literary Review*. 2: 1.5 (Fall 2011): 17-24. Print.

A Note of Thanks

It's been a long road to this book, but I have been supported at every turn by family, friends, mentors, and well-wishers. You know who you are.

But a few I must name: Rajini Srikanth—friend, collaborator, and chief instigator—who coaxed the first personal essay out of me for the tenth anniversary of 9/11. lawrence-minh bùi davis, who published it in the *Asian American Literary Review*. CSU Summer Arts, hosted by Fresno State: coordinators, guest artists, and cohorts who gave so generously of themselves in Fresno's ungenerous Julys. In particular, Doug Rice, who coordinated the first creative writing workshop I ever took, and from whom I learned the moral and aesthetic imperative of seeing. My first writing group, which became my first AWP panel: Jackie Heffron Williams, Phyllis Brotherton, Armen Bacon, and Sally Vogl.

My colleagues Linnea Alexander, Connie Hales, and Cheng Lok Chua for early and enthusiastic support of my writing. And Steven Church, who read my 40-paged essay all those years ago (and pretty much every essay I've published since) and told me I was writing a book. Melanie Kachadoorian, Lucilia Valério, Zhou Xiaojing, and others for bringing my essays into their classrooms early on. The Chicanx Writers and Artists Association (CWAA)—especially my former students Erin Álvarez and the late Mia Barazza Martinez—for hosting my very first readings. Hedgebrook, for residency and fellowship. Sage and gentle Janice Lee, who gave three of my essays a home in *Entropy*.

The brilliant Theo Nestor, writing coach extraordinaire,

who read an early version of this book and said, "Free the poet." Shadab Zeest Hashmi, for reading the essays with great heart and understanding. The entire Trio House Press team, who have been a marvel to work with—especially Kris Bigalk and Cynthia Via for lavishing their insights and love on the manuscript, Joel W. Coggins for the cover design, and Natasha Kane for seeing it through production.

Azfar Najmi, for his creative, critical, and caring eye on my website.

To all my students, through tendrils of time—in Karachi, Boston, and Fresno: I'm ever grateful that you challenge me to grow, even as you give me roots.

And for cheering me on through it all, and sometimes propping me up: my two-in-one California family, beautiful and beloved. Writer-mothers, Suraiya Jabeen and Mah Talat Shazi. My siblings and their partners: Amir and Linda, Azfar and Meherwan, Sadia and Kip, and the star of the Najmis, Sheba. Our children, who inherit these stories as they create their own: Maya, Cyrus, Naïla, Armaan, and Amara.

No longer earthside, but inspiring these pages: my Abbu, Professor Haroon Najmi, the keeper of keys. My Chotepapa, Ilyas Najmi, the seeker. Kaneez Fatima, my Amma, the family memoirist. Anjum Ara, known to the world as Apa. And forty years gone, Rubina Najmi, whose absence has shaped all our becomings.

Finally, a writerly debt to Suraiya Jabeen, Sadia Najmi, and Maya Bina Vannini. Mother, sister, daughter—my first readers of everything.

About the Author

Samina Najmi teaches multiethnic US literatures at California State University, Fresno. A scholar of race, gender, and war in US literature, her articles include "Narrating War: Muslim and Arab American Aesthetics" in the *Cambridge History of Asian American Literature*. She has coedited three volumes of critical essays and midwifed the reissue of a 1903 novel, *The Heart of Hyacinth*, by Onoto Watanna, Asian America's first known novelist. Samina was among twenty-one writers nationwide to contribute an address on the state and future of Asian American literature for the twentieth anniversary of the Smithsonian Asian Pacific American Center in 2017. Samina is a founding faculty advisor for the annual Undergraduate Conference on Multiethnic Literatures of the Americas (UCMLA) at Fresno State and helped to establish the Cheng Lok Chua Scholarship for students of multiethnic US literatures.

Samina's personal essay commemorating the tenth anniversary of 9/11 ushered in a new era of creative nonfiction in her writing. Her personal essays have been published widely, including in *World Literature Today*. Among the honors she's proud to claim: Penguin Random House's site, Signature, lists "Triptych" as an example of the possibilities of the triptych form; Roxane Gay selected "Greenford's Gift" for publication in The Rumpus and the essay remained on the website of a high school in Greenford, UK, for three years; "Abdul" won *Map Literary*'s creative nonfiction prize, and "Trinita" was nominated for a Pushcart.

Daughter of multigenerational displacements, Samina grew up in Pakistan and England, spent eighteen years in Massachusetts, and, since 2006, calls Fresno, California, home. Here she has watched with wonder her two children, her many students, and her citrus grow.

Samina believes in Fresno's sunsets; in everyone's three feet of influence, and in the power of language and literature to extend our reach beyond it.

About the Book

Sing Me a Circle: Love, Loss, and a Home in Time was designed at Trio House Press through the collaboration of:

Cynthia Via, Editor
Kris Bigalk, Editor
Natasha Kane, Interior Designer
Joel Coggins, Cover Designer
Azfar Najmi, Author Photographer

The text is set in Adobe Caslon Pro.

About the Press

Trio House Press is an independent literary press dedicated to discovering, publishing, and promoting books that enhance culture and the human experience. Trio House Press adheres to and supports all ethical standards and guidelines outlined by the CLMP. For further information, or to consider making a donation to Trio House Press, visit us online at triohousepress.org.

www.ingramcontent.com/pod-product-compliance
Lightning Source LLC
Chambersburg PA
CBHW060513080526
44586CB00012B/475